The Human Science of Communicology

THE HUMAN SCIENCE OF COMMUNICOLOGY

A Phenomenology of Discourse in Foucault and Merleau-Ponty

Richard L. Lanigan

 Duquesne University Press
Pittsburgh, Pennsylvania

Published in the United States of America
by Duquesne University Press
600 Forbes Avenue, Pittsburgh PA 15282

First Edition

Library of Congress Cataloging-in-Publication Data

Lanigan, Richard L.
The human science of communicology : a phenomenology of discourse
in Foucault and Merleau-Ponty / Richard L. Lanigan. — 1st ed.
    p.   cm.
Includes bibliographical references and index.
ISBN 0–8207–0242–0 (cloth) : ISBN 0–8207–0243–9 (paper)
    1. Communication—Philosophy.   2. Merleau-Ponty, Maurice,
1908–1961—Contributions in philosophy of communication.
3. Foucault, Michel—Contributions in philosophy of communication.
4. Phenomenology.   I. Title.
P91.L338   1992
302.2'01—dc20   91–47094

In memory of those students and workers
peacefully communicating a desire for the power of
freedom and democracy
who died in the massacre by government troops
in Tiananmen Square at Beijing, China
on 4 June 1989

And,
For my colleague and friend from the
People's Republic of China,
Guo Rui-hong, Ph. D.

And our son,
James Guo Lanigan

Contents

List of Figures, Plates and Tables

PLATES

TABLES

Acknowledgements

Research and writing is a time-consuming activity, but in my case the practice has been made considerably easier by my Research Assistants for 1990-91, Thomas Puckett and Ian Henderson. I thank them for the continuing dialogue on semiotic phenomenology and the problematic of postmodern discourse. Their aesthetic text discoveries of the document in the Library have made their way into the Museum as a monument of the sign "communication semiotic."

The dialogue among scholars is a reflexive and reversible process from which I have benefited immensely over the years. But in the particular context of the present book, I am especially indebted for the research collaboration of four colleagues: Professor Jenny L. Nelson, Director of Graduate Studies in the School of Telecommunications at Ohio University, and her colleague in the Philosophy Department, Professor Algis Mickunas; Professor Henri Quéré at the Institut du Monde Anglophone, Université de la Sorbonne Nouvelle (Paris III); and, Professor Lenore Langsdorf, my departmental colleague at Southern Illinois University.

Regarding the text itself, chapters 3, 7, 8, and appendix B are published here for the first time. Chapter 3 is drawn from research completed while I was Institute Professor at the Ohio University Summer Institute for the Human Sciences in 1986 at the kind invitation of Professor Algis Mickunas, and it was subsequently presented as a paper at the Sixth International Human Science Conference at the University of Ottawa, Canada, in May 1987. Chapter 7 is based on a paper presented at the 1989 conference of the Semiotic Society of America held at

Indiana University-Purdue University, Indianapolis, Indiana. Chapter 8 was originally presented to the Japanese-American Joint Seminar: Japanese and Western Phenomenology, held at the Kansai University Seminar House near Sanda-city, Japan, in October 1989 under the auspices of the Phenomenological Association of Japan and the Center for Advanced Research in Phenomenology (USA) coordinated by Professors Hiroshi Kojima and Lester Embree. Appendix B is based on a study guide annually revised during the last for years in my graduate course "Communicology as a Human Science" at Southern Illinois University.

The remaining chapters (1, 2, 4, 6, 9, and appendix A) in the present volume are extensions and revisions of pieces published earlier and used by permission from the publishers as noted. Chapter 1 from *The Humanist Psychologist*, 15, no.1 (Spring 1987), pp.27–37; chapter 2 from *Critical Studies in Mass Communication*, 5, no. 4 (December 1988), pp. 335–345; chapter 4 from *Hermeneutics and the Tradition* (Proceedings of the American Catholic Philosophical Association, Vol. 62), Daniel O. Dahlstrom (Ed.), 1988, pp. 124–135; chapter 5 from *Semiotica*, Vol. 81 (1991); chapter 6 from Ian Angus & Lenore Langsdorf (eds.), *The Critical Turn: Rhetoric and Philosophy in Contemporary Discourse* (Carbondale: Southern Illinois UP, 1991); chapter 9 from the *Gebser Network Newsletter*, vol. 6, no. 2 (1989), pp. 4–8; appendix A from *International Journal of Intercultural Relations*, 10, no. 4 (1986), pp. 512–516.

Plates 1, 2, and 3 are the original photography of artist Joel Feldman and are published by permission. Plates 4 and 5 are reprinted from Suzi Gablik, *Magritte* (New York: Thames & Hudson) copyright 1970, 1985 by Suzi Gablick and used with her permission. All figures and tables are my own creations based upon the particular text being discussed. In particular, the quadrilateral model as a *thematic paradigm* in figure 5 is constructed according to Foucault's own verbal description given in the *Order of Things: An Archaeology of the Human Sciences* (p. 115ff) and as applied to two empirical examples showing a *problematic paradigm* of discourse (p. 201); (1) Tropes, Verb, Names, and Primitive Names in the Seventeenth and Eighteenth Centuries, and (2), Syntax, Formalization, Phonetics, and Interpretation in the Nineteenth Century. An early, partial version of Figure 11 appeared in my *Semiotic Phenomenology of Rhetoric: Eidetic Practice in Henry Grattan's Discourse on Tolerance* (Washington, DC: Center for Advanced Research in Phenomenology & UP America, 1984), p. 32.

Preface

For those who are familiar with my most recent book, *Phenomenology of Communication,* the present book will be a sequel. For those unfamiliar with that volume, the present book may serve as an introduction to my thinking about semiotic phenomenology and the process of human communication in the shadow of what Hegel called "absolute freedom and terror". For everyone, the book will be the unabashed re-introduction of the term *Communicology* to name the discipline which studies *human discourse.* We may expect it will generate some of the same sort of discussion that greeted the disciplinary study of ethical human practice when Auguste Comte suggested the name Sociology to his colleagues. In the age of philology, his academic critics at the universities riled at the use of a Latin-Greek compound word as a *name.* Yet, almost no one remembers his critics and Michel Foucault has deconstructed and demystified the modernist rationality of the name. There is a lesson in that, perhaps best captured by Umberto Eco's close to *The Name of the Rose*: "stat rosa pristina nomine, nomina nuda tenemus" [yesterday's rose endures in its name, we hold empty names.]. The lesson is repeated in *Foucault's Pendulum* for those who cannot give up "the forgetfulness of rationality," to borrow the Other Foucault's phrase.

Perhaps more controversial in the chapters that follow is my argument that Maurice Merleau-Ponty and Michel Foucault are linked in very important intellectual and philosophical ways that are often obscured by the *tout Paris* mentality that sweeps from France to America with much lost in the transatlantic translation. The argument locates itself in the shadow of the medieval Sorbonne with its legacy of the *trivium* in which grammar, logic, and rhetoric secured the study of discourse as a human practice. It is the brilliant talent of Merleau-Ponty that his discourse is an "incarnate logic enveloped" in the play of grammar and rhetoric. His writing speaks our mind *in communis*. Equally so, Foucault's discourse is a rhetoric diagnosing the foundational deception of *grammaire générale* and its facade of positivistic logic. His writing speaks our mind *in proprius*. The constitution of Self-Other-World and its rupture as Subject-Power-Knowledge is an ambiguity of *desire*: for Merleau-Ponty, the phenomenological ambiguity of the *flesh*, and, for Foucault, the semiotic ambiguity of the *nameless voice* (*énoncé; logos*). Thus faced with naming the unnameable discourse of *power* (the aporia which Plato confronts in the *Sophist*), I am prompted to suggest that we should use the name Communicology to mark the flesh of the nameless voice, lest the anonymous practice of discourse as *terror* in Modernity continue to subvert the discourse of choice in Postmodernity that Merleau-Ponty was first to call *freedom*.

1

On the Foundations of Communicology as a Human Science

Can an American do Semiotic Phenomenology?

Q ualitative methods, the interpretative approach, the narrative model, and similar names for the inappropriately
labeled, but commonly so-called, "naturalistic" paradigm approach to research in the human sciences are all too familiar
these days. These names mark out an apparently new and politically fundamental shift in the contemporary currents of research practice generally in the traditional arts or humanities
disciplines and specifically in the discipline of Communicology.
This shift is supposed to be in conflict with, or at least different from, quantitative methods, the measurement approach,
the observation model, and like names for paradigm procedures in the social sciences. In my characterizations of both
methodological paradigms, I use the disciplinary name "Communicology" and shall continue to do so throughout my present analysis and in subsequent chapters because, for the time
being, it is a name whose time is "just now" in the academic
world, as it were. It does not yet represent an established
paradigm label with disciplinary political overtones as do the
names "Speech Communication," "Communications," "Mass

1

Communication," "Telecommunication," "Intercultural Communication," or any of the other "communications" we communicologists formally entitle with existence in our professional associations, whether it be the International Communication Association, the Speech Communication Association, or the World Communication Association. This disciplinary category was essentially initiated with the 1989 publication of the *International Encyclopedia of Communications*, which displaced the lonely disciplinary entry on "communication" written by Edward Sapir for the inaugural 1931 edition of the *Encyclopedia of Social Sciences*. Indeed, the discipline of communicology now contending with three separate professional associations and their political labels (hence, "communications") is itself a testament to the psycho-sociological shift from the failed "unified science" paradigm to the human science paradigm. The idealization of "society" in an increasingly unified "social science," a direct analogy to its mentor concept of a "unified science of physics," has failed. It is an intellectual embarrassment that we still find "communications" textbooks using the physics exemplar to suggest some vague analogy (often little more than a notion of idealized behavior based on the asserted introspection of the so-called "objective" researcher) to thinking about linguistic competence and performance. Fortunately, the return to the human science paradigm is refocusing attention on the performance and practice of persons communicating at the intrapersonal, interpersonal, group, and cultural levels of context for affective and conative meaning along with the traditional cognitive meaning orientation. The human scientist is "taking reality" (*capta*) as the valid source of evidence in research, rather than falling victim to the "Postmodern Condition" of positivism in which the assumption of a "given reality" (*data*) indexes the subsequent representations of judgment ("making it operational"). This comparison of views first emerged in the early part of this century in the discourse initiated by the human science research of Lucien Lévy-Bruhl. This discourse surrounded the birth of the discipline of Sociology and the field research of Franz Boas, which largely accounted for the birth of the discipline of Anthropology. Now in the later part of the twentieth century, ironically, the contrast of human and social science theory and methodology is repeated in the emergent discourse surrounding the discipline of Communicology (see appendix A).

Communicology is certainly not the name of a new paradigm in Kuhn's sense of the term,[1] nor is it yet the mark of a "community of interpretation" in Peirce's sense.[2] However, we might take note that in the international cultural context of the communication discipline, the existing English "communicology" functions as an appropriate translation for the new French "*comunicologie*" and the German "*Kommunikationgemeinschaft*," terms used increasingly to suggest a qualitative and human signification as opposed to the quantitative and technological reference of "cybernetics," "communications," and "*informatiques*." In short, "communicology" is a neologism of American (USA) scholars writing during the 1950s, and in this discussion of paradigmatic theory and method, it should afford all scholars a certain amount of academic detachment, since nobody "owns" it yet. Let me note in passing that the entry for "communicology" in appendix B gives a short history of the term's use. I am not going to praise or blame any perspective in the ubiquitous "communications" discipline by name, at least not any more than I have already.

That general difference of orientation aside, I propose to focus on three items for analysis and discussion. First, I offer an account of *semiotic phenomenology* as a theory and research paradigm for communicology which has its origins in the mother of all art and science disciplines, philosophy. Second, I want to make a suggestion about how this paradigm would function in human and social sciences in general. Third, I am going to suggest what this paradigm might do for the study of communicology as human discourse. My overall intention is to do these things in a reflexive way, i.e., so that the chapter itself is an application and illustration of theory.[3]

SEMIOTIC PHENOMENOLOGY AS A PARADIGM

If we are to speak of semiotic phenomenology as a communication paradigm, we must begin with the recognition that there is both an American (USA) and a French origin. The American version is virtually unknown outside of historical philosophy.[4] The French version is badly misconstrued by interpreters and commentators in the United States. A recent example of such aberrant research is a small group communication study where human groups are hypostatized as structural *channels* of communication.[5] This article reports its representational data according to a classic positivist view of human "behavior." By comparison, a correct understanding of the human group *in situ* as conduct, as a *medium* of communication, has long been available in McFeat's work on small group cultures.[6] In addition, Lyons's work on semantics offers a complete discussion of the communication theory distinction between the human channel ("transmission" of a message) and medium (memory function and judgment structure of a message, i.e., "storage and retrieval"), and their empirical research consequence.[7] First, a word about the French version of semiotic phenomenology, which will be examined in detail in chapter 4.

In France, there has been a debate for several decades between the phenomenologists who argue for the speaking subject as the key to understanding human communication as *parole* (the embodied act of speaking) and the structuralists who advocate understanding communication as *langue* (speech as social practice) through the agency of the speech community. This debate between the phenomenologists and structuralists involved both groups with *semiology*, and a second generation of scholars argued the resulting issues, especially in literature, anthropology, history, psychology, and sociology, under the respective names of *hermeneuticists* (or hermeneutic phenomenologists) and *poststructuralists*.[8]

At the moment, we are witnessing the return to semiology and its assimilation by both sides. For example, we see in the work of A. J. Greimas a semiotic and hermeneutic phenomenology and we find a semiotic poststructuralism in the work of Jacques Derrida. We do not need to dwell on the specifics of these paradigmatic trends, except to acknowledge that they are grounded in more than a century of theoretical and applied communication research. Even a cursory reading of the linguists Ferdinand de Saussure, Roman Jakobson, Louis Hjelmslev,[9] Emile Benveniste, and John Lyons confirms this fact, and this is true for the philosophers of the same period who are fascinated with communication, especially the early work by Karl Jaspers and Martin Heidegger in Germany, and that of Jean-Paul Sartre and Maurice Merleau-Ponty in France.

In more recent work, we are all familiar with the schools of thought represented in Germany by Jürgen Habermas, Niklas Luhmann, and Karl-Otto Apel and in France by Roland Barthes,[10] Michel Foucault, Pierre Bourdieu,[11] and Jean Baudrillard.[12] Nor should we forget the special insights about human discourse that come from Freud and his French critic, Jacques Lacan. In my view, it is regrettable that more (U.S.) communication scholars have not taken better advantage of this overall rich resource of European thought. The exception, I must note, is the early use of the phenomenological research model, developed in the Department of Psychology at Duquesne University, that stimulated the growth of a similar tradition in the Department of Communication at my own institution, Southern Illinois University.[13] All too frequently, I believe, communicologists have assumed that paradigmatic strength comes by counterdistinction to the theories of other disciplines; researchers are much too facile at adopting their methodologies in a theoretical vacuum.

As a matter of focus, let me suggest that what Communicology as a discipline borrows from phenomenology is the methodology of description and empirical constitution. What it fails to borrow is the normative logic of the phenomenological theory. The result is an atheoretical description of the worst sort: subjective introspection—ironically the very thing that Edmund Husserl, the founder of phenomenology, attacked in the nineteenth century as the cause of a crisis in science.

What Communicology borrows from structuralism is the methodology of deconstruction and empirical description. Communicology also fails to appropriate the logic model of structuralism's concomitant theory. Again, the result is an atheoretical description in the worst context: individual behavior claimed as social practice—ironically as well, this so-called naturalistic method is anything but a model of physical nature;

it is properly the cultural model of empirical human discourse. Recall that the Poole, Siebold and McPhee article illustrates this confusion of the distinction between nature (the person as human channel) and culture (the person as human medium).[14]

Let me now turn briefly to the less well known (U.S.) tradition in semiotic phenomenology. The nineteenth century contributions of John Dewey, William James and George Herbert Mead are generally familiar at least in the applied traditions that survive them, progressive public education and political democracy from Dewey, interpersonal and humanistic psychology from James, and Mead's symbolic interaction model in sociology and psychology with its "concern with the inner, or phenomenological aspects of human behavior [that] has both substantive and research implications."[15] Manis and Meltzer characterize the phenomenological influence in symbolic interactionism with these basic propositions describing the researcher's human science research focus:

1. The meaning component in human conduct.
2. The social sources of humanness.
3. Society as process.
4. The voluntaristic component in human conduct.
5. A dialectical conception of mind.
6. The constructive, emergent nature of human conduct.
7. The necessity of sympathetic introspection.[16]

Little appreciated (with the exception of William James) is the great theoretical debt that the American pragmaticism movement owes to Charles Sanders Peirce. His systematic presentation in eight volumes of semiotics and phenomenology (later called *phanerscopy*) and his four volumes on mathematical logic make him the American pioneer in the study of human thought, language, and communication. If there is an American founder of communicology, it is C. S. Peirce.[17] With the current republication of his complete collected works in a chronological edition, we are only now becoming aware of Peirce's importance to the discipline of communicology, especially in theory construction. Let me now turn to my second point, the application of semiotic phenomenology as a theoretical paradigm per se.

THE PARADIGM AS DEFINING EXEMPLAR

As a contextualized research question, "Can an American do semiotic phenomenology?" expresses a research problematic that bears on the human sciences in general, and on the discipline of communicology in particular. This problematic has several paradigmatic (i.e., in-class transformations) and syntagmatic (i.e., among-classes transformations) characteristics: (1) the word "can" signals an orientation in research that focuses on possibility of depiction/description, rather than on probability of prediction/ascription; (2) the phrase "an American" refers to those positivist researchers in the United States who claim to represent "dominant" or "main stream objective" practice, which argues that symbolically mediated and generalized research judgments tend to be individual in nature, and this individualism is heavily constrained by a psychocultural and sociocultural view of science as positive technology, i.e., the modernity notion that representation derives causally from "reality"; (3) the verb "do" indicates this "American" preference for technological application that is, at least, atheoretical and, at most, prior to theory statement; and (4) the phrase "semiotic phenomenology" specifies a contemporary theory and praxis approach to human communication that constrains the uncritical use of the atheoretical positive science just explicated. That is, phenomenology is the study of human conscious experience and semiotics is the study of signs and sign-systems. Phenomenology is, first, an examination of the discursive models of being human and, second, the examination of normative logics as communicological theory.[18] Semiotics is, first, the examination of human models of discourse and, second, the examination of normative logics as communicological praxis.[19]

What I propose to explicate in my analysis is the paradigmatic consequence of answering the research question posed, "Can an American do semiotic phenomenology?". I am particularly concerned with the process of legitimation, the illusion of positive practice irregardless of one's theoretical commitments of preferences. I want to explore the dangers of the very notion of a paradigm so expressed. Or, to describe it in a more subtle but accurate way, I am concerned to step outside of Kuhn's positive notion of being confronted with either paradigm evolution or revolution, both of which seem to be no more than paradigm legitimation when Kuhn's theory per se is explicated by its own normative criteria!

By way of briefly illustrating what I mean, consider this: you answer the question I pose in this chapter with a simple "yes" or an equally comforting "no." In either case, your answer legitimizes or norms the question: (1) by *granting* the question its own discursive reality—it is a well-formed, clear question and thereby illustrates that science has a psychological rhetoric; (2) by *acknowledging* the validity of an answer as a normative, parsimonious extension of both the theory and practice embedded in the question and thereby illustrating that science has a logic—it is, as Searle[20] would argue, a well-formed speech act that entails a propositional act, along with an intentional practice; and (3) by *discounting* any expectation of a differently formed answer, thereby granting that science has a psychological grammar with all its ontological anonymity. It is at least ironic, then, to note that such an uncritical answer to my question enlightens us about the power of legitimized knowledge as opposed to understanding. As Merleau-Ponty and Foucault[21] remind us, (1) legitimate(d) knowledge is no less than the voice of science that is no particular embodied person, but merely rhetoric as a psychological representation of that voice (rhetorically, a *prosopopoeia*; see chapter 8), (2) legitimate(d) knowledge is no less than the judgment of science which is no particular human, embodied act, but merely logic as a psychological and inferential representation of that act or action (logically, an *asyndeton*; see chapter 8), and (3) legitimate(d) knowledge is no less than the discursive origin of science which is no particular human, embodied person, but merely the grammar (*langage*) as a psychological representation of "person," that is to say, the subject (grammatically, the "subject" of nomination, ascription, or predication in a sentence; see chapters 5 and 9).

In short, there are two answers to the question, "Can an American do semiotic phenomenology?". *Either* yes *or* no is one of such response. *Both* yes *and* no is the second possibility. Both answers represent thematics, i.e., propositions which are a positive expression of the research norms contained in the problematic. These are the norms of legitimation we just reviewed: *understanding* (*savior*) versus *knowledge* (*connaissance*). The essential characteristics of each are: (1) possibility versus probability, (2) particular versus universal (or singular versus general), (3) praxis versus practice, and (4) conscious experience versus the experience of conscious (or perception/expression as theoretical versus sensation/observation as atheoretical—however, observation is a modality of expression because expression is reflexive to perception!). These four conditions as a system constitute a normative logic model by which any answer to the question is constrained in its phenomenological constitution. To express such an argument is to clearly identify my research approach in this chapter as a qualitative theory and methodology that is concerned with *understanding*, with describing, and thereby constituting, the condition, relation, and consequence of human norms (hypothesis; Peirce's *abduction*). My approach is not a quantitative theory and methodology that is concerned with knowledge, i.e., with norming ("inventing" in its technical theory construction sense) assumed constituents of psychological or sociological representation in human action (hypostatization; deduction or induction).

Having described the manner in which problematics constitute thematics, and how thematics entail the normative, prescriptive conditions for any constitution (description with the ontological force of depiction), I now take up the two possible answers to the propositional question. They are the combinatory (analogue) normative answers "both yes and no," and, the exclusionary (digital) norming answers "either yes or no" (see appendix B). As a narrative proof of the problematics and entailed thematics, consider the legitimation of the understanding paradigm that occurs as you pragmatically link the semantic force of "both yes and no" with "both true and false," "both valid and invalid," "both significant and insignificant," "both sense and nonsense," and "both sincere and insincere." Understanding not only requires but is a human participation in the phenomenon. Understanding is science *in situ* and is properly called *human science*. Now consider the equally forceful legitimation of the knowledge paradigm as you link "either yes or no" with "either true or false," "valid or invalid," "significant or insignificant," "sense or nonsense," "sincere or insincere." Knowledge not only requires but is science *de natura* and properly called *natural science*. Hence, the ironic and puzzling nomination of the contrasting qualitative human science approach as "naturalistic."

I began the preceding analysis by exploring the consequences of a "yes" answer and a "no" answer as a praxis condition from which I can abstract the thematic theory conditions which ground all possible answers. Explicitly stated, such an abstraction is a communicological process of theory construction in which a *differentiation by combination* (both/and analogue logic) produces and, thereby, expresses a set of metatheory conditions that subsequently create a substantial description of the phenomenon under investigation. In short, the constitution of norms proceeds from a discovery of sufficient conditions in perception to the necessary conditions of description as expression (depiction). Put in plain language, I am arguing that a "both yes and no" answer entails a "because . . ." predication, or ascription, as sufficient condition for perception by a person, be it as listener reader, or viewer. Likewise, the "because . . ." entailment is a necessary condition for the person as speaker, writer, or image maker.[22] On these positive theoretical conditions, it is clear to us that the absence of the "because . . ." entailment is necessary condition for theory on the model of the natural sciences: Nature either is or is not; at least, we are asked to assume so in this century. Therefore we are confronted with the discovery made popular by Karl Popper, that theorizing about Nature is a counterfactual business. That is, hypostatizations are assumed "positive" when we fail to produce an empirical counterexample. On these negative sufficient conditions we posit knowledge, but it is a "we" that has already started from the theoretical ground of the understanding paradigm. Without wanting to labor the place of theory construction in the discussion of paradigms (see appendix B for that), I now turn to my third and last, point.

SEMIOTIC PHENOMENOLOGY AS COMMUNICOLOGY

Recall the four propositions I used to define the paradigmatic status of semiotic phenomenology; as a paradigm for theory and research, they are:

1. A discursive model of being human.
2. A human model of discourse.
3. A normative logic in communicological theory.
4. A normative logic in communicological praxis.

Propositions one and three are *necessary* conditions for any research which purports to depict (describe) or predict (ascribe) *discourse as a human practice* (a phrase I prefer to "behavior") of communication. Propositions two and four are *sufficient* conditions for the same inferences. In the context of the first proposition, Merleau-Ponty, in the area of perception, and Foucault, in the area of expression, demonstrate the empirical and eidetic meaning of discourse as an existential and structural model of being human. Language, discourse, gesture, all psycho-social practices, are lived experiences of the person; they are not anonymous objects in Nature[23] nor are they are the constructs of the mystic forces of authority, whether sacred or secular.[24] With regard to the third proposition, Husserl, Apel, and Greimas each explore the normative logics necessary to any understanding of communicological theory. Husserl tests the transformations of the eidetic and empirical conditions for communicative phenomena, while Apel explores such communicative transformations as they constitute disciplinary studies and institutions. Greimas works to separate out the transformations in language from those in speech. With Greimas, we hear the voice of narrative, but we do not yet understand who is speaking, or, to use Foucault's telling phrases, it is the discourse of the "nameless voice" confronting the "voiceless name".[25]

Turning to the second and fourth propositions (a human model of discourse and a normative logic in communicological praxis), these are the human models of discourse that occupy Ruesch, Jakobson, and Benveniste. Discounting the cybernetic analogy of Weiner and the mathematical analogy of Shannon and Weaver, Jürgen Ruesch studies the intentional practices of persons as individuals, as participants in group culture, and their role (albeit idealized) in the institution of social organization. Jakobson begins with the comparative structure of languages, generalizes to folktales, and then to all semiotic practice as a logical necessity, whether formalized as a logic, mathematic, or linguistic phenomenon. Jakobson's discovery of the distinctive features in human language as an eidetic condition of empirical existence is, perhaps, the most significant discovery in the twentieth century regarding our understanding of the nature and function of human discourse.[26]

Benveniste traces the history of language as a record of human practice.[27] In that record, he discovers the meta-communication feature of all human discourse. These normative logics in communication theory are subsequently the focus of study by Habermas and Luhmann. Habermas explores the universal pragmatic feature of speech as a communicative action in the lifeworld of the person. Luhmann explores the macrostructures of society and culture which contain the possibilities of such a lifeworld. With the insights of Jean Baudrillard, we enter the world of mediated and exchanged human reality, where the dialectic between a choice of context and a context of choice becomes the political economy of the lifeworld. In practice, normative logics come to constitute the theory of communication as lived: mediation is praxis.

I close my introductory analysis now, not with a theoretical summary or a master proposition, but with the conscious experience of mediated human discourse. In the film *Tender Mercies* (1983), the actor Robert Duvall plays the part of a down and out alcoholic country-western songwriter and singer named Max Sledge. As Sledge comes out of the feed store in small Texas town, a woman on the sidewalk, a stranger, asks him: "Mister, did you use' to be Max Sledge?" He answers: "Yes, I was him" We, you and I, here and now in the narrative of this chapter, stand on the same sidewalk as Max Sledge. Someday a stranger will ask us, "Mister did you use' to be a communicologist?" Because our lifeworld will come to displace our professional paradigms, we will be able to answer: "Yes, I *was* one."

2

Irving Goffman and the Attempt at a Phenomenology of Mass Media

T he question "Is Erving Goffman a phenomenologist?" is more than a rhetorical device implying an appropriate answer of "yes," "no," or "maybe." In the tradition of Gregory Bateson's theory of human communication, according to which persons constitute cultures of meaning,[1] Goffman's own conditions for the analysis of discourse fall within the category of human conscious experience that he calls *frame analysis*.[2] In short and in part, my question is a frame. The exploration of this theoretical frame first leads to Bateson's specification of communication as a human practice.[3] That is, Bateson offers us the phenomenological notion of a frame of discourse as a unique practice of *hysteresis* or learning, the record of which is culture as it is embodied in the lexicon of human speech. As Bourdieu also confirms,[4] hysteresis is the uniquely human condition of communication as *practice* in which a meaning is created by a message, whether or not that message is understood as intended or not, i.e., a differentiated conjunction of meaning functions that Michel Foucault calls respectively "desire" and "power."[5] The effect of each message is information theoretic, as understood in terms of Shannon and Weaver's 1949 historical reference to information theory as a mathematical, digital system of choice.[6] "Communication" (information per se) in this information theoretic view is a choice made in a *given* context and it is susceptible to an either/or logic of digital selection. Here, the process of signification as the "reduction of uncertainty" provides a referential practice (probability as a signifier), but no referent (signified). In fact, we should realize that the formal and operational procedures of information theory require a symbolic equivocation of the signifier and signified in the conception of the sign. From a postmodern perspective, then, expression and perception are collapsed into the operational concept of *representation* and it empirical manifestation as the *symbol* in speaking and writing.

Second, my question asks us to entertain the epistemological problem of analysis as a phenomenological procedure in the human sciences, i.e., the Goffman notion of the *strip* that is "any arbitrary slice or cut from the stream of activity."[7] Here, according to Bourdieu, the methodological problem of analysis is the theoretical problem of *hexis* [L. *habitus*], i.e. the *problematic* of habit in which the choice made (consciousness) demands that its own context (experience) be *taken* as thematic.[8] This way of formulating the issue of analysis is strictly phenomenological. A *problematic* is a description of a phenomenon from which essential characteristics are abstracted as the criteria for defining that concrete example of the phenomenon. Where such criteria (a token with a tone, in Charles Saunders Peirce's sense)[9] are used to define a typology, a *thematic* is constituted or realized. The validity of the eidetic realization can be checked by locating the original phenomenon or one like it as an empirical actualization in experience.[10] Thus with the eidetic notion of hexis, the empirical practice of habit becomes a message that is communication theoretic. The meaning of the message is communication theoretic in the communication theory sense of an embodied choice of context that is manifest in an analogue logic of both/and selections.[11] Here, the process of meaning as the "constitution of intentionality" (conscious experience) provides a referential *practice* (i.e., possibility) as its own reflexive referent (i.e., the sign as signifier and signified). We discover the hierarchy of human meaning precisely in this ideological function of discourse by which both frame and strip are linked as cultural values, i.e., the communicative boundaries of hysteresis and hexis, desire and power that Husserl calls a "*factum*".[12]

As I proceed to explore these two notions of frame and strip, the methodological similarity of Goffman's research orientation to phenomenology will become increasingly clear. At the same time, this explication allows us to understand that, unlike the rich phenomenological tradition of theory upon which he depends for ideological guidance, Goffman's "ethnomethodological" work is per se largely atheoretical.

Goffman's approach to methodology ignores the fact that meaning, as the embodied performance of speech, exemplifies the distribution of *human desire* and *social power*. Such desire begins as a message within social interaction, sustains its force in communication, and legitimizes itself as power in such practical institutions (codes) as *cultural demand* and *social preference*. Recall that each message is communication theoretic; it is a choice of context. For example, human communication locates itself within the context of: (1) Consciousness, (2) Culture, (3) Civilization, and (4) Nature. These epistemological concepts are insightfully illustrated, for example, in the many works of Foucault that provide a theoretically informed diagnosis of institutions such as the hospital and the prison,[13] organizations Goffman has characterized as the "total institution."[14] These institutions are, of course, discovered in the practices of social communication and in the contributing discourse of the person. Foucault notes that (1) *communication* actualizes the cultural demands of human interaction (e.g., the concepts of person, society, physical reality, and myth) which display human *choice* in the form of desire (e.g., values that are human, group, material, and spiritual) and (2) communication concretizes the *practice* of *culture* (e.g., the negative social preferences manifest in xenophobia, alienation, ethnocentrism, and anomie) as the *context* of *power*.[15] Figure 1 (see Appendix D) illustrates this dynamic of the practice of choice. While Foucault's interests are similar to Goffman's, Foucault's work is theoretically informed by an explicit view of semiotic phenomenology.

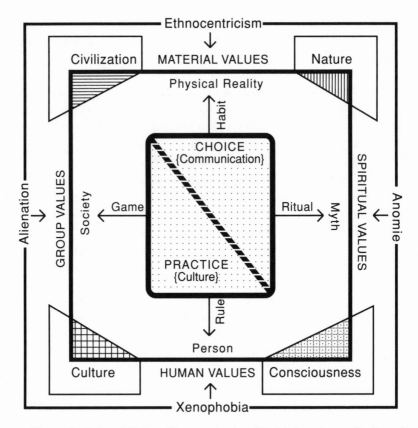

Figure 1. Cultural Values Communication Model (see Appendix D and Table 1).

Legend:

Choice and Practice operate according to a digital and analogue logic of differentiation.
Digital Logic:
1. Two values in disjunction [true or false, good or bad, etc.],
2. Choice establishes differences [either/or, neither/nor].
3. Practice establishes form [knowledge; "way to do it"].
4. Information Theory: Context of Choice for Choosing.
Analogue Logic:
1. Two or more values in combination [more and less, great and small, etc.].
2. Choice establishes similarities [both/and, in/out, up/down].
3. Practice establishes structure [understanding; "know how"].
4. Communication Theory: Choice of Context for Choosing.

THE QUESTION OF METHOD AND THEORY

Following the theory and application of human science research by Maurice Merleau-Ponty, the phenomenological method consists of a three step procedure: phenomenological description, reduction, and interpretation.[17] *Reflexitivity* where each step of the method is entailed in every other step, is a necessary theoretical condition of phenomenology.

Thus in the frame of theory, Step One, a description is an initial account of (1) the depiction (description per se) that accounts for a human awareness of *what* a phenomenon is, (2) the reduction of that description to an essence (a fundamental account of *how* the description has meaning), and (3) the interpretation that is implicit practically in the description or *why* a meaning is manifest by the analysis of the description. In turn, Step Two, the *reduction*, entails a second reflection and analysis repeating each step of description, reduction, and interpretation. Although it is most difficult part of the theory, the reduction step is also the most insightful stage of understanding (*savoir*). It amounts to a precise definition of the necessary condition (e.g., a typology) of the subject matter that is merely a sufficient condition under description (e.g., a token). Last, Step Three, the *interpretation*, is the concrete application to which the combined description and reduction point (e.g., a tone or contextual style of awareness in which the realization of a phenomenon as belonging to a particular typology is constituted by our awareness of this particular, concrete phenomenon as a token per se). Once again, the interpretive or hermeneutic step consists of a phenomenological description, reduction, and interpretation. A simple and familiar language example of the overall three-step theory is the eidetic model of the linguistic meaning of words (an empirical experience) in which connotation (a description) is linked to denotation (a reduction) and is the basis of all meanings (an interpretation) for the given word (type) as used in a certain situation (token) by a specific person (tone). The reflexivity of analytical categories in phenomenological theory has the following structure:

1. Phenomenological Description:
   a. Description;
   b. Reduction;
   c. Interpretation.
2. Phenomenological Reduction:
   a. Description;
   b. Reduction;
   c. Interpretation.
3. Phenomenological Interpretation.
   a. Description;
   b. Reduction;
   c. Interpretation.

In other words, every category is entailed by every other category. The procedure by which these theoretical conditions are implemented in methodological terms will be discussed momentarily, because the methodological arrangement of categories represents a variation of sequence from that of the theory I have outlined. But before considering the methodological perspective, a brief comment must be made about research perspective.

In the rhetoric of "normal science," in which "scientific method" is assumed to be its own theoretical explanation, positivist researchers assume that the order of analysis (OA) is identical to the order of experience (OE). This view allows the so-called "objective" condition where the researcher is assumed not to be present, not to be an influence on the research act (figure 2). By comparison, the phenomenologist is directly concerned to account for the researcher in the activity of doing research. As Don Ihde demonstrates, the phenomenologist approaches the situation with true objectivity (accounting practically for subjectivity) by carefully following out the sequence of experience being examined in contrast to the experience of doing the research per se.[18] In short, the phenomenologist reverses the order of experience and the order of analysis to make the experience of research practice match the practical order of the lived through experienced under investigation. Thus in the phenomenological procedure, the positivist's preconceived "logical" sequence of experience is backtracked (Husserl's *epoché* or "bracketing") in analysis (figure 2).

In a strictly *methodological* sense that incorporates the theoretical conditions just explained, we can make three procedural statements. These criteria state the semiotic code (communicative message) conditions for the phenomenology of the situation as lived by a person. The phenomenology quite literally becomes the logic of a governing *phenomena* found in the meaning of the situation under study (see Appendix E). Meaning, the signs composed of signifiers and signifieds, constitute the subject/object matter under analysis. Signifiers are simply the expressions or expressive elements in communication that contain the *symbols, index, or icons* of the context, message, contact, and code communicated by one person (addresser) to another (addressee). By contrast, signifieds are the perceptions or perspective functions in communication that contain the *referents or interpretants* of the context, message, contact, and code communicated by one person to someone else. Roman Jakobson's well known model of human communication[19] and its semiotic grounding in Pierce and Hjelmselv[20] are usually assumed as definitional in such analyses (figure 3).

Phenomenologist's Paradigm

[experience = that which is *taken* in analysis: *Capta*]

OE --------------------------------->
{experiencer > experiencing > experienced}

<--------------------------------- OA
{experiencer < experiencing < experienced}

Positivist's Paradigm

[experience = that which *given* prior to analysis: *Data*]

OE --------------------------------->
{experiencer > experiencing > experienced}

OA --------------------------------->
{experiencer > experiencing > experienced}

Figure 2. Comparative Research Procedure Involving the Order of Experience (OE) and the Order of Analysis (OA).

CONTEXT
[*referential*]

MESSAGE
[*poetic*]

ADDRESSER — — — — — — — — ADDRESSEE
[*emotive*]   [*conative*]

CONTACT
[*phatic*]

CODE
[*metalinguistic*]

Figure 3. Jakobson's Semiotic Phenomenological Model of Human Communication Theory indicating ELEMENTS and [functions] respectively.

In this communication theory context, therefore, phenomenological methodology has the following structure:

1. Description (Thematizing the)
    2. Interpretation (of the)
    3. Reduction (of the)
    4. Description (of the Sign[s])
5. Reduction (Abstracting the)
    6. Interpretation (of the)
    7. Reduction (of the)
    8. Description (of the Signifier[s])
9. Interpretation (Explicating the)
    10. Interpretation (of the)
    11. Reduction (of the)
    12. Description (of the Signified[s])[21]

Within this schema, we can correctly surmise that Goffman follows the first four steps, known as *descriptive phenomenology*. The Goffman schema of frame, strip, and analysis (as presented in his book *Frame Analysis: An Essay on the Organization of Experience*) roughly corresponds to the phenomenological description, reduction, and interpretation. If we correlate Goffman's steps and the phenomenological schemata, a taxonomy emerges in which a research project description consists of (a) the *frame* or method steps one and two—"thematizing of the interpretation," (b) the *strip* or method steps two and three—"interpretation of the reduction," and (c) the *analysis* or method steps three and four—"reduction of the description [of the Sign]."

Goffman does not use the phenomenological method steps five through eight. Adding these steps to the first four would constitute a theoretical base for the descriptive phenomenology, by way of historical comparison, and the resulting model would constitute what is called an *eidetic (transcendental) phenomenology* in the tradition of Husserl and James. Nor does Goffman use steps nine through twelve as a supplement to the model, which would be to adopt the semiotic phenomenology illustrated in the present book and by the work of Schütz, Merleau-Ponty, and Foucault.[22]

We should note that in the quasitheoretical discussion that constitutes the introduction to Goffman's book, *Frame Analysis,*

he does provide a pointed discussion of his debt to the phenomenological tradition, mentioning by specific chronology
the heritage of Franz Brentano, Husserl, James, and Schütz. He
suggests that he follows the phenomenological concepts of
"bracketing" (description), "typicality" (reduction), and "code"
(interpretation). Yet all these affirmations of the primacy of
phenomenological method are clearly not a theoretical priority. As Goffman says of his book and the model it expresses, "I
personally hold society to be first in every way and any individual's current involvements to be second; this report deals only
with matters that are second."[23] In the context of contemporary
thought, such a statement accords with a *structuralist* position
that champions the analysis of *langue,* or the speech community dialect of individuals, over the study of *parole,* or the individual and interpersonal speaking action (Husserl's *factum*) of
the person that constitutes culture (the interpersonal transmission of meaning as human choice and practice). Goffman
merely generalizes the theoretical distinction of Saussure's
linguistics to the broad realm of social action. But the structuralist distinction is still operative in Goffman's applications,
a particular example of which is his inductive generalization
of "radio talk" to the processes of everyday interpersonal
communication in *Forms of Talk.*[24]

The methodological judgment that we can render is this:
Goffman is a methodological "phenomenologist," but at the
price of being atheoretical. The reason is quite clear. To adopt
the communication theory of phenomenology (which I
designated as communicology in chapter one), would require
a focus on the human conscious experience (choice and practice) of the person, of one who cannot be conceived as an
isolated sociological "individual" merely interacting with other
isolated individuals, or as Jakobson would describe it, as an
addresser only among other addressers. On the other hand,
Goffman cannot adopt the structuralist theory that would be
compatible with his claim to privilege methodologically the
action of society and its members as a collective constraint on
the individual, an addressee only among other "addressees."
Such a stance would require that he abandon the lived-world
context of everyday experience in which he conducts all his

field research, albeit at a distance of supposed detachment characteristic of the positivist spirit. As even Goffman's unabashed admirers concede, this tension of theory versus method is ever present. For example, Christopher Ricks, referring to the *Forms of Talk* chapter entitled "Radio Talk: A Study of the Ways of Our Errors," notes that "after all, his witticism 'the ways of our errors' depends upon our momentarily blinking at what might itself be an error."[25] No matter how rhetorically appealing Goffman may make the imputed claim, method is not theory and technique is no substitute for the reality of conscious experience.

LISTENING TO THE RADIO: AN EXAMPLE OF APPLICATION

In order to illustrate the consequences of Goffman's atheoretical approach to research, I am selecting a brief section of the *Frame Analysis* book in which he analyzes the "radio drama frame" as a particular case of the more general idea of "the theatrical frame."[26] Goffman beings his research report and analysis with the suggestion that radio (a phenomenon of human expression and perception) is a special frame inasmuch as we are concerned with sound perception while we attend to the mechanical aspects of radio transmission.

We are apparently listening under a very special condition or *strip* of consciousness unfolding as a perceptual experience. As he says, "a basic feature of radio as the source of a strip of dramatic interaction is that transmitted sounds cannot be selectively disattended."[27] In other words, the dramatic frame only permits the listener to have a *diachronic notion of time* in which one event follows another in the sense of a linear historical series of events. This is true of all basic sound expressions in the phenomenology of a message, whether they be the sound expression of an objective situation (the scene of action; a description), the expression of human speech (actors as characters in the story; a reduction of description) or in that of music (the mood for affective meaning; the interpretation of the reduction of the description).

First, it seems true that in the dramatic presentation of the radio program, the "multiple channel effect" of ordinary everyday life sound perception is destroyed. This is to say, in the "multiple reality" of everyday life (to borrow a phrase from Schütz), we are simultaneously listening to the sounds of many different sources—other people talking at once, the noise of machines and activities, the sounds of animals and nature, and so on. Yet, in all of this apparent cacophony, a human being has both (1) a focus on sound—one thing or person is listened to and has our attention as a source of expression—as an addresser, and (2) a locus of sound—one thing or person is the referent of our perception—as an addressee. A radio transmission cannot duplicate this human conscious experience as a multichannel transmission (although stereo or quadraphonic audio transmissions gives a "magic act" illusion by dividing the apparent directional source of sound). In point of fact, human listening and human speaking are empirical examples of the "law of participation" that flies in the face of the positivist belief in a deductive model of reality (see appendix A). The radio presentation must convert the embodied awareness (focus and locus) of human sound expression/perception into a complex, but linear, progression of sound that moves our focus (*what* we pay attention to) from place to place in order to create the illusion of one locus (*how* we attend, i.e., listen, see, touch, imagine we can speak, etc.).

As a quick illustration, let me recall Goffman's discussion of the combination of the human voice and music. In a radio drama, a story is told through the voices of characters in a play or other radio drama. The "sound effects" person creates the noise of nature and social activity as a background for the actor's voice. A character in a scene emerges in these sounds to create a sense of focus and locus: we known who is talking and where the character is. But the problem of time, the problematic of consciousness per se as an experience remains.

How can the radio drama create a sense of time that is not bound to the expected linear progression of temporal history that moves from past to present to future? The production answer is music used as a symbol with its own referential value as meaning. Musical sound can play the symbolic role of time and move the required referential scene of action and people from place to place in any *time order*. As Goffman notes, there is the "realm status of an event."[28] The realm is the basic notion of a foreground and background combination of speech versus music. For example, an impression of "actual" experience is signaled by loud foreground music (with a quite background of human voices) that is slowly muted in order to reverse the situation. Human voices become louder as a foreground perception and the music quiets into the background. The radio program staff has thereby created an "actualization" of conscious experience.

A "bridge" occurs in radio program production when music is suddenly foregrounded and we all know that the scene of action is changing; we expect new characters saying new things. We are willing, therefore, to accept any time change using the basic elements of present or past or future. Music can also be a message that "foretells" or codes events. In this case where we see Jakobson's communication element of "contact" at work, music is used as a signature to any event, i.e., every time we hear the same music the process of locus and focus are reversed. Music causes a locus; we know the same thing is about to happen again, and how is not in question. Yet we still do not know what will happen to whom this time; we have no focus.

If the radio program director wishes to reverse our understanding of these instrumental musical cues for time in the drama, the human voice can simultaneously become the music. In a "musical" performance the characters break into song at various points in the dramatic action. With this signing technique, the character is an immediate focus, and we lose locus. We have a brief moment where we are suspending the space of the situation in order to engage a moment of pure time. While the character sings, we are involved with her in the social understanding of affective meaning; we are concerned with emotion as a function of communication. We forget the aspects of space and location; we suspend cognitive meaning and its imperative demand for a sense of "reality."

Given Goffman's analysis of the radio frame, we immediately can see that the analysis is phenomenological in method, but atheoretical. The radio frame is an accurate description and depiction of the experience people have when they, as addressees, listen to radio dramas. It is phenomenological description. But there is no reduction and interpretation because these steps would lead to individual interpretation of a given radio frame, and Goffman wants to avoid that possibility. Indeed, Goffman wishes to avoid any consideration of the embodied audience: the people, individual persons, experience the radio frame as a lived-experience, as a personal and *not* a public experience as Goffman supposes.

At this person/group juncture in the analysis, it is important to point out that even in the "microsociology" of the radio audience that Goffman gives us in *Forms of Talk*, the audience is given as a holistic collective entity and at the very least is preconceived to be an aggregate displaying group typicalities in society. Indeed, "radio and television audiences are not only large but also heterogeneous in regard to 'sensitivities': ethnicity, race, religion, political belief, gender, regional loyalties, and all the physical and mental stigmata."

It is unfortunate for us to realize that Goffman's radio frame description, while it accords with the possibility of personal experience, is in no way reduced and interpreted as the "typicality" that you or I can experience. To be specific, I mean the typicality of *my experience* (or yours) as a person, an experience which is the consistency of my process of awareness as I repeatedly live through similar listening experiences with the radio. I do not mean the typicality of social experience as a collective category that we all can agree fits the *conception* of what is typical in a speculative sense of assumed practice (the positivist notion of a "social convention"). Rather, and on reflection of the phenomenological reduction and interpretation type, it becomes obvious to each of us as a person in the audience (not as audience members) that the "multiple channel effect" dismissed to easily by Goffman is still with each of us, personally considered, compared, and constituted. Our consciousness is a phenomenology of description (consideration), reduction (comparison), and interpretation (constitution) of the sound phenomenon we call "radio".

When you and I listen to a particular radio drama and experience it as a frame (context), it is in the real world of other "channel" and "media" influences. We hear other sound messages in our personal listening situation and that is precisely why the radio sounds can have foreground focus and locus. Indeed, our sensations and intellections are a *synergism* of perception (recall Merleau-Ponty's many demonstrations in his *Phenomenology of Perception*) in which our embodied experience is always that of explicit *synesthesia* (one encoded sense is decoded by integration in another sense; e.g., to "see texture" or "sing the blues"). As persons in the audience listening to the radio program, we bring a theory to the situation. From our social and cultural background experience, we perform a phenomenological reduction on the radio frame. We select it as the signifier in the situation. We accept the radio message (the radio drama frame) as the expression of meaning that is the essence of the description of human life (i.e., *our* life, our conscious experience of the meaning that these radio sound typifications express).

When we accept the "code" of the radio drama frame, we go along with the narrative structure of the story and accept it as drama. We allow our personal interpretation of the message to be the one with *our* meaning.[30] We understand in the way that we as persons *desire to understand*. We are choosing the context of our meaning as we live it. For example, one of the best relevant illustrations of this phenomenological procedure is *Radio Days*, the 1987 film by Woody Allen. This film is another example of synergism and synesthesia inasmuch as it expresses visually for the eye the same phenomena that the radio drama expresses aurally for the ear.

To make such an analysis as I describe it, Goffman would have to accept a theory of the person and the primacy of Schütz's multiple reality as lived by the person and not as a structural artifact (the "individual" or "member") of society. Goffman rejects such a view except insofar as he looks upon it from afar with a positivist's assumed objectivity and imputed generalization. How Goffman would theoretically justify the validity of his methodological description, in the radio drama frame for example, is an open question—by choice. His atheoretical research leaves us without an answer. At best, we might conclude that method alone is a sufficient theory. In following such a view we cannot fault Goffman, for this argument is, needed, the atheoretical sophism by which much of positive science also justifies its claim to objectivity. Ironically, Ricks uses just such an explanation to justify Goffman's work as belonging to literary criticism, not to social science.[31]

So, just as I began my analysis in this second chapter with a question (Is Erving Goffman a phenomenologist?), I could end with the question unresolved. In that case, I should be accepting Goffman's methodology as a sufficient theory. Systematic description of *ritual* (see figure 1) would have occurred, but our desire to *understand* cultural meaning, and to *recognize* the exercise of social power in communication would remain undisclosed as a *game*. Instead, I have taken Goffman's frame analysis into the theoretical arena of phenomenology proper by providing both the reduction (an account of *habit*) and interpretation (an account of personal *rule*) steps to his description step of method. In so doing, I illustrate how the phenomenological theorist can improve on the legacy of Goffman. Yet I am also forced to conclude on theoretical grounds that Goffman is not a phenomenologist in the traditional and usually accepted meaning of that name, because I insist on cross-checking his research conclusion with persons in their lived-world, not that world formed (even at the micro-level) by the naive realism of the researcher. Thus to reverse Goffman's paraphrase of his own perspective and thereby state the phenomenologist's perspective, I am suggesting that as a phenomenologist "I personally hold the *person* to be first in every way and any of society's current involvements to be second; this chapter deals only with matters that are first." In this reversal, we are motivated to keep straight the theoretical applications of choice and practice, desire and power. Communicated messages are evidence of a *subjectivity* (choice, desire) that *is* (law of participation) coded as *intersubjectivity* (practice, power) which is, of course, the provocative original thesis of the founder of the reflexive theory and method of phenomenology, Edmund Husserl.

3

Silent Science

On the Semiotic Phenomenology of Cultural Media (Art vs. Television)

T elevision exemplifies both a problematic and a thematic for the appreciation of the communicative elements that constitute cultural media. Television is a medium for transmitting the message of human values that is Culture per se. Our familiarity with television, however, tends to obscure the fact that there are other media which better inform the paradigm of communicated cultural meanings. The fine arts like painting and sculpture are an especially good example of the media accounting for what anthropologists (see Appendix C) call "cultural transmission."[1] Television in its practical function as an "ascetic imperative" can also obscure the affective richness with which culture transmits its meaning in the medium we call *people*.[2] In fact, Langsdorf argues that "certain ideas, which are foundational for our sense of value, are intrinsically absent in the video text."[3]

We often forget in the naive realism of our everyday lives that our own particular cultures, whether oriental or occidental, make *us* the media of communication per se.[4] We are just beginning to explore theoretically the human meanings of televisual experience within the boundaries of such an embodied "phenomenology of media."[5] Tom McFeat's extraordinary small group culture research on the human *group* as a *medium* of communication notwithstanding, more attention needs to be paid to the media of the masses within the context of cultural transmission.[6] That is, we should look to the typicality to be found in the social collection of personal practices, arts, and artifacts used as channels of expression and perception. The fine, performing, and visual arts are the media which constitutes a *silent science* of personal and social practice that accounts for the lived-reality we call "Culture" (see appendix E). In the qualitative research tradition of the human sciences (*Geisteswissenschaften*) this appreciation for the value of everyday practices remembered as, and in, art is the teaching of Lévy-Bruhl's cultural "law of participation" (see appendix A). And I think it is worth remembering as a resource for the integration of communication and cultural studies.[7]

Semiotic phenomenology is a human science research methodology within the discipline of Communicology which begins empirically at the point of human meaning, self-expressed and self-perceived in the *person* (see chapter 9). It is unlike positivist notions of "media culture" that hypostatize a "mass media or information society" as a theoretical condition of social analysis.[8] The three part phenomenological procedures of description, reduction, and interpretation, combined with the semiotic view of meaning as constituted in coded signs (signifiers/signifieds), offer a theoretically established and empirically illustrated research approach in the human sciences. The many applied studies of cultural practice by Maurice Merleau-Ponty and Michel Foucault are especially good illustrations, as is shown in chapters 5 and 6 especially.

In this third chapter, I first illustrate briefly these methodological themes phenomenologically developed as a cultural discourse within the communicative media of painting (a two dimensional medium). In a second section, I explore the theoretical connection of television and painting (as two dimensional) to sculpture and human interaction (both three dimensional media). As Langsdorf insightfully suggests, "In regard to visual experience, our inventions allow us to see what is too far or too small to be seen naturally, as well as to see what cannot be seen naturally: ourselves in a range of activities."[9]

Semiotic phenomenology is surely a method with theoretical commitments in the study of communicology, the most important of which is that human beings expressing themselves in their own lived-discourse are the best source of facts when it comes to analyzing why they are creators and beholders of meaning.[10] Let us begin here, now, with ourselves by undertaking a practical and empirical (i.e., experienced by people) illustration of applied qualitative research. First, I offer a brief illustration of applied research using the methodology of semiotic phenomenology. With Merleau-Ponty, we discover in this example that art in its communicological modality as culture is a practice of "silent science."[11]

THE METHOD OF SEMIOTIC PHENOMENOLOGY

As a way of facilitating the methodological discussion of semiotic phenomenology, I shall in due course want to situate the explication in the context of an interpersonal communication textbook commonly used in the discipline of communicology, Gail and Michele Myers' 1985, *The Dynamics of Human Communication: A Laboratory Approach.*

At this juncture, let me make an important comment for contextual purposes. Another textbook that offers a more advanced theoretical parallel to semiotic phenomenology is the 1977 Smith and Williamson *Interpersonal Communication.*[12] Chapter 4 of this text presents the Laing, Phillipson, and Lee 1966 model of interpersonal perception and expression based on an *abductive logic* consisting of the "direct perspective" (phenomenological description), the "metaperspective" (phenomenological reduction), and the "meta-metaperspective" (phenomenological interpretation).[13] From a qualitative research point of view, it is important to note that the Laing, et al., model has been validated using a Boolean logic transformation in deductive logic.[14] While this fact is theoretically contrary to Lévy-Bruhl's "participation" thesis, I note it simply to remind readers that logic (necessary and sufficient condition

rule) has always been a preferable theory construction procedure to that of mathematics/statistics (truth condition rule)
in the empirical study of interpersonal human communication, as we just saw in the review of Goffman's methodology in
chapter 2. Let us now return to the Myers' textbook and its
model of communicology where I am explicitly taking the "real
world" approach explaining how the phenomenological method can be used in the study of art (exemplified in the fine art
of painting) as aesthetic communication (one level of symbols)
linked to the representation of interpersonal communication
(a second level of symbols).

The Meyer define one dimension of human communication
as *interpersonal communication*. This dimension is characterized
by the fact that there is "a transaction between people and
their environment."[15] Of course, the environment most nota-
bly contains other *people* in particular, or a general (generated
by Rationality) concept of the *Other* such as "God," "Nature," or
the humanistic invention of "Man." Yet it is more likely to
contain additional and important contextual *representations* of
other people. Most of what we come to know about another
person is semiotic in an obvious sense. That is, we note the
symbolic, iconic, and indexical import of the person's clothing,
their manner of speaking and gesturing, and so on, as system-
codes in our society and culture. We tend to pay less attention
to how those persons are situated in the world, how the system-
codes are embodied by all of us as conscious experience in the
choices we make and in the practices we perform (see figure
1). We tend to assume a positivistic "natural attitude" about the
context in which we perceive them: their "environment" is just
"there," as it is supposed to be. What we lack is the phenomenological sensitivity of a person living in the complex sign-
system of Self-Other-World described by Merleau-Ponty, and
the parallel system of Subject-Power-Knowledge depicted by
Foucault, that is the everyday social reality of humanity.[16]

As the Meyers explain in the introduction to their book,
interpersonal communication is a dimension of human communication that is differentiated from technology and mass
media. Media is a *symbolic presentation* of communication behavior. Technology is a *channel* of communication in which

images of behavior *re-present* the actual conscious experience you or I live through as a human being. For example, the mass media present me with visual and sound images, whereas by contrast, I am witness to actual interpersonal communication events and situations: I experience transactions between people and their environments. Because these media images are *active* and *dynamic* (video tape and pictures appear true),[17] I shall tend to think that my witnessing experience is passive and static. Apparently, I just sit there watching and listening.

Rather, my perception is a parallel process to that of expression. Because I am watching a representation (perceived as presentation) of interaction that is active and dynamic (e.g., an event on "video"), the understanding (*savoir*) that I bring to my interpretation of the representational images (visual or oral) is also active and dynamic (Jakobson's distinctive feature).[18] The presentation, my lived-through-experience, a *memory* in consciousness, matches the representation, an image or symbol of such an experience that I recognize as my own, as one I have had (Jakobson's redundancy feature). Schütz calls this phenomenology of meaning the "we experience."[19] That is, I see (image) my experience in the behavior of another person. This experience can range from simply understanding what someone else is doing at the moment that I see them do it to the *desire* to be like, and live like (*power*), another person that I perceive as special in some way. In most instances, that "some way" is a shared experience, our World, the shared cultural experience of living a moment together, or, in the long term, of "growing old together" in Schütz's epigram. Or the "some way" can take on a negative dynamic of rhetoric or ideology in the forms of xenophobia, alienation, ethnocentrism, and anomie (see figure 1).

One way to perceive that my perception of representational images is active and dynamic is to experience a communication image that is static and passive in presentation (e.g., in a work of art like the painting *Las Meninas* that Foucault uses as a thematic subject matter in *The Order of Things*). Such a painting is the reverse of the television or film experience where the image is *experienced as* (but is not in fact) an active and dynamic discourse. For this reason, I shall turn in a moment directly to

the less complex experience of painting to illustrate the semiotic phenomenological method in communicology.

By using a "semiotic square" (cf. Figure 5) in which we are
using the value judgments of the the system (static : dynamic::
passive : active), a similar comparison might be made between
the usual television experience of a photograph (static-passive)
and a motion picture (dynamic-active). A more complex comparison is evident in Umberto Eco's *hypercoding*, where watching a black and white film on television with musical sound
(static-active) is compared with the experience of a television
program in color with stereo sound (dynamic-passive).[20] Remember at this point, I am not interpreting what different
television program images and formats are or can be as significations, but rather how persons are able to interpret them
as meanings, i.e., as images (a representation) based on our
own lived-through experience which is always with us in our
memory as a coded presentation of meaning.

Such memories of desire and power are the criteria we use
to decode the representation and make the image have a
meaning. It is not just the idea of a meaning (i.e., a signification), but *my meaning* as an interpreting act. An excellent illustration of this process of differentiation is the current contro-
versy about "colorizing" old black and white movies for television. It does not matter whether you are "for" or "against" the
process, since in either case you perceive *correct meaning* as a
presentation-representation linkage in your primary lived-
experience as cultural memory. That is, younger persons raised
as children on color television tend to like (perceive as normal)
colorization of movies for TV: a positive, analogue *comparison.*
Their parents, who were reared on color movies and black and
white television do not like (perceive as abnormal) colorization
generally: a negative, digital *contrast.* I might suggest the parallel example of language perception, examined in detail in
chapter 8, in which a child is likely to see nothing wrong with
the aphorism: "I lie, I speak." No adult will hear that comment
passively.

As we will note later in the analysis of the painting *Las
Meninas,* to encounter a painting is to have an *aesthetic* experience (meaning in presentation) and, second, a *communica-*

tion experience (meaning in representation). The painting (passive, static) becomes an aesthetic experience (active, dynamic) as I intersubjectively encounter it. Of course, the process is transactional and reflexive: my discourse becomes a communication experience (passive, static, representation) of the aesthetic experience (active, dynamic, presentation). Thus, my communication always has an aesthetic consequence for me and the people I encounter; I constitute meaning in a cultural medium which is my own embodied practice (see figure 1). Fine art becomes an excellent example of this phenomenology of communication, the conscious experience of presentation and re-presentation in which the painting per se and the aesthetic experience are a discursive transaction between people and their environment.[21]

At this point, I want to be careful not to confuse semiotic phenomenology with traditional notions of positivist "art criticism." Art criticism as an academic genre is a very legitimate goal, but not the one with which I am concerned. As Isenberg points out, there is

> a theory of criticism, widely held in spite of its deficiencies, which divides the critical process into three parts. There is the value judgment or *verdict* (V): 'This picture or poem is good—.' There is a particular statement or *reason* (R): '—because it has such-and-such a quality—'. And there is a general statement or *norm* (N): '—and any work which has that quality is *protanto* good'.[22]

This "natural attitude" theory of art criticism illustrates the positivist view of *media culture* as it may be found in the fine arts, especially in painting. You may also recognize it as descriptive of more positivistic approaches to the critical study of television and other visual "mass media."

By comparison, the semiotic phenomenological approach (literally the "sign logic of a phenomenon") to the communicological analysis of meaning in cultural media procedurally requires the three steps, sign description, signifier reduction, and signified interpretation. Now, let me describe the method of semiotic phenomenology in a self-reflexive theoretical manner for which discourse practice is simultaneously an example of itself in presentation.

1. DESCRIPTION: The procedure is one of describing the interpersonal experience of encountering the phenomenon as a re-presentation of a signification that you recognize in the situation, in others and yourself (such as a painting—my referential example for continuing analysis). Ask yourself: *What am I experiencing?* Try starting with "I am conscious of . . . ", or, you might begin by completing the sentence: "To *me*, it is. . . . " When you engage the "to me" or *direct perspective*[23] on meaning, you are using facts to describe, a practice usually referred to as "cognitive meaning" or the "world perspective" of the "natural reality." Recall the Meyers' definition of interpersonal communication: "a transaction between people and *their environment.*" (emphasis mine) The description, in other words, specifies those discursive *signs* or Hjelmslevian *relations* that depict the signifier/signified (expression/perception) elements and functions of *human* communication.[24] Here I refer directly to Jakobson's model (based on Hjelmslev) of communication theory, whereby *elements* consist of the addresser, addressee, context, message, contact, and code, and the respective *functions*, emotive (expressive), conative, referential, poetic, phatic, and metalinguistic (see appendix B).[25]

2. REDUCTION: This procedure is one of abstracting or reducing to a definition of communication your description (the statements made in #1) of the interpersonal experience of encountering the painting. Ask yourself: *How* am I experiencing? Try starting with "Other people, who know me, would say I am conscious of. . . " or, you might try completing the sentence: "To me, *myself*, it is. . . " "Myself" in this context is used to voice the alterity viewpoint that another person would take; it is, if you will, an "alter ego" or "*metaperspective.*" When you use the "to me, myself" perspective, you are basically using the perspective of personal *emotions* to define—and this definition is usually referred to as "affective meaning" or the "other's perspective" in the "social reality."

Do not forget that the phenomenological analysis is *synergistic* (the whole is greater than the sum of the parts) and *syncretic* (the whole is a higher type than the parts in a normative logic), so in the Reduction step of the analysis, you are using emotions to define the facts you described.[26] This is another way of saying that you are discovering that "facts" are more complicated than they seem—the conceived "facts" are mediated or "filtered" through the "fact" of your emotional (expressive) perspective. This emotional perspective is literally imagination, an imaging (or expressive perception) that you construct by code to represent the view of an other person, modeled on your own constituted view of your Self.[27] Your comparative interpersonal experience of writing and reading personal letters is another ready illustration of this symbolic process. Return again to the Meyers' definition of interpersonal communication: "a transaction *between people* and their environment." (emphasis mine) Thus, the reduction specifies which signifiers or discursive elementst express the essential meaning of the description.

3. INTERPRETATION: This procedure involves interpreting the meaning of the reduction of the description. Ask yourself: *Why* I am I experiencing? Try starting with "I, who know myself, would have said I am truly conscious of . . ." or, you might try completing the sentence: "To me, myself, *I* judge it to be. . . . ." When you use the combined "to me, myself, I" perspective on meaning (*meta-metaperspective*), you are using vaues to judge or choose. This is usually referred to as "conative meaning" or the "self-perspective" in the "personal/existential reality." Here again, you should remember the synergistic effect, namely, that in the interpretation step of the analysis, you are discovering a value judgment by using emotions to define the facts you described in your analysis. At this point, you have explicated the very complex phenomenon called "aesthetic judgment" in "interpersonal communication." That is, facts, emotions, and values do not occur in isolation—they are constituted reflexively by human interaction in both the Self-Other-World and Subject-Power-Knowledge communication system. Consider the Meyers' definition of interpersonal communication with yet a third emphasis: "*a transaction* between people and their environment." In short, the interpretation step of the analysis allows the researcher to specify the *signified* or *perceived* element in the reduced signs of the description.

The Meyers' discussion of the "Communication Case" offers a parallel, analogical explication of the phenomenological approach.[28] They call their steps (1) The Description of the

Problem; (2) The Analysis, and (3) Your Reactions. Please note that this "case" discussion is meant as a phenomenon displaying validity: a typical and, therefore, definitional experience. Validity is defined by the logic of typicality (sufficient condition) in a category (necessary condition) and is *not* an illustration of a "case study" as a statistical notion where a population "n of 1" is hypostatized for generalization.

Thus to summarize, the conceptual and applied phenomenological relationships, as Foucault would say, name a "discourse" within which choices, practices, and meanings are constituted as follows:

Step 1: DESCRIPTION [Laing's direct perspective]

= Fact	= Cognition	= World; Knowledge	= Me	= Case Description

Step 2: REDUCTION [metaperspective]

= Definition	= Affection	= Other; Power	= Myself	= Case Analysis

Step 3: INTERPRETATION [meta-metaperspective]

= Value	= Conation	= Self; Subject	= I	= Case Reactions

Please note that there is not some timeless single "correct" answer to a phenomenological analysis, such as the positivist's assumption that only one "interpretation" is correct. Even the most positivistic of sciences no longer purport to accept such an idealistic standard for either a "unified science" or a "single reality." Any such universal answer would simply bypass the meaningful human acts of analyzing, choosing, and understanding in order to posit a signification external to the analyzed phenomenon. You can do this sort of analysis, but it becomes positivistic art criticism, or another example of media culture at work as an imposing institution. As Baudrillard suggests, you will simply place your analysis in a context where "information devours its own contents." That is to say, "instead of causing communication, *it exhausts itself in the act* of staging the communication; instead of producing meaning, it exhausts itself in the staging of meaning."[29] Thus, Baudrillard recommends that we stop making sense in communication to forestall the media system operation of re-presentation.

In short, we need to avoid idealist standards for reality whether in a positive science or in a positive politics. Rather, the valid methodological use of phenomenological description, reduction, and interpretation allows the *constitution of meaning* (i.e., a communication theory depiction by abstraction, not an information theory prediction by generalization). This usage can be shown as valid by locating a sufficient and/ or necessary condition in the *abductive logic* (rule + result = case) of the situation described.[30] Oral or written explications of how you constituted your meaning, thereby, can be tested against the *conditions of discovery* where the criterion for analytic validity is the presence of typicality.

Typicality is the ability first to abstract from an empirical exemplar those eidetic (conceptual) characteristics which define it and, in turn, to confirm the process by using the eidetic features to specify a second empirical example or the spatial/ temporal endurance of the original exemplar. These verbal *capta* (discovery; facts as taken) may be obtained using *topical protocols* in interviews with research respondents or from original protocol statements (which is what I use in the Levi example of painting below) that are descriptions of meaning as lived.[31]

A "sufficient condition" is an *experience* in the description that justifies the *understanding* (read: "reduction") of the *value judgment or conation* (read: "interpretation") that any person can make. That is, we make a judgment that we understand as possible in a defining way as a concept (eidetic) or as an experience (empirical). Do not confuse this sufficient condition with the positivist sociological view of a "situational definition." Rather, the sufficient condition is a *lived-through meaning* described by the *respondent,* not you. We sometimes refer to (merely signify) such "lived-through" sufficient condition experiences in our communication with others by saying, "You had to be there to understand" or "You won't understand until you do it yourself." The idea of meaning in practice is implicit here, even if the practice is conceptual or eidetic. But with a proper use of the phenomenological method, the meaning can be expressed as a discourse phenomenon. Your communicative discourse can create the meaning as a conscious experience for your listener. For example, we all know when our communication is successful in a practical sense, either because we are understood (eidetic) or the response behavior is appropriate (empirical); typicality validates our interpretation.

By comparison, a "necessary condition" is an idea or concept in the description that justifies our understanding of a value judgment: it is both a choice that we can see and one that we are all capable of making. Necessary conditions allow us intuitively or conceptually to understand possible situations where immediate experience is not yet a possibility. The syllogism is the most familiar example of necessary conditions at work. Although occasionally referred to as "thought experiments," necessary conditions are not just conceptual tests that substitute for the empirical tests researchers would run if they had some way of experiencing the phenomena existing beyond the range of human sensation. The necessary condition is the *meaning to be lived through,* a meaning that we now see as "what will have been," (to quote Schütz).[32] The necessary condition is a criterion without which a judgment cannot be made.

PAINTING: A FINE ARTS EXAMPLE
OF SEMIOTIC PHENOMENOLOGICAL ANALYSIS

The following example is a brief application of methodology using as a capta source the case protocol description written by a painter to depict the typicality of the aesthetic meaning he finds in his own lived through experience.

DESCRIPTION: In a protocol about himself, the French painter Julian Levi writes the following description of his lived experience of painting in his essay *Before Paris and After.*[33]

> I find it rather difficult to write about my own painting. Briefly, I am seeking an integration between what I feel and what I have learned by objective criteria; an integration between the tired ex-perienced eye and the childlike simple perception; but above all I hope to resolve the polarity which exists between an essentially emotional view of nature and a classical, austere sense of design. *"In truth, I have painted by opening my eyes day and night*

on the perceptible world, and also by closing them form time to time that I might better see the vision blossom and submit itself to orderly arrangement." This quotation from an article by Georges Rouault, which appeared in *Vevre*, is to me rich in meaning and summarizes, with Gallic brevity, precisely what I have been driving at.

It seems to me that almost every artist finds some subdivision of nature or experience more congenial to his temperament than any other. To me it has been the sea—or rather those regions adjacent to the sea—beaches, dunes, swampy coasts. I haven't the space to go to the roots of this particular nostalgia but it has been part of my life since early childhood.

As a secondary interest, I cherish the human physiognomy, the painting of people who, for diverse reasons, I find arresting. I seldom find my models among people of superlative beauty or symmetry. I am often fascinated by "brats" of eight or nine with stringy hair and querulous expressions. . . .

REDUCTION: Levi cites two definitions, one that is a denotative signifier (an eidetic reduction) and one that is a connotative signifier (an empirical reduction). The denotative or "dictionary-like" conceptual definition is the quotation in italics from Georges Rouault. Rouault expresses the idea of which Levi wants to be conscious (the eidetic signifier; a necessary condition). The connotative or "encyclopedia-like" experiential (empirical) definition is (1) his description *the shape of the sea* (or its mirror: the land) expressed in "those regions adjacent to the sea—beaches, dunes, swampy coasts" and (2) *the shape of people* expressed in "the human physiognomy. . . people. . . I find arresting." Levi expresses the experiences he has (the empirical signifier; a sufficient condition). Note the definitional use of the "to me" perspective and the first person narration.

INTERPRETATION: Why is there a signifier connection between the denotative and connotative meanings in the reduction? Why is Levi linking the shape of the sea recorded ("arresting") in coast lines with the shape of people recorded ("arresting") in body lines? Why is there (in English translation, which is our lived experience) an implied phonological game played with the words "sea" and "see"? Can it be that for

Levi (and us?) the "sea" of nature expresses a shape *that the art-ist must perceive*, while the vision (the "see" of humans—whether as "seeing" or being "seen") of the artist (and us?) is to perceive a shape that an artist must express (artistic vision stops, arrests)?

The essence (phenomenological meaning) of Levi's description and reduction is, therefore, taken from one of his *revelatory phrases* (see appendix B), namely, "find arresting." Just as Levi finds the quotation from Rouault "arresting," just as Levi finds coast lines and body lines "arresting," it is the unique "find" that is arresting in Nature. And, yet the "arrest" in personal experience is the human finding: "the querulous expressions." In fact and in deed, may we not rightly think of aesthetic perception as the complaining expression? In his autobiographical account, we come to realize what, how, and why Levi has signified an aesthetic consciousness of his artistic work. At the same time, we communicatively learn what it means to experience the aesthetic. The value judgments named by the words "find" and "arresting" are simultaneously sufficient and necessary conditions of meaning as signified.

Other meanings can be found to constitute the possibility of lived experience. You can justify yours by tracing out another "sign logic in the phenomenon" (phenomenon = Levi's "description" above), i.e., a reduction and interpretation that each of us personally can understand as an essential analysis of what Levi may mean by what he writes. The criteria for the constitution of meaning is to show that the analysis is justified by sufficient and necessary conditions abstracted directly from the described capta or data. As McLuhan argues, "Consciousness itself is an inclusive process not at all dependent on content" and "Consciousness does not postulate consciousness of anything in particular."[34]

By way of conclusion with this example analysis, I need only add that consciousness does constitute itself semiotically (the erroneous assumption made by Goffman as we saw in chapter 2). So the phenomenological condition of any eidetic or empirical phenomenon analyzed is an essential description of the possible phenomenon as lived. In other words, consciousness is itself an objective experience of participation in the

Self and stands in the position of the unseen spectator (an Other in the shared World). For example, there is the phenomenological analysis of the painting *Las Meninas*, and Foucault suggests that the same empirical argument for the rules of expression/perception is constituted in the viewer's encounter with René Magritte's painting titled discursively *Ceci n'est pas une pipe* [This is not a pipe] painted in 1926 (illustrating McLuhan's first comment), and in its own latter-day commentary entitled *Les Deux mystères* [The Two Mysteries] painted in 1966, which pictures a painting of the 1926 painting (illustrating McLuhan's second comment).[35] In Magritte's case the semiotics of language and image are intentionally called into question by the phenomenological reflexivity of expression and perception simultaneously actualized as presentation and realized as representation.[36] As we shall see momentarily, these Magritte paintings, like *Las Meninas*, are rare paradigms by which we may interrogate and concretize more complex images like those of television.

TELEVISION AS AN INTERPERSONAL METAPHOR OF ART

In the next paragraph, I offer a concrete event taken from the popular discourse of television. As a practice, this popular culture discourse-image constitutes a phenomenological description of a perceived television experience ("signs" in discourse). It is a phenomenological reduction of the description as an expression of human consciousness (the "signifiers" of discourse are presented in my ongoing parenthetical narrative beginning with this comment). And the example is a phenomenological interpretation.

MAX HEADROOM ON TV

Television viewers like us throughout the world, for the most part, now know that the name "Max Headroom" is a popular culture name for one's participation in television as a synthetic experience of expression and perception. For example, a recent issue of the popular French news magazine *L'Express* declares "We have been entertained with astonishment for four years now. Max was born as the perfect son of a computer, the pure synthesis of an immaterial face."[37] The article then explains that "the true face of Max" is *not* the "real life" comedian Matt Frewer (the series actor), but rather that "Matt" was sought out as a look-alike for "Max." This particular name, "Max Headroom," as a cultural medium, nominates a general experience (Matt Frewer is acting) best described phenomenologically as a semiotic fantasy or *media culture* phenomenon of a maxim (somebody real must look like the fictitious Max, if we can only find him). It is no accident here that a maxim is a commonplace in the rhetoric of popular culture in which, indeed, we are meant to experience the max image "max-im" as the "maximum immanence" or "maximum implosion" (Baudrillard's phrase) of everyday practice as mediated by technologies (on air, Max looks like the character *cum* reporter Edison Carter who really is Matt Frewer, a comedian now turned serious actor). As Foucault cautions, and yet again reminds us, "To *name* is at the same time to give a *verbal representation of a representation,* and to place it in a general table."[38]

"Max Headroom" is such a name; it becomes fantastic because the semiotic rule for interpretation of a sign (first level representation) and its meaning is reversed (second level representation). Todorov gives us the rule for fantasy: "What in the first world was an exception here becomes the rule."[39] In short, we have the *cultural practice* in which the fiction becomes the fact by a process in which metaphors "die" and become literal significations. Connotation takes up denotation as a practice phenomenon: Matt Frewer comedian for Matt Frewer actor; Matt Frewer actor for Max Headroom; Max Headroom substitutes for Edison Carter; Edison Carter for TV viewers; and so on. Another excellent example is the cartoon character analogue named *Max Headrest* (an icon fiction for Ronald Reagan, actor and President) who frequents the *Doonesbury* comic strip by Gary B. Trudeau.

As in all media culture, with Max we slip into the progressing metaphorical narrative (which like *this* nameless voice, this very parenthetical comment in this sentence which you are

now reading/hearing, comments on itself in your own conscious awareness! Warning! Like Max Headroom in the television network system, "This narrator's voice will continue to
appear as you continue to read."). This "I lie, I speak" narrative/
metanarrative problematic is explored further in chapter 8.
Since you have just experienced the verbal representation of
representation, we can "look at" the television example now,
and then at its relationship to the fine art of sculpture.

As a metaphor or first level narrative representation of the
"named voice," we can ask: What is the world of Max? The
narration begins. A parking garage traffic gate with the literal
message, "MAX HEADROOM 5 FT. 10 INS.," is the last message
perceived before a motorcycle rider crashes into it—he just
happens to be an action news television reporter, a job requir-
ing an illiterate talent for presenting images without words
(voiceless names or the trope *asyndeton*; see chapter 8), trying
to escape death at the hands of two other illiterates who are
hitmen from the hypercapitalist network. My narrative, like
this insertion is, and will continue to be, a second level narrative representation of "nameless voice" or the trope known as
prosopopoeia.) The gate is violently smashed into his head (literally, allegorically, morally, and anagogically a *media implosion*;
see table 1 for Foucault's parallel model). The reporter has
come too close to seeing and videotaping the absent audience, an illiterate viewer who suddenly becomes the literate
presence of a mere cipher (the spectator's body exploded
when subliminal advertising signals became too intense, an
example of Merleau-Ponty's "degree zero spatiality" or Roland
Barthes's "writing degree zero"). A computer hacker (a literate
illiterate; information requires no experiential referent) attempts to duplicate the persona of the reporter with a simulation computer program. The simulation is incomplete, partial,
and prone to superficial change (illiterate to the third power;
we are supposed to notice that the Max Headroom TV screen
"image" is a crude rubber head foregrounded on two dimensional graphics, an "immaterial face"–note the contraction here
between "immaterial" as connotation and "face" as denotation;
the TV image-frame is not art; merely two dimensions do not
make a painting).

To summarize precisely, we have in Max a simulacrum that is a mirror image of an automaton whose coding is aberrant.[40] In other words, as television viewers, we witness in Max the primordial computer birth, death, and rebirth of television literacy: an image expression that becomes the perception of the perception of. . . as the sign becomes a sign of the sign of. . . in an apparent condition of unlimited phenomenology and semiosis where the public space envelops the private: Max Headroom on TV as TV names the fantasy of computer "reality." Indeed, we encounter the maximum maxim in the persona of Max (especially when as a new media "personality," he tries in "classic" fashion to sell us New Coke). This process is the conscious experience of technological audiovisual communication that a person lives in a mass society. Gerstlé characterizes this axiological phenomenon as the "public/private duality" in which "communication, in effect, accepts two principles of structuration that one can identify symbolically in the opposition between the sign and the practice."[41] As Baudrillard summarizes the phenomenon for us, "thus, the media do not facilitate socialization, but rather the implosion of the social in the masses."[42]

CULTURAL MEDIA (VERSUS THE MEDIA CULTURE)

Given the previous discussion of phenomenological methodology and our immediate conscious experience with the Max Headroom example of media discourse, I now propose to explore briefly the general problematic of "media culture" or "cultures" manufactured by "media events" (compared to art as "cultural media") as a way of thematizing certain aspects of current theoretical debate. On the one hand, I want to thematize the beneficial model of *cultural media*, i.e., the practices of people that create culture in the best sense of art as volitional contribution and appreciation. The practices I have in mind are those that constitute what we live as the *human*, that chosen human practice of dynamic speech. In addition, I am especially concerned first, with exposing the narrow theoretical misconception of *television* as synonymous with *media* in both academic analyses and as embodied in everyday discourse, and, second, with expanding the idea of media to all the arts, painting and sculpture in particular, as exemplars of human *embodiment as a signifying medium* of communication.

COMMUNICOLOGY AND VIDEOLOGY

Communicologie has achieved some currency in popular French usage as the designation of *human communication*, in deliberate contradistinction to the cybernetic usage of communications, informatics, telematics, and telecommunications (see appendix B). Just as I have used *communicology* as a new descriptor term, I adopt the term *videology*, first used by the artist Nam June Paik to describe the attempt by artists to make video creations information theoretic; i.e., to outproduce the producers of videotape or continue to "reduce uncertainty" by further and further divisions resulting from mere increased production of the endless representation of representation exemplified in videos of videos. Since the rule of selection operates in an assumed context or "situation" in information theory, it finally cannot be discovered. We know that there is a rule, e.g., a cultural norm, but we do not what it is (Eco's "undercoding"). As Paik warns about our ability to select presentations of reality from among the levels of representation, "We should be more conscious of the situation that we are in the era of information overload and it means information-retrieval is more tricky than information recording."[43] For example, in a typical "music video" we are confronted with an intentional loss of referent (there is no-particular-thing-to-see, only image-things located in my multiples of other image-things) in the video of the video of, etc., for the precise reason of creating a focus on the musical sound and a parallel gesture of human movement (keep in mind that movement is not a reification).

Unfortunately, Ihde's initial phenomenological study of communication media falls victim to such an information theory error of mere "information recording" by adopting the digital context of Husserl's transcendental distinction between real and ideal objects. Husserl's digital distinction gets "overloaded" in Ihde's analysis when the media ideal (recording) is derived from the real (information), yet the ideal remains only in the "vicinity" and cannot be made real. As Ihde comments,

> Cinema and television are still primarily entertainment devices or information devices that can be seen to be most clearly use situations appropriate for the aesthetic stance. But telephones, the increasing use of other communication media, and even the communications uses of television-mediated interpersonal engagements bring this stance to the vicinity of action.[44]

In short, we need the reversibility of the real (information) and the actual (retrieval) as an example of mediated human communication. "Recording" (state) is not "retrieval" (action) as Ihde suggests, as, for example, people who use telephones and trains in the third world already know. Their real phones seldom actually work (messages cannot be retrieved) and, actual trains are seldom functioning as "real" in any expected sense of available space or punctuality (an old General Semantics proposition: "the map is not the territory"). Or in the first world, for another example, the French "mini-tel" telephone system for popular consumer voice and data transmission, together with public monitors for Metro train arrival times, records a great deal of information, yet the system is hardly experienced as aesthetic (retrieval).

I propose to follow the theoretical usages for "communicology" and "videology" in the comparative explication of cultural media (aesthetic communication) and media culture (information). I hope to extend the little noticed, but insightful, analysis of this differentiation of the aesthetic function in cultural media made by Christopher Finch.[45] Namely, I want to accept the possibility of making the experience of art creators and spectators transactional through the work of art as communicological (analogical combination of the actual image and the real), rather than as videological (digital separation of the ideal image and the real). Such an analysis allows us to understand how the *object world* contextualizes the *subject world* without the hypostatization of positivist science and its assumptive negation of the human self.

Finch reminds us that the encounter with art is an engaged

human action, not merely an object seen in the sense of Ihde's "vicinity of action." That is, artists create works that require *participation* (practice and choice) by the spectators so that the experienced work of art is as much *spectator created* (the actual) as it is an artist's creation (the real). Creator and beholder role reversibility is required so that artist and spectator give up the passive visual choice to be either in one role (the ideal) or the other (real) by becoming both in lived-through activity that engages the body in trans-action (retrieval) as a practice. For the purpose of explicating the creator-beholder transaction as embodied communication, I am using the two counterposed concepts of media culture (information theoretic creations of a digital either/or logic of the ideal versus the real) and Cultural Media (communication theoretic creations of an analogue both/and logic combining the actual and real). I capitalize "Cultural Media" since this is the affirmative view for which I am arguing and I want to mark it as such. This distinction of media culture and Cultural Media specifies respectively the *problematic* and *thematic* of what Lévy-Bruhl was first to call "collective representations" in his *Les fonctions mentales dans les sociétés inférieures*, originally published in 1910 (appendix A). Himmelstein also draws this type of distinction in his very useful comparison of *High Art* (my "media culture" of aesthetics as communicology) and *Popular Art* (my "Cultural Media" of information as videology) as praxis artifacts in cultural media discourse.[46]

In his philosophico-anthropological volume, Lévy-Bruhl advances his *Law of Participation* by which "social aggregates," i.e., audiences or creator-spectator groups in a mass sense, can be described and interpreted. He has two primary theses in his classic book: "(1) The institutions, customs and beliefs of primitives [social aggregates] imply a mentality which is prelogical and mystic, oriented differently form our own."[47] This category corresponds to my designation of the problematic of media culture as information theoretic. As a typology of human experience, the category is information theoretic because the typology is geared to "reduce uncertainty" in the creative act, a fact characterizing, for example, the cultural transmission research of Lévi-Strauss.[48] Lévy-Bruhl continues: "(2) The collective representations and interconnections which constitute such a mentality are governed by the law of participation and is so far as they take but little account of the logical law of contradiction."[49] This statement characterizes, for example, Foucault's work.[50] This collective representation category is the thematic of Cultural Media and it is communication theoretic. It is the human experience typology directed to the "constitution of meaning" in the artistic creation and spectacle by combining the image of the actual (signifier; appreciation) with the real (signified; constitution).

A particularly appropriate exemplar analysis of the aesthetic differentiation between information theory and communication theory is the Australian cultural studies example noted by Fiske, Hodge and Turner: the shift of displayed aboriginal art from the historical museum (information context: real made ideal) to the art gallery (communication context: real made actual) thereby creating a new rule of semiotic reality.[51] In Canada, an analogue example showing phenomenological reversibility exists, according to the rule of semiotic fantasy, in the display of John Hooper's outdoor sculpture *Balancing*, a lifesize work featuring five figures (a businessman, two teenage male students, a woman in casual dress, and a male jogger) all standing on a "Y" shaped beam projecting out of the lower canal bank near the Rideau Bridge (communication context: actual made real), rather than displayed *inside* the National Art Gallery (information context: ideal made real), located on the upper bank of the canal in downtown Ottawa.

Part of my analytic intention for examining art in culture and communication is to respond to Lévy-Bruhl's challenge (repeated by Foucault) concerning the nature of cultural transmission through participation: "A vast field for positive research into the mental functioning of aggregates of various kinds, as well as into our own laws of thought, is thus laid open to us."[52] In Appendix A, I have described the place of Lévy-Bruhl's logic in contemporary human science; I will not repeat it here. In the present context, let us recall that qualitative research which is both eidetic and empirical has a phenomenological grounding in Lévy-Bruhl's creator-spectator law, later exploited to advantage by both Merleau-Ponty and Foucault.[53]

The Law of Participation describes quite simply a human consciousness that perceives a reality of beings related to phenomena (subjects and objects) that are intuitive to the senses, because the experience is *lived through* (presentation; sign experience) before it is conceived sensually (representation; signifier/signified consciousness). "In varying forms and degrees they [the relations] all involve a 'participation' between persons and objects which form part of a collective representation."[54] Quite understandably, an encounter with works of art provides an excellent illustration of this participation. This is especially true where the art-work is sculpture, and the encounter takes the form of interpersonal engagement, where self and alterity are mediated by symbolic objects.

For example, Joel Feldman, my colleague and an associate professor in the School of Art at Southern Illinois University, and are engaged in such an ongoing research project. Rather than focusing on painting, with its two dimensional constrains, we are using sculpture, with its three dimension advantage, for comparison with interpersonal communication. We ask students to do several projects, including (1) a phenomenological case analysis of the art per se from their individual experience, (2) a phenomenological analysis of their behavior in comparison to other students while doing the first analysis, and (3) a phenomenological analysis of what the artist is trying to communicate.

Feldman's life-size sculpture, *A Family Unit*, is installed in a normal second floor office area of our Communications Building, rather than in a traditional museum or gallery context which can corrupt the intrinsic human values in the art.[55] The art work is, thereby, made to oppose the semiotic idealism of modernity enshrined in the institutional notion of the museum-gallery. The art work becomes, in the fashion of a postmodern discourse, explicitly a message in the process of communication, i.e., a phenomenon actually engaged as real by a person in an unmediated here and now conscious experience. A similar effect exhibits itself in the photographic art

Plate 1. Feldman's Art Installation *A Family Unit* (Exterior Room view)

Plate 2. Installation Viewpoint from Exterior to Interior

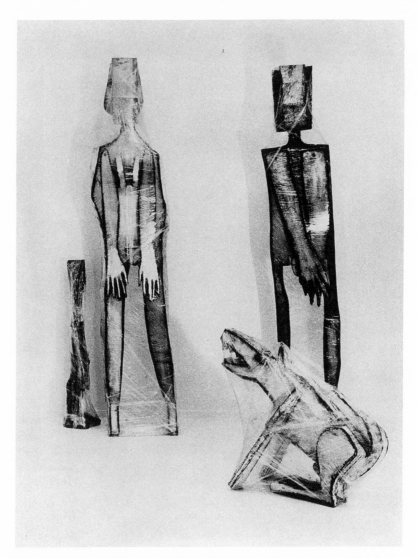

Plate 3. Feldman's Wood and Plastic Sculptures (Interior Room View)

of Richard Ross whose book *Museology* (the title itself is deliberately postmodern) consists of images depicting the depictions offered by the world's more famous art and "natural science" museums.[56] Nude Greek statues stand in corners only, as if too ashamed to stand in the middle of the room; stuffed animals crafted into an apparent natural landscape are made surreal by the glass case that holds them; drawers full of rare stuffed birds awaiting exhibition time are, indeed spaceless and timeless life. But let us return to Feldman's art as choice and practice in the communication of values.

The sculpture (plate 1) includes a room which with the door closed, requires the use of a "peep hole," security door lens reversed to view the room interior. The room measures ten feet wide by twelve feet long by eight feet high. The room (plate 2) can also be viewed with the door open. The closet style door is slightly smaller than normal (suggesting that a person might look in or reach in, but probably not step in, thus avoiding a body-risk choice of practice) and it is covered with lead sheathing to make the door and peephole a progressive point of use focus and locus (recall the chapter 2 discussion of these perspectives as created on the radio). The interior is lit by two 100-watt bulbs that viewers may switch on from the outside. The room (plate 3) contains life size figures that are carved from poplar wood, painted, and covered with plastic shrink wrap. The plain white interior walls of this life size office-like room contextualize its sculpted pieces which consist of a child, an adult female, an adult male, and a dog, together with an empty metal folding chair.

For persons encountering *A Family Unit,* participation is the essence of cultural media as communicology. All the communication theoretic choices of *both* depiction *and* description are counterposed in ambiguity with the information theoretic elements of *either* prediction *or* ascription of practice.

Two other artists, in particular, have also brought their sculpture to bear on this aesthetics of transactional participation between human being and art, subject and object. Nam June Paik's current work is, in the public/spectator experience of it, the literal/metaphorical use of television sculpture to substitute and reverse the *person/family* analogue (iconic signs taken as indexical; actual to real) with the *television/image* analogue (indexical signs taken as iconic; real to actual).[57] In the communicology world of Paik's art, the person/group sculpted for old TV sets replaces the videology world of tape program producers who make videotapes from videotapes. Or, from a different experiential perspective on Paik's sculptures, seeing television as myself embodied in an art work (a Cultural Medium experience) replaces the "entertainment" of watching a TV reporter interviewing another TV reporter about an event neither one is experiencing (a media culture event) because the person that they want to interview refuses the "media opportunity."

And yet again, the experience of the Kienholz's (1986) *The Art Show* (researched and created over more than a decade; art's answer to the positivist's longitudinal study) illustrates the very powerful meaning constituted by giving "human" sculptures the audiovisual function (practice) of responding on their own terms to the viewer.[58] Optical switches in the eyes of the statues start and stop tape recorders that playback (through speakers in the mouth) ensemble tapes of comments made by previous spectators who walked among the sculptures at past exhibitions in other museums or galleries. Complete Cultural Media reversal occurs between the human (gallery spectator) and the representation of the human: the life-size sculptures of people representing (depiction, description) spectators at a gallery. Who the show is, and who is at the show, becomes an ontological exercise in social and culture, choice and practice. In this contemporary genre of sculpture, we confirm Merleau-Ponty's comment about the artist: "Inevitably the roles between him and the visible are reversed. That is why so many painters have said that the things look at them."[59] Is such participation in art the essence of television? Max Headroom tells us "Yes!"

Contrary to Flusser's hypothesis that "TV is a technique of manipulating images in lines, and it therefore permits the imagination of concepts,"[60] the media culture proposition is that *television is a participation in imaging-imagination*. Television is an imaging-imagination in which actualizations (= eidetic objects of consciousness as representations) and realizations

(= empirical objects of experience as representations) are reversible. Television is, in every sense of the word, a reflection of, and on, the *image* of the viewer's consciousness of self experience. This image is intuitive and participatory. It does not have to, but it may, become an experience that can be conceived *either* as a possibility of living (actualization), *or* a conceived experience of consciousness already lived through (realization). Yet again, the image can be *both* actual *and* real, which is precisely the rule of fantasy that allows us to participate in the experience as literally meaningful.

The best empirical evidence and illustration here, as Jenny Nelson argues, is any viewer's personal attachment of the actual (personal accounts of watching) to the television phenomenon as real (what is "seen" while watching) that is depicted in the *revelatory phrases* of his or her own discourse about television where the actual and the real are reversible.[61] In Nelson's "televisual experience," there is in Lévy-Bruhl's terms, simply *participation* that is lived through as *a constituting meaning* before there is any situational call for conscious reflection on the experience. No idealization is abstracted from the actualization or the realization. Here, we see the sense in which theory choice emerges from practice and vice versa, precisely what phenomenologists refer to as the "embodiment" of consciousness (actuality) or a "lived-through" experience (reality).

Flusser bases his positivistic argument on the construction of a metaphoric analysis of media culture in which the cinema film image has the attributes of a wall in a room, whereas television is like a window in that wall. Either you see the wall or the window; it does not matter which since the information value is the same. Media culture gives values as data; data is signification. Television is not a door in the wall because "the door is a tool which allows man to transform window visions into practice." Yet a wall may be covered in paint (the icon for film) or with pictures (the television icon as a filmic alternative to the "window," i.e., a little wall on the big wall). "This is what the world 'television' means: a better vision that [n] (*sic*) is provided by conventional windows."[62] The uncertainty of signification is reduced. What Flusser fails to discover in his metaphoric model is the very point made so explicitly by Foucault in his discussion of Cultural Media within which speaking and painting are the human paradigms for *expression* and *perception*.[63] Although first used extensively by Merleau-Ponty, speaking and painting play a key semiotic role in all contemporary French thought.[64]

For example, Foucault demonstrates that the painting *Las Meninas* by Velasquez contains the icon of participatory imagination, a mirror. The mirror is, of course, the icon of dynamic imagining of unlimited temporal dimensions captured in a viewing of the painting, yet it is also the index of a static image as reified in the painting per se. This dialectic is the beginning of the silent science. With Merleau-Ponty, we realize that "a Cartesian does not see *himself* in the mirror; he sees a dummy, an 'outside,' which, he has every reason to believe, other people see in the very same way but which, no more for himself than for others, is not a body in the flesh."[65] Phenomenologically of course, participatory imagination is simply another semiotic name for *discourse* where the discursive function is the "nameless voice" that narrates the story (*prosopopoeia de l'histoire*). In *Las Meninas* (printed as the frontpiece in Foucault's *The Order of Things*), we spectators observe from behind the painter's easel and canvas a scene in which a painter portrays a group of adults and children. Note that this voyeur aspect of looking at art is a fundamental part of Feldman's installation, as well as the Paik, Kienholz, Hooper, and Ross examples. In the background on the wall, we intuitively focus on a mirror that reflects the image of a spectator who is not visible in the frame of the picture proper. We have ignored the small picture on the wall next to the mirror; its focus is not clear by comparison to the mirror (a locus). It seems necessary to forget the rest of the painting per se in order to concentrate on and conceive this smaller "picture painting" on the wall. As Foucault suggests, in the "forgetfulness of rationality," we intuitively realize and concretize our Self as the absent spectator whose image we see present in the mirror. The portrayed spectator (an image) is a participation (a mirror) of imagination (a person). The spectator is "that space in which we are, and which we are."[66] In *Las*

Meninas, the rupture of conscious experience (Lacan's "symbolic") becomes a discourse of fantasy ("imaginary") in which we see the "real."[67] A similar, but fantastic, reversal occurs as *we* focus on the artist in the picture, brush in hand, who focuses *his* gaze on his work—unseen by us—on a canvas of which we see only part of the back frame (itself completely framed by the picture per se that we see).

Thus by parallel dialectic structure, we realize how Max Headroom can become an icon of our own consciousness in the midst of experiencing the real as fantastic. We become the *televisual experience*, we are a semiotic phenomenology of discourse. A *telos* or culturally constrained media constitutes the existential grounding of vision, i.e., the reflexivity of human perception and expression is created.[68] Televisual experience as perception becomes a genealogy (paradigmatic shift of typology) and, as expression, it marks the loss of mass memory. Televisual experience is participation in consciousness where my values are constituted in place of mass values; I invent a discourse, a Cultural Media, to stand in place of media culture. The semiology becomes coterminus with the phenomenology. In Foucault's words, "Let us give the term *genealogy* to the union of erudite knowledge and local memories which allows us to establish a historical knowledge of struggles and to make use of this knowledge tactically today."[69] This is why I can today watch "Max Headroom" now that he (we?) has his (our?) own regularly scheduled television show and "personality" (*sic*) commercials (read: media culture), thus demonstrating Umberto Eco's thesis that:

> The mass media are genealogical, and they have no memory (two characteristics that ought to be incompatible). The mass media are genealogical because, in them every new invention sets off a chain reaction of inventions, produces a sort of common language. They have no memory because, when the chain of imitations has been produced, no one can remember who started it, and the head of the clan is confused with the latest great grandson.[70]

Eco rediscovers Lévy-Bruhl's proposition that the Law of Participation cancels Aristotle's Law of Contradiction. We should note here that the Law of Participation has subsequently become, i.e., is an alternative name for, the redefined law of Non-Contradiction (it has rhetorical priority over the Law of Contradiction and the Law of Identity respectively) specifically in Foucault and in communication theory generally.[71] To redefine Aristotle's original is to understand the Law of Non-Contradiction; I must first (a necessary and sufficient condition) intuit that it is not true in human conscious experience that the law of Non-Contradiction states that something cannot both be and not be at the same time and place. The obvious counter example is human language; as symbolic, language both is and is not when a person uses it. This essence of discourse is what Foucault constantly returns to in his research studies.

We rediscover that "local memory" becomes a conscious experience intuitively brought to the televisual image. Memory as such does not exist in the image per se; human memory is not mass rationality, not the *experience of* consciousness (this was Goffman's mistake, as we saw in chapter 2). Thus, the television "audience" is a social aggregate (McFeat's small-group culture) that is little more than the collective representation of the person, an individual who is not yet a conceived subject of rationality.[72] Eco merely brings to television what Foucault first described in his analysis of Raymond Roussel's surrealist literary writing and later explicated in his analysis of the surrealist painter, Magritte.[73]

The message of "Max Headroom" as a popular culture consumer icon becomes a *discourse event* that is both a rupture, *a chiasm* and a *catachresis* where the tropes name the narrator, and a narrative reflection, a *prosopopoeia* and *persona* where the tropes present a nameless narrator. By way of definition, the trope *chiasm* is a special case of *irony* (negative) or *simile* (positive) in which there is a comparison by degree (binary analogue) of presence (part) and absence (attribute). In a similar fashion, the trope *prosopopoeia* is a special case of *metonymy* in which there is a comparison by degree (binary analogue) of the real (substance) and the imaginary (attribute). In this context, I should also note that the trope *catachresis* is a special case of *metaphor* in which there is a comparison by degree (binary analogue) of the proper (substance) and the insipid (whole).

And last, the trope *persona* is a special case of *synecdoche* in which there is a comparison by degree (binary analogue) of the appearance (part) and the concrete (whole). The operation of these tropic functions in the abductive logic of *le même et l'autre* (self-other—same-different) is an extended technical issue in itself, and I shall save that discussion for chapters 6 and 7.

Returning to the example of the painting *Las Meninas*, the message as the window in the wall *combines* with the mirror. Because I either choose the painting (an undercoded window; a signifier without a signified) or the mirror (an overcoded window; a signified with too many signifiers), the information value is the same: the painting or mirror signifies by being a choice, but aberrantly because we do not know what is chosen (signified); thus, it does not create a meaning. Therefore, I immediately intuit the prior condition posed by the communication theoretic value of the phenomenon I observe in *Las Meninas*.

That is, the painting as a whole creates meaning because I constitute the image of the spectator in the mirror as *me*. Meaning is a mirror (me) reflecting a mirror image (the "spectator" in the mirror in the painting), which in turn allows my conception of the "painting/portrait" next to the mirror on the background wall in *Las Meninas*. In Merleau-Ponty's celebrated *system of four terms* (Je, Moi, Tu, Vous) "I" constitute the meaning of "Me" so that "You" (personal) can construct the signification of "You" (public).[74] Or, as we might formulate the system according to Foucault's *quadrilateral model* (see figures 5 and 6; table 1): The "I" as "Self" constitutes the meaning of "Me" as "Other" so that "You" (personal) as the "Same" person can construct the signification of "You" (public) as "different" from yourself. The mirrored image is the Self as creator-spectator (*that* is television), not the spectacular image of the Other in the window (*that* is cinema). Thus, the mirror message illustrates the communication theoretic condition of a *metagram* because, as Foucault remarks, it "is both the truth and a mask, a duplicate, repeated and placed on the surface. At the same time, it is the opening through which it enters, experiences the doubling, a separates the mask from the face that it is dupli-

cating."[75] A more familiar example of a metagram is the following sentence: There is nothing written here. Or we might
cite Magritte's painting title: This is not a pipe. Max Headroom
is a *visual metagram.*

Television, conceived merely as a window message, creates
the discourse of a media culture (a media event) by setting the
normative and normalizing conditions of a choice in context
where the viewing audience as spectator "reduces uncertainty"
(the content is not entertainment, but information that is
always consumed). In this discourse, the rhetorical tropes of
chiasm and catachresis are the value judgment of differentiation: a combination that inappropriately separates. The
dead reporter (Edison Carter) is not just Max, the image,
and I am not just the image viewer. Max gives me good existential evidence that I am a person, because he is not: he is
no body's image, but I am/have some body.

At the same time, my discursive response to the message
creates the Cultural Media (aesthetic communication) by
constructing the semiotic conditions that are a choice of
context where I "constitute meaning" (not information, but
communication that is prereflectively always reflexively
existential in the embodied practice that performs it). As a
figure in the Cultural Media discourse, prosopopoeia is the
combinatory value of judgment, the "nameless voice" as Foucault says, that articulates the existential person who is prior
to the subject of discourse (persona).[76] Because my conscious experience is lived out, I do not confuse myself with
the TV character Edison Carter (an image, a sign of a person)
or with Max (an image of an image, a sign of a sign). Max
Headroom is a name, a verbal representation of a representation. As Foucault argues, "The figures through which
discourse passes act as a deterrent to the name, which then
arrives at the last moment to fulfill and abolish them. The
name is the *end* of discourse."[77] An *archaeology* (syntagmatic
shift of category) that discovers the end of the name (Eco's
loss of mass memory) is reflexively a *genealogy* (paradigmatic
shift of category) of the person (Foucault's loss of the subject
or persona). The tropic formulation is a clear abductive logic
of ontology: The discourse of chiasm (rule) and prosopo-

poeia (result) signifies the person (case), just as catachresis (rule) and persona (result) creates the image (case).

As a matter of theory construction, it is critical to note here that for Foucault, archaeology (Jakobson's "syntagmatic axis"), and therefore, the "subject" is the image of discourse: a metagram, a rupture of that "subject" in *grammaire générale*," a break that constitutes the chiasm. From the chiasm, an unnamed voice speaks with the voice of *local memory*, it is *the birth of the person*.[78] As Baudrillard confirms, "Silent and withdrawn, the masses are no longer a *subject* (certainly not of history); they can no longer, therefore, be spoken, articulated, represented, cannot pass through the political mirror-stage nor the cycle of imaginary identifications."[79]

Television, then, is no mere voyeuristic adventure with a window, as Flusser would have it. Television is the "good ambiguity" of a narcissistic encounter with the mirror of consciousness: the body (a sign) of the Other (a signifier) is made flesh (a signified) in the Self as "bio-power" (lived-meaning), to cite Foucault's version of Merleau-Ponty's formulation.[80] Television becomes for us what discourse is for Roussel, when Foucault says of him "He doesn't want to duplicate the reality of another world, but, in the spontaneous duality of language, he wants to *discover* an unexpected space, and to *cover* it with things never said before."[81] In the parallel experience of television, as in all cultural media, especially the fine art of painting as we have seen, the chiasm combines with the prosopopoeia to articulate the existential essence of a person that I can *discover* as signification (data as the given) or *cover* with meaning (capta as the taken). *Signification* becomes the use of the Law of Contradiction to separate the Self and Other, social aggregates are, or become, rational collections of individual subjects; the group, the class, the mass are the absolute predication of the Other. The media culture of videology signifies the individual as a subject in search of a persona to be exploited, the subject as mere information. "That is why", according to Longinus, "the best use of a [rhetorical] figure is when the very fact that it is a figure goes unnoticed."[82] This approach is the ideological stuff of raw capitalistic consumerism in the media that is so often criticized.[83] Indeed, Baudrillard's well-

known prolegomenon expresses the political consequence of
this view of media culture as media events:

> The current strategy of the system is to inflate utterance [*parole*]
> to produce the maximum of meaning [*sens*]. Thus, the appro-
> priate strategic resistance is to refuse meaning and utterance, to
> simulate in a hyper-conformist manner the very mechanisms of
> the system, itself a form of refusal and non-reception. This is the
> resistance strategy of the masses. It amounts to turning the
> system's logic back on itself by duplicating it, reflecting mean-
> ing, as in a mirror, without absorbing it. This is the dominant
> strategy at the present (if one can call it strategy) because it is
> this particular phase of the system that has triumphed.[84]

A word of caution here. While most American (USA) readers
take Baudrillard's comment as the statement of a political
program for strategic action—[a politics ironically coopted,
before it could begin, by such commercial forms as music
television (MTV) and Cable News Network (CNN)—I think it
important to note that this interpretation is dangerous at best.
Although he has obvious critical theory (neo-Marxist) beliefs,
Baudrillard is nonetheless writing within the *tout Paris* tradition of French intellectual life with its *l'histoire* connotations
of "history" versus "discourse" a tradition I shall discuss more
fully in chapter 4. It is not all that clear whether he is describing a failed action program (history) or calling for a new
action program (discourse). And for that reason he deliberately
creates a positive ambiguity in his diction that contextualizes
this passage, whereby his intellectual roots are both everywhere
and nowhere. In the phenomenological tradition of Merleau-
Ponty, he chooses *parole* or "speaking" to imply he is neither
a structuralist, who would have used *langue* or "the speech community," nor a poststructuralist like Derrida who would have
used *écriture* or "writing," nor is he a contemporary semiotic
phenomenologist like Foucault who would use *énoncé* or "stat-
ing/expressing." On the other hand, Baudrillard does not
follow the distinction between the structuralist *signification* (the
same as the English) and the phenomenologist's *sens* or
"meaning" (connoting a "sense of direction" in the signification).
Instead, he uses the *avoir du sens*, a colloquial construction

meaning "to make sense"; this is something halfway between "signification" and "meaning" with their political baggage. It also implies strong agreement with Foucault's distinction between *savoir* or "know how" [= power] and *connaissance* or "conscious knowing" [= knowledge]; thus, *sens* would be akin to *savoir*. All this to say that Baudrillard is best read as calling for an end to "signification" (a better translation of his *avoir du sens*) and its cybernetic ideology of informatics, but one does *not* do so by "not making sense." Rather, as Merleau-Ponty already demonstrated, a person makes sense by exposing "signification" as *non-sense* in the media praxis of human communication, shown in chapter 2 with Goffman's work on media.

By comparison to the staged and subsequently staging media event, the experience of *meaning* is a use of the Law of Participation to conjoin Self and Other in the communicology of Cultural Media (aesthetic communication) like television, writing, painting, speaking, and so on. Social aggregates (spectators) become social selves (creators), persons whose own lived consciousness of their selves is simultaneously an ascription of meaning to Others. This point was illustrated previously in detail in my example of methodology using the existential discourse of the French painter Julian Levi. In addition, a particularly good illustration of my point is the communicological experience of the *calligram* noted by Foucault as a comparison with the information theoretic metagram.[85] A calligram mixes the graphic and the visual in double reverse levels of signifying combination, as does, for example sculpture in nontraditional settings, or Ross's photographs displaying the museum displays ("media event") meant to be displayed as real. The absolute use of culture for media emerges in the choice of practice as the practice of choice, as anyone will note when confronted with a visible/invisible message like a rebus calligram (see figure 7).

As a brief conclusion for the issues raised throughout the analysis in this third chapter, let me note that I have worked through a pedagogical example of the method of semiotic phenomenology using the theoretical propositions of a typical interpersonal communication textbook. The example is explicitly related to the artist's personal narrative about his painting, both to show the method as empirical and to introduce the topic of painting as a form of mass media communication. Building upon the analysis of painting as an exemplar practice in communication, I turned to the relationship displayed in the comparison of sculpture and television as media in cultural transmission. The parallel structure of sculpture and television as mass message systems provided a useful base from which to make a theoretical analysis of expression and perception from the perspective of semiotic phenomenology. Here, I especially focused upon theory derived from the applied empirical work of the French theorists Maurice Merleau-Ponty and Michel Foucault. While art as a medium of cultural transmission operates as a "silent science" in many contexts associated with human communication, particularly in areas like television, we are just beginning to understand the methodological richness of phenomenology for the semiotic task of analysis in the discipline of communicology as a human science. But before I continue my explication of this human science, it will be useful to construct an historical background for the convergence of the work by Merleau-Ponty and Foucault. That background, the subject of chapter 4, begins with Saussure.

4

From Saussure to Communicology

The Paris School of Semiotics

C ontemporary semiotics in the European tradition begins
by common acknowledgement with the teaching of the
Swiss linguist, Ferdinand de Saussure. I say "teaching" since,
contrary to the promises he gave to his students, he neither
wrote nor published an account of the course he gave three
times, in 1907, 1909, and 1911. That course was entitled *Cours
de linguistic générale* [Course in General Linguistics]. From their
notes and his, Saussure's students subsequently published a
volume with the same name in 1916, three years after his death.
While the usual professor may shudder at the contemplation
of being remembered through the notes of his or her students,
not just in one course, but as a composite of three courses given
in three different years, Saussure did in fact become the person
with whose research we mark the beginning of contemporary
European semiology.[1]

Saussure gave his famous *Cours* after 1906 as an alternative
to his regular course in Sanskrit and historical linguistics while
professor of linguistics at the University of Geneva, the city of
his birth. Between 1878 and 1887, just prior to his Geneva professorship, he was a professor in the École Pratique des Hautes
Études in Paris, which incidentally even today maintains a

course of study in semiotics. I should pause a moment here to add that the semiotic influence in Paris moved several blocks toward the River Seine during 1988, inasmuch as Henri Quéré was elected professor in comparative literature at the *Institut du Monde Anglophone of the Université de Paris III (Sorbonne Nouvelle)*. Professor Quéré's election, thus, represents the final conservative mark of acceptance of semiotics within the intellectual life of France. Quéré along with Algirdas J. Greimas and Joseph Courtés, both at the *École des Hautes Études en Sciences Sociales*, are the founders of the original *Groupe de Recherches Semiolinguistiques* (Paris). Under the leadership of Greimas, this group developed and has created an entire research program around the semantic, hermeneutic model of the "Semiotic Square," radically different from, yet nostalgic for Aristotle's logic square.[2]

Having mentioned Saussure and Quéré, I have now marked the beginning of semiotics in the nineteenth century up to the present in Paris. In order to account for the intervening years and their key personalities in the development of a semiotic influence on philosophy and the human sciences, I shall make use of Michel Foucault's Quadrilateral Model of Discourse. I have often glossed this model by using the contemporary nomination "human science of communicology." With this usage which I introduced in chapter 1, my intention is to include all these influences within the study of discourse and its practice, especially the phenomenological influence. But before I begin this review, let me remind you of Saussure's basic theory, the elaboration on it made by Louis Hjelmslev, and finally the reformulations introduced by Roman Jakobson, a onetime student of Edmund Husserl.

THE LEGACY OF SAUSSURE

The revolution in historical linguistics that Saussure introduced was the idea that the unit of discourse is the *sign*. A sign is composed of two parts, a signifier or element of expression and a signified or element of perception. Saussure wanted to eliminate the standard usage in historical linguistics of the term "concept" as the expressive referent of a word, and at the same time he wished to eliminate the use of a word's "sound-image" as the perceptual, i.e., merely sensate, referent. Rather than a concept linked to a sound-image as the definition of a "word," Saussure invoked a *logic of values* (parallel to Peirce's notion of a *normative logic*) grounded in human communication practices. This linguistic logic, ocassionally referred to by Saussure as *signology*, is a system in which oppositional values allow us to understand linguistic meaning.[3] The logical concept of "opposition" should not be taken casually as a synonym for "contradiction" since opposition is a positive value (as noted by Hjelmslev, an *analogue relation: Both / And*) and not a negative value (*a digital correlation: Either / Or*). Saussure gave the expressive value the name "signifier" and, in turn, the perceptual value became the signified. *Semiology* (now replaced by *Semiotics*) is the name of this new human science of signs.[4]

Saussure defined signs within the general context of human communication (i.e., semiology) by arguing that human discourse has certain characteristics. First, speech (*parole*) is distinguished from language in the sense of a social dialect (*langue*). Speech is a linguistic utterance that represents a person speaking in a private sense that individualizes meaning; speaking produces connotative meaning in *praesentia*. By comparison, language dialect is a linguistic norm that is intersubjective and promotes a unifying social process of shared meaning in *absentia*; language or dialect produces denotative meaning in the conversational world of society. Second, Saussure gave priority to the study of language which is itself temporally differential. Language is either *synchronic* as a here and now linguistic practice, or, language is *diachronic*, showing a temporal ability to project future meaning in which case it is "prospective", or to recover past meaning in which case it is "retrospective." Saussure gave his primary concern to synchronic linguistics. In consequence, he came to view the system of sign relations as completely arbitrary. Any signifier may be attached to any signified, and conversely.

In short, Saussure conceived of semiotics as the study of sign systems where language has priority over speech, because language is differential in being synchronic, social, and arbitrary. In Saussure's theory, semiotics is prior to linguistics. The fact that speech is diachronic, personal, and motivated remains as a phenomenological concern, however.

HJELMSLEV

The contribution that Louis Hjelmslev made to Saussure's semiotics is to attempt its expansion as a deductive logic.[5] While his research model fails as an empirical project in descriptive linguistics, the formal system offers a set of very important theoretical insights about how semiotic systems function. That is, we discover how communication and information systems operate when not assumed to be dependent on one or more particular human natural languages, nor on a mathematical formalism indebted to deductive inference. We need to note two basic ideas here. First, Hjelmslev demonstrated that signs cannot be simply constructed as the differential combination of a signifier and a signified, i.e., only conceived as an opposition by contradiction or disjunction. Rather, a sign is self-reflexive in the sense that a signifier and a signified respectively must each be capable of expression and perception by combinatory opposition in a logic of conjunction. This to say, a signifier itself consists of *both* a signifier *and* a signified. The same requirement holds for the signified. In other words, Hjelmslev is accounting for the symbolic function that exists in language where there is both an eidetic and an empirical representation of meaning moving from a connotative semiotics, to a denotative semiotics, and finally to a metasemiotic level of "real" reference, i.e., our usual notion of the reality or world to which we refer when we predicate a meaning. In terms of linguistic theory this insight is the now commonplace hermeneutic observation that an *object language* always entails a *metalanguage* function (see Appendix B).

The second basic idea that Hjelmslev added concerns the nature of a sign in its logical connection to other signs. Hjelmslev again showed that the Saussurian digital logic of either/or differentiation ("correlation") defining a "system" is incomplete. He suggests that differentiation can also be accomplished by combination in which an analogue logic of both/and differentiation establishes "relations" in a "process" (see part two of Appendix B).

Hjelmslev conceived of semiotics as the study of sign systems and processes where language or speech may have priority, because language is differential in being both synchronic and diachronic, personal and social, and yet, arbitrary. In theory, for Hjelmslev, semiotics is still prior to linguistics because language is not exclusively prior to speech.

JAKOBSON

Elmar Holenstein, in his summary discussion of Jakobson's phenomenological structuralism, gives us the third stage of the theoretical development in the history of Saussure's semiotics.[6] Jakobson's contribution consists of two models, one for the organization of the human sciences (figure 4) and the other for the system and process of human communication. In brief, he

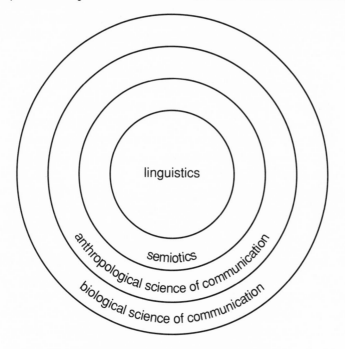

Figure 4. Jakobson's Human Science Model

argues that the human sciences model is theoretically ordered by an eidetic constraint of "redundancy features" and an empirical constraint of "distinctive features" in human discourse. The result is an explicit hierarchy of the human sciences: (1) Linguistics, (2) Semiotics, (3) Communication Science (anthropological) and Exchange Systems (economics), and (4) Life Science systems and processes (biology).

In addition, the human communication model (see figure 3) is a composite of six elements (addresser, addressee, context, message, contact, and code) and their respective six functions (emotive, conative, referential, poetic, phatic, and metalinguistic). The key features with respect to redefining the Saussurian models are these: *Langue*, or social dialect, is redefined as *code* and becomes part of a *static system.* The term "synchronic system" is dropped because we are not longer limiting the scope of analysis to linguistic systems (all nonverbal systems are to be examined). *Parole*, or speaking, is now defined as a *message* within a *dynamic system.* The term "diachronic system" is dropped because we are now concerned with all exchange systems, not just the linguistic system.

One other special hermeneutic principle is developed, the *poetic function* of discourse in which code and message are interchangeable, thereby establishing a logical hierarchy (see figure 3). This poetic function has become the hallmark definition of human communication in which "communication theory" as an analogue logic of both/and combination entails "information theory" with its digital either/or logic of exclusion. Simply put, the priority of linguistics over semiotics requires that a choice of context (distinctive feature) always precede a choice in context (redundancy feature). Chapter 8 is a detailed example of this point.

Given this review of the semiotic foundation for developments on the French scene, I now turn explicitly to Foucault's quadrilateral model of discourse to briefly sketch the conjunction of philosophy and human science in Paris as it develops during the time interval between Saussure's professorship and that which Quéré has come to occupy.

THE PARIS SCHOOL OF SEMIOTICS

Let me initially suggest what I am going to say about the Parisian intellectual scene. First, I want to take up the development of French philosophy as it moves progressively from Existentialism to Phenomenology to Structuralism, and finally into the current arenas of Poststructuralism. Second, I shall take a quick look at the same type of emerging concerns on the part of the human sciences, moving in order from Structural Linguistics to Semiology to Psychoanalysis and then finally to Hermeneutics.[7] However, I shall run these two traditions together as a milieu in which we have the progressive development of the *philosophy of the human sciences* as it more or less occurred, and is occurring, in the French context of *tout Paris,* the ontological aphorism that French intellectuals use to describe what is current, what is important to know, what, indeed, all Paris is talking about. In short, I shall be using Foucault's quadrilateral model of discourse to talk in turn about four other discourses: First, the combinatory discourse of Existentialism and Structural Linguistics, i.e., the respective problematics of "attribution" and "representation"; second, the discourse of Phenomenology and Semiology, i.e., the problematics of "designation" and "substitution"; third, the discourse of Structuralism and Psychoanalysis, i.e., the problematics of "articulation" and "specification"; and fourth, the discourse of Poststructuralism and Hermeneutics, i.e., the problematic of "derivation" and "combination."

Foucault, in his *The Order of Things: An Archaeology of the Human Sciences*[8] and *The Archaeology of Knowledge,*[9] uses his quadrilateral model of discourse to show that the hermeneutic of a tradition in discourse is, in practice, the tradition of a hermeneutic. His *reflexive and reversible* discourse model is an attempt to show the semiotic function of the communication process, what he calls the "law of communication."[10] Discourse is the condition of the name, that is to say, discourse is itself a general taxonomy of representations that nominates meaning. As Foucault says, "to name is at the same time to give the verbal representation of a representation, and to place it in a general table."[11] A table consists of one series (that can be defined as Jakobson's paradigmatic axis or Foucault's *genealogy* method) intersecting another series (the syntagmatic axis or Foucault's *archaeology* method). This space of time is what Foucault calls an *interstice*, the location of the discourse system where conscious experience is a meaning.

To understand Foucault's overall semiotic taxonomy, we must confront another French aphorism that is part of the *tout Paris* discourse, namely, the phrase which is used, for example, by Vincent Descombes as the title of his history of modern French philosophy: *Le Même et L'Autre* (see figure 6). We are forced to deal with the ambiguity of this phrase which in its reversibility gives it an unquestioned phenomenological precision of signification. In one context, we translate it as "Self versus Other," only to realize that it also must be translated as "Same versus Different." The semantic dynamics of this aphorism are a linguistic equivalent to an "optical illusion" which has an infinite regress of reversibility as between foreground and background focus in visual perception. And so, here is our quadrilateral of discourse in which the Self is Same and the Other is Different or conversely in all the quadratic ratios that are possible. I have already mentioned the "semiotic square" model of Greimas as being one hermeneutic and semantic application of this positive ambiguity of the Self/Other—Same/Different semantic ratio. Let me now turn to the application of the Foucault model, because it applies more generally than does the technical semiotic square at the level of discourse as a general system and process of human communication.

Existentialism and Structural Linguistics

What both Existentialism and Structural Linguistics have in common is the semantic ratio of "Self versus Other," i.e., the tropic sign of the part/whole combination: synecdoche. What better illustration of this philosophic pair than Jean-Paul Sartre's well-known aphorism "We are condemned to choose"? The existential condition is always one of choosing between the self and the other. And in parallel fashion, we have already seen in Saussure's structural linguistics the bifurcation of signifier and signified, the diacritical approach to human communication in which speaking and language are the embodiment of Self as expression versus the Other as perception in discourse. In terms of Foucault's model, existentialism illustrates the discursive process of "attribution" in which self is marked by otherness. We need only recall Sartre's analysis of the "gaze" as proof in point. In parallel fashion, structural linguistics illustrates the discursive process of "representation" for Foucault. Saussure's very definition of the sign as the diacritical separation of expression (the signifier) and perception (the signified) is a manifestation of the Self (the synchronic) divorced from the Other (the diachronic).

Phenomenology and Semiology

With phenomenology and semiology, there is a commonality in the semantic ratio of "Same" versus "Other," i.e., the tropic sign of the substance/whole combination: metaphor. The best illustration here is the work of Merleau-Ponty and his response to the Sartrian aphorism with one of his own: "we are condemned to meaning." With his well known distinction between authentic speech (*parole parlante*; speech speaking) and sedimented discourse (*parole parlée*; speech spoken); Merleau-Ponty exemplifies the sameness of embodied discourse as being-in-the-world that is yet Other in the constitution of being-at-the-world.[12] In his unequaled skill at stylistic French, Merleau-Ponty has given us an existential phenomenological reduction, *le même et l'autre* has become *être-au-monde*.

In terms of a parallel example in semiology, we may turn to the work of Roland Barthes.[13] For Barthes, the dynamics of the philosophic pair "same" versus "other" are directly incorporated into the Hjelmslevian model of discourse. The signifier system becomes for Barthes the operation of rhetoric where the system of expression remains the same as it moves through the levels of connotation, denotation, and realization. Yet, the counterpart signified system of ideology offers us the perception of the Other as a difference by similarity in the three semantic levels. In short, Barthes's semiology offers us rhetoric as the name of similarity in expression, while ideology names the differential consistency in perception. Again in terms of Foucault's model of discourse, phenomenology is a "designation" of similarity while semiology is the "substitution" of the Other. In authentic speech, a rhetoric of existential sameness designates the Self, while it is the ideology of sedimented speech that substitutes for the Other.[14]

Structuralism and Psychoanalysis

In the comparison of Structuralism and Psychoanalysis as a discursive example of *le même et l'autre*, we have the semantic ratio of "Same" versus "Different," i.e., the tropic sign of the substance/attribute combination: metonymy. The best example for structuralism in this case is Claude Levi-Strauss.[15] His structural anthropology as summarized in the last chapter on "The Principles of Kinship" in his book *The Elementary Structures of Kinship* is an overt use of information theory. Here, the digital logic of either/or judgments is put in the service of a similarity based on difference: *kinship*. Within a given context of judgment, whether I make a correct or an incorrect choice, I still have the same information value although each choice is different. Probability becomes the reduction of uncertainty, i.e., pure information. In Foucault's model, we have in such anthropological discourse an "articulation" that is its own "specification" that we know as kinship rules in a given culture.

By comparison, a good example of psychoanalysis is the work of Jacques Lacan and his well-known statement that "the *unconscious is structured* in the most radical way *like a language*, that a material operates in it according to certain laws, which are the same laws as those discovered in the study of actual languages, languages which are or were actually spoken."[16] We might translate this proposition in terms of the "same" versus "different" discursive rule by saying that the consistency of the unconscious, its "sameness" is guaranteed by a relationship analogous to language which is only symbolically different. For Lacan, the hierarchy of meaning proceeds from the symbolic, to the imaginary, and then to the real (a parallel to Hjelmslev's connotative, denotative and metasemiotic categories of meaning; and to Peirce's notion of abduction in which a rule plus a result yields a case or fact). A quick, but apparent, illustration of this abduction model is the example of phonological coding in schizophrenic language given by Gregory Bateson. One of his patients continually uttered the phrase "manzinnita wood" (the symbolic; a "rule") which Bateson took to be a naming reference to the common California bush growing on the hospital grounds. Only later while having a meal with the patient at a restaurant (a choice of different context) did Bateson hear anew the phonological coding of the sentence "Man is an eater, if he would" (the imaginary; a "result") which became the clinical insight to therapy (the real; a "case"). In the context of Foucault's discourse model, what Levi-Strauss and Lacan jointly illustrate is the sameness to be found in "derivation" because of the equal difference to be found in "specification."

Julia Kristeva must be included here as a summary theorist whose work (following from Lacan) on the symbolic, the semiotic, and the *chora* spans all the categories I have covered thus far, namely, her commentaries on, and analysis of, Existentialism and Structural Linguistics, along with phenomenology and semiology (including the practice of discourse as rhetoric), and finally, on the present discussion of structuralism and psychoanalysis.[17]

Poststructuralism and Hermeneutics

By comparing poststructuralism to hermeneutics, we shall examine the discursive semantic ratio of "Self" versus "Different," i.e., the tropic sign of the part/attribute combination: simile (positive signification) or irony (negative signification). Let me turn in a general way to Jacques Derrida for an illustration of deconstruction.[18] In his work on grammatology, we have a return to the primacy of inscription as the symbolic act. In this view of discourse, the Self is destroyed, deconstructed, and discovered in the "trace" left by the act of "erasure." *Différance* is the Self deferred by a differential act that is not the sign of speech, but the sign of language. There is an allusive sense here in which Saussure's personal fascination with anagrams (simile) and his apparent arguments against logocentrism (irony) indeed, have become a post-trace in Derrida. I turn now to the parallel situation with hermeneutics by citing a distinction made originally by Emile Benveniste and then taken up by Paul Ricoeur.

Benveniste has pointed out, following Jakobson, that there is a distinctive feature of redundancy in the French verb typology that can be categorically illustrated with the ambiguity of the French word *l'histoire*.[19] We must variously translate this word either as an oral discourse, in a word, a "story," or we have to translate it as "history" in the sense of a narrative. A story is not inscribed, a history is. Discourse and narrative are the voice of a "Self" yet they are "different" voices, the story is embodied orality and the history is disembodied inscription, i.e., symbolic *erasure* is the Self found in the symbolic *trace*.

A somewhat clearer version of this mechanism, albeit by counterpoint to Derrida, is Ricoeur's explication of Benveniste's discourse/history distinction. Ricoeur offers us a model of narration as human time in which he distinguishes "public time" and "private time."[20] Public time emerges as "public narrativity" or what Benveniste calls "history." Public narration is a time of hermeneutic *regeneration*, a narrative that continues after the death of the individual because we are dealing with the time of language. By comparison, private narration is a mortal time of hermeneutic *generation*, the living discourse of a story being told which is closed off finally by death. Here, Ricoeur thinks in terms of Heidegger's being-toward-death (*Sein-zum-Tode*). To summarize once again in terms of Foucault's model of discourse, Derrida's post-structuralism views the Self as a "derivation" of the combined elements to be found in that which is "different," just as Benveniste and Ricoeur find the Self derived from a discourse that combines the elements of history as temporal differentiations of lived experience.

As I included Kristeva at the close of my previous category, I now must mention Pierre Bourdieu who in many ways represents a bridge between post-structuralist and hermeneutic concerns with his theory of embodied *habitus* (*hexis*) as a socio-anthroplogical model of communication practice.[21] He is, at the present time in Paris, widely acknowledged as the person to read, especially following the death of Foucault. Pierre

Bourdieu is at the moment *tout Paris*. Of particular interest to my argument is the fact that he suggests rather clearly that (American attitudes to the contrary) the application of semiology

> does not strictly speaking contradict phenomenological anal-
> ysis of primary experience of the social world as immediate
> understanding; but it [semiology] defines the scope of its [pheno-
> menology] validity by establishing particular conditions in which
> it is possible (that is, perfect coincidence of the ciphers used in
> encoding and decoding), which phenomenological analysis
> ignores.[22]

My analysis in the present book seeks to demonstrate the many ways in which Bourdieu's thesis, long since present in the work of Merleau-Ponty and Foucault, is correct in both an eidetic and empirical application.

Let me close my analysis in this chapter by citing a passage in which all the semantic ratios, all the combinatory oppositions of signification that I have mentioned are used as a self-reflexive discourse intended to show *le même et l'autre*, to show Self and Other as the Same and Different. The passage is the opening comment in Foucault's inaugural lecture (*éloge*) at the *Collège de France*. In this classic oration, you will hear a chain of signifiers and signifieds. The *genealogical* signifiers are the expressive series: (a) attribution, designation, articulation, and derivation which function to symbolize (b) existentialism, phenomenology, structuralism, and poststructuralism. The *archaeological* signifieds are the perceptive series: (a) representation, substitution, specification, and combination which function to symbolize (b) structural linguistics, semiology, psychoanalysis, and hermeneutics. These signifiers and signifieds are the signs, the table of semiotic of discourse that is *le même et l'autre*, the name that "represents representing." Thus, Foucault's inaugural lecture is speech speaking (parole parlante), a taxonomy for the philosophy of the human sciences, and yet the lecture, the discourse, is a semiotic phenomenology of meaning which begins with its own title as an *aphorism* of what we are about to hear: *The Order of Discourse*.

> I would really like to have slipped imperceptibly into this lecture, as into all the others I shall be delivering, perhaps over the years

ahead. I would have preferred to be enveloped in speech, borne away beyond all possible beginnings. At the moment of speaking, I would like to have perceived a nameless voice, long preceding me, leaving me merely to enmesh myself in it, taking up its cadence, and to lodge myself, when no one was looking, in its interstices as if it had paused an instant, in suspense, as a sign beckoning to me. There would have been no beginnings: instead the discourse would proceed from me, while I stood in its path—a slender gap—the point of its possible disappearance.[23]

5

Somebody Is Nowhere

Michel Foucault On Rhetoric and the Discourse of Subjectivity in the Human Sciences

F oucault's master methodological work, the *Archaeology of Knowledge*, is a phenomenology of semiotics operating in the discourse of the human sciences. This book, published in 1969, gives us a revolutionary insight into the capta of discovery, literally, that which we may *take* as evidence in scholarly inquiry. Foucault gives us a new domain of research that we may call communicology: a rhetoric of the person situated within a discourse on the human sciences. It is remarkable that, after almost twenty years, no major philosophical commentary on Foucault's work addresses "the recovery and restoration of the subject within the folds of the space of communicative praxis" prior to Calvin O. Schrag's explication, although it is noted partially in the historical commentaries offered by Hayden White.[1] This prior silence is almost imperceptible among the popular flood of books, the data, devoted to Foucault. The silence *given* is just the short of failure, of rupture, with which Foucault finds delight in his own research. "In this shift of concern from the reality talked about in discourse to a concern with the persons addressed there is a concomitant shift from discourse as referential to discourse as persuasive."[2] In short, Schrag offers us his view of a Postmodern rhetoric in *Communicative Praxis and the Space of Subjectivity*, which constitutes a thematic explication paralleling Foucault's own *L'Archéologie du Savior*. Schrag's thematic discussion completes an earlier project in which his *Radical Reflection and the Origin of the Human Sciences* was largely a parallel explication for the problematic of Foucault's *The Order of Things: An Archaeology of the Human Sciences*.[3]

Given such a comparative context, my approach in this fifth chapter to Schrag's *Communicative Praxis and the Space of Subjectivity* is articulated in the spirit of the project which Foucault and Schrag share: a return to the discourse of the speaking subject. Thus, I am concerned to explicate the speaking subject that emerges as the person in the discourse that we understand (*savior*) as the work of Foucault, and, as we come to know (*connaissance*) through the voice of Schrag, "so expressive discourse has been assigned the task of delivering the subjectivity of the subject."[4] I am concerned with the analysis of four topics: (1) Foucault's view of *discourse* as a problematic and thematic in the human sciences; (2) Foucault's semiotic phenomenology as a method; (3) the grounding of Foucault's rhetoric in the Law of Communication (as itself a ground of logic in Heidegger's sense) which is a rhetorical intuition and constitution of the traditional Law of Non-Contradiction; and (4), Foucault's existential case studies of René Magritte's surrealistic painting, which continues the earlier discussion begun in chapter 3, and the sexual ontology of the hermaphrodite— mademoiselle Adélaïde Herculine Barbin—who became monsieur Abel Barbin by force of the discipline of communication.

FOUCAULT'S PROBLEMATIC AND THEMATIC

In the world of modernity, Foucault's four *epistemes* (16th to 19th centuries) where discourse is too quickly equated with "ordinary language" as given, and its current stepchild "conversation analysis," Foucault reminds us that the factual presence of language is a positivity, a datum. The blunt fact is that modernity offers us an "ordinary language" which is no less than positivism in the disguise of symbolic presentation. Thus for Foucault, the choice of the ritual, game, habit, and rule embody a practice of representation whose rupture locates the crisis in modernity (see figure 1). There is symbolic *disguise* because the linguistic representation is neither "ordinary" as a consensus of legitimation, nor is it a "language" because the symbolic makes no presentational relation (Jakobson's familiar "poetic" function in communication is not present). We shall analyze a specific empirical example of this problematic in chapter 7 when we encounter the Chinese encyclopedia. But first, the explication of the theoretical problematic.

The close study of discourse, i.e., the "name" as the general taxonomy of representation, unmasks the *deception* of conversational grammar and we dis-cover (or "uncover" in the sense of *aletheia*) the dis-course of positivism, i.e., the false re-presentation of "ordinary" language as a parallogism. Thus Schrag reminds us, "The new emphasis on language and discourse has, not unexpectedly, led to a resurrection of the medieval trivium in which grammar, logic, and rhetoric were accorded their respective and combinatory functions."[5] In his work also, Foucault utilizes fundamental thematic concepts of rhetoric to redefine and value the discourse (problematic of grammar and logic) in the human sciences by decentering the spoken subject in language as ontological grammar and by reconstituting the speaking subject in discourse as an ontological rhetoric. Foucault finds his problematic in the "subject" of positive discourse ("general grammar") where the "social subject" of the social sciences is a disguised object. The person is reified as the object of study in the positive regard of the neomodern social sciences. The "ordinary language" of the social sciences is, in deed as it is in theory, an account of the objectified "subject." The social sciences are a study of "individuals," anonymous analytic objects to which the practices of discourse point (recall Goffman's approach discussed in chapter 2), but which we do not and cannot understand in our lived-world of existential choice and practice. The positivist's "individual subject" of discourse is a deictic ghost: The "subject" is a representation of the unknown. In Julia Kristeva's sense, the speaking subject of positivism, of ordinary language, and of conversational analysis, is in *Language: The Unknown.*[6]

While we might invoke the discourse of modernity and hypostatize the unknown as Nature or Civilization, thereby inventing science or society as normative, we do better to accept the discourse of Postmodernity with its culture of persons (see figure 1). We do better to discover the *discourse of the subject* (the language of the ordinary as originary; a semiotic in lived phenomena) and reject the positivism of a "subject of discourse, a subject to discourse" (the ordinary in language; an epiphenomenon in the semiotic system, whether grammar, or logic, or both). Schrag gives us a clear statement of the problematic: "What manner of 'subject' is implicated in the speaking and writing that comprise the ongoing conversation and *écriture* of mankind (*sic*)? And what shape would discourse about this *subject* assume?"[7] Foucault's statement of the thematic is equally concise: "There are two meanings of the word *subject*: subject to someone else by control and dependence, and tied to his (*sic*) own identity by a conscience or self-knowledge. Both meanings suggest a form of power which subjugates and makes subject to."[8]

This analysis, then, is a discussion of the communicative function of *desire* contained in the problematic of discourse as analyzed by Foucault,[9] i.e., an *archaeology of the name*: the account of rhetoric as the subject of control and dependence where *subjectivity is embodied intersubjectivity,* and, a discussion of the communicative function of *power* as the thematic of discourse in Foucault's analysis, i.e., a *genealogy of the name*: an account of rhetoric as the *intersubjectivity of embodied subjectivity* reflecting the influence of Merleau-Ponty and his critique of Husserl. By taking this perspective, I am agreeing with Kristeva that "we would like to insist upon structuralism's unacknowledged debt to phenomenology."[10] I shall examine the two most famous examples of each discourse that Foucault cites as rhetorical typologies of discourse.

First, an exemplification of the problematic of discourse is the eidetic case discussion by Foucault of Magritte's painting

Ceci n'est pas une pipe (rhetorical typology: the failure of positivism discovered (capta) and realized in the discourse of a represented object). Second, the thematic of discourse in the empirical study of *Herculine Barbin: Being the Recently Discovered Memoirs of a Nineteenth-Century Hermaphrodite* (rhetorical typology; the failure of positivism discovered (capta) and actualized in the discourse of a represented subject). In this process of moving reflexively and reversibly from problematic to thematic, object to subject, Foucault surely meets John Nelson's criteria, the six principles of validity that would be "basic to a general rhetoric of inquiry" in the human science of Communicology:

1. Literality has a figurative basis.
2. Reality has a figurative basis.
3. 'Literality' and 'reality' are implicit plurals.
4. Combinations of figurative modes may occur.
5. The best single basis for demarcating paradigms of inquiry is tropal prefiguration.
6. Proliferation of paradigms is good for inquiry.[11]

Or as Schrag summarizes, the explication is "a pondering of how one can best enter the ongoing *concretion* of thought and action, interests and concerns, in such a way that their configurations and disjunctions, directions and misdirections, can be noted and described." Because, "persuasive discourse is thus already inscribed into the wider text of discourse, in which world, self and other are reciprocally involved."[12] Our task, then, is to draw out the combinatory relation between Merleau-Ponty's Self-Other-World model of discourse and that of Foucault contained in the Subject-Power-Knowledge model.

FOUCAULT'S METHOD: SEMIOTIC PHENOMENOLOGY

The problematic and thematic illustrate the primacy that Foucault gives to the "Law of Communication"[13] in discourse that has its archaeology grounded in the failure by rupture of the Aristotelian Law of Identity (along with those of Contradiction and Excluded Middle), and that has its genealogy in the continuous intuitive success of rupturing the Law of Non-Contradiction by the practice of symbolic representation.[14] In

this context, where the grammatical logic of modernity is replaced by the rhetorical logic (tropes) of Postmodernity, Foucault
practices a semiotic phenomenology of speech and discourse;
"it is revelatory rather than referential" says Schrag.[15]

> The opposition between Foucault's genealogy and phenom-
> enological archaeology, therefore, is not an absolute one. Both
> of Foucault's moves—toward power relations and toward the
> infinity of interpretations—can be seen as a radicalization of the
> twin phenomenological themes of the lived-body and historicity.[16]

The semiotic phenomenological method Foucault employs
is, of course, taken from his teacher, Merleau-Ponty, from
whom he takes the methodological metaphor of *archaeology*:

> There is truly a reversal when one passes from the sensible world,
> in which we are caught, to a world of expression, where we seek
> to capture significations [capta] to serve our purpose, although
> this reversal and the "retrogressive movement" [Husserl] of truth
> are solicited by a perceptual anticipation. Properly speaking, the
> expression which language makes possible resumes and amplifies
> another expression which is revealed in the "archaeology" of the
> perceived world.[17]

As a context for this thematic archaeological thesis on the
reversibility of perception and expression, we should recall in
particular the specific program of semiotic phenomenology
Merleau-Ponty describes in his Inaugural Lecture at the *Collège
de France*,[18] his essay "On the Phenomenology of Language,"[19]
and his preface to the *Phenomenology of Perception*[20] where the
triadic method of description, reduction, and interpretation
detailed throughout the main text is announced.[21] Recall that
in the French human science context, discourse is distinguished from natural language in that discourse is the natural
language "assumed and transformed by the speaking subject"
such that "natural language provides a new dichotomy, that of
enunciation [*énonciation*] and of utterance [*énoncé*] which are
two complementary aspects of speech for Saussure."[22] Enunciation is the expressive modality of perception usually characterized by the phenomenological term *intentionality*, where
one's "consciousness of. . ." is, indeed, the expression that
"resumes and amplifies another expression."[23] In comparison,

utterance is "the state resulting from enunciation, independently of its syntagmatic dimensions (sentence or discourse). So defined, utterance has to do with elements that point us toward the domain of the enunciation."[24] Thus for Foucault, the problematic of discourse is a phenomenological description of language as a sign-system pointing to the speaking subject. In this first methodological step, recall that "formations" are based in the emergence of certain "relations" in discursive communication. These formations have three forms in semiotic communication, i.e., the modalities of "statement," "event," and "discourse." The *statement*

> is a function of existence that properly belongs to signs and on the basis of which one may decide, through *analysis or intuition*, whether or not they "make sense," according to what rule they follow one another or are juxtaposed, of what they are the sign, and what sort of act is carried out by their formulation (oral or written).[25]

Second, the thematic of discourse is a phenomenological reduction of language as a signifier or plane of expression. This thematic is located in the utterance (*énoncé*) of the statement as a discursive *event*. As Foucault says of the enunciated statement:

> It is certainly a strange event: first, because on the one hand it is linked to the gesture of writing or to the articulation of speech [sign description], and also on the other hand it opens up to itself a residual existence in the field of a memory [sign reduction], or in the materiality of manuscripts, books, or any other form of recording [sign interpretation]; secondly, because, like very event, it is unique, yet subject to repetition [signifier description], transformation [signifier reduction], and reactivation [signifier interpretation]; thirdly, because it is linked not only to situations that provoke it [signified description], and to the consequences that it gives rise to [signified reduction], but at the same time, and in accordance with a quite different modality, to the statements that precede and follow it [signified interpretation].[26]

Third in the procedural process is the essential conjunction of the problematic and thematic, i.e., description and reduction, as a phenomenological interpretation of the signified or the plane of content in discourse. Note that the situation of everyday discourse (the utterance of "rules") is an ongoing process of communicative transformations (the "result" of utterance) from which are taken discourse formations in the form of events (the "case" of utterance). Following Peirce, this is an abduction (Rule + Result = Case) and not either a deduction or induction where formation leads to transformation. It is on this logical ground that Foucault separates his approach from that of the German critical theorists like Jürgen Habermas.[27]

> One might say, then, that a discursive formation is defined (as far as its objects are concerned, at least) if one can establish such a group; if one can show how any particular object of discourse finds in it its place and law of emergence; if one can show that it may give birth simultaneously or successively to mutually exclusive objects, without having to modify itself.[28]

In summary, Schrag reminds us that "Foucault's archaeology of the human sciences culminates in a shift of focus from the being of man (*sic*) as historical subject to the 'being of language'."[29] Rhetoric (*parole parlante*; speech speaking) is thereby the discourse (*parole parlée*; speech spoken) constituting the subject in representation (*langue*) and his/her intersubjectivity in presentation (*discours*; *langage*). As Kristeva confirms,

> the term *discourse* designates in a rigorous and unambiguous fashion the manifestation of *la langue* in living communication. Clarified by Emile Benveniste, discourse is contrasted with *la langue*, which thence designates language as a collection of formal signs, stratified in successive layers that form systems and structures. Discourse implies first the participation of the subject in his language through his *speech, as an individual.* Using the anonymous structure of *la langue*, the subject forms and transforms himself in the discourse he communicates to the other. *La langue*, common to all, becomes in discourse the vehicle of a *unique* message. The message belongs to the particular structure of given subject who imprints a specific seal upon the required structure of *la langue*. Without being aware of it, the subject makes his mark on *la langue*.[30]

TABLE 1. Desire-Power: Foucault's Intertextuality of Medieval Hermeneutics and Rhetoric; Heirarchy of Theory is 1 -> 4, Hierarchy
of Practice is 4 -> 1.

Scholastic (Medieval) Models:

Interpretation [herméneutikos]	*Rhetoric [logos]*
1. **Anagogical Interpretation** [collective/mystical referent; anagógé = referent; rhetoric = logic of discourse]	1. **Articulation** [lectio; articulus] {Foucault: **Designation***} * the problematic of "name" at each level.
2. **Moral or Tropological Interpretation** [individual/subjective referent; tropic = logic of speech]	2. **Judgment** [disputatio] {Foucault: **Nomination***}
3. **Allegorical Interpretation** [interpretative/code referent; kinship = logic of exchange]	3. **Generalization** [quaestio] {Foucault: **Description***}
4. **Literal Interpretaton** [textual/media referent; grammar = logic of language]	4. **Concept** [lectio] {Foucault: **Classification***}

Foucault's (Quadrilateral) Rhetoric Models:

Desire: Archaeology of the Name[1]	*Power: Genealogy of the Name[2]*
1. **Articulation** by Rhetoric[3] {Isomorphism*} [Metaphor]	1. **Specification** by the Other {Reversal*} [Ethnocentrism]
* = Foucault's thematic procedure of methodology at each level	
2. **Designation** by Sophistic {Models*} [Metonymy]	2. **Substitution** by the Same {Discontinuity; "Rupture"*} [Alienation]
3. **Derivation** by Dialectic {Shifts*} [Synecdoche]	3. **Element** (**Combination**) by the Different {Specificity*} [Xenophobia]
4. **Attribution** (**Proposition**) by Maieutic {Correlations*} [Simile (Irony)]	4. **Representation** by the Self {Exterority*} [Anomie]

Notes:

1. A general taxonomy (symbolization) of representation; *Law of Representation* = Subjectivity is embodied intersubjectivity; the contingent Flesh.
2. A specific taxonomy (consciousness) of representation; *Law of Communication* = Intersubjectivity is embodied subjectivity; the universal Flesh.
3. The problematic of the contingent subject [subject to discourse] is made thematic as a universal subject [subject of discourse] in the combination of "archaeology" and "genealogy" as a *Critical Genealogy* where the rules of discourse operate as *both person and persona* (Foucault, 1980, pp. 98–102):

    (1) **Rhetoric** "Rule of Immanence": "The Theme of the 'flesh' that must be mastered, different forms of discourse—self-examination, questionings, admissions, interpretations, interviews—were the vehicle of a kind of incessant back-and-forth movement of forms of subjugation and schemas of knowledge" (p. 98); this rule illustrates Merleau-Ponty notion of *freedom*.

    (2) **Sophistic** "Rule of Continual Variations": "Relations of power-knowledge are not static forms of distribution, they are 'matrices of transformations'" (p. 99); this rule illustrates Merleau-Ponty's notion of *terror*.

    (3) **Dialectic** "Rule of Double Conditioning": "the specificity of possible tactics, and of tactics by the strategic envelope that makes them work" (p. 100); this rule illustrates Foucault's notion of *desire*.

    (4) **Maieutic** "Rule of the Tactical Polyvalence of Discourse": "discourses are tactical elements or blocks operating in the field of force relations; there can exist different and even contradictory discourses within the same strategy; they can, on the contrary, circulate without changing their form from one strategy to another, opposing strategy" (p. 102); this rule illustrates Foucault's notion of *power*.

Foucault illustrates his point concerning discourse as an event with a discussion of the four hypotheses, which we will come to in a moment, by which a discursive formation might be tested.[31] He accomplishes this analysis by relying on the phenomenological description or "field of presence" that is produced in any discourse by the four part medieval view of hermeneutic, e.g., Guibert de Nogent's *Liber quo ordine sermo fieri debeat* (A Book about the Way a Sermon Ought To Be Given).[32]

As Umberto Eco confirms, the quadratic description is a discursive hierarchy of hermeneutic interpretation that progresses from the *literal* (text/media referent), to the *allegorical* (symbolic/code referent), to the moral or *tropological* (individual/subjective referent), and to the *anagogical* (collective/mystical referent).[33] Eco's applied concrete example here, of course, is not his novel *The Name of the Rose* illustrating the sign of a sign, or the literal "name" in modernity that Foucault would describe as "Desire: an archaeology of the Name" (see table 1). Rather, Eco's example is *Foucault's Pendulum*, a novel illustrating the symbol of a sign, or the allegorical-moral-anagogical "name" in Postmodernity that Foucault describes as "Power: a genealogy of the Name." In this second novel, there is a further illustration of phenomenological reversibility and semiotic reflexivity embedded in the example itself. Thus, we should note in passing that the "invention" of the literal pendulum, a sign (motion) of a sign (analytic harmonic), in 1851 by Jean Bernard Léon Foucault to show the formation (e.g., desire) of organization (e.g., power) can also be "ruptured,"[34] a human subject made into a dead body "object" on the pendulum wire thus restructures the pendulum (motion) to illustrate a "transformation of organization"[35] in Michel Foucault's sense of an allegorical—moral—anagogical pendulum, a symbol (dialectic harmonic = discourse) of a sign (motion = speaking). For those readers who do not follow this mathematical example illustrated by the "communicative praxis of subjectivity," Eco kindly embeds yet another hermeneutic layer in the "space of subjectivity."[36] To wit: the dead body hanging in place (literal referent) from the roof of the *Conservatoire des Arts et Métiers* (allegorical referent), a museum building that used to be the abbey church of Saint-Martin-des-Champs (moral-tropological referent) and is now the true "Solomon's Temple" (anagogical referent) as described in the "narrative utterance" (Greimas' term) of the novel.

Michel Foucault's phenomenological reduction or "field of concomitance" for his four hypotheses is also a function modeled on medieval rhetorical practice,[37] e.g., as practiced at *L'Université de Paris*, with a hierarchy parallel to that of interpretation (table 1).[38] The rhetoric progresses from inscribed *lectio* (concept as read), to *quaestio* (generalization), to *disputatio* (judgment) to oral *lectio* (articulation of the concept). As Eco so pointedly summarizes this type of procedure, "This means that, since there are rhetorical rules, tropes and allegories can be interpreted univocally as if they were literal expressions. Rhetoric is a natural language."[39] It is Foucault who brings the analysis of utterances (*énoncé*) to bear on this "natural language" enunciated as discourse.

Third and last, Foucault's phenomenological interpretation or "field of memory" is recorded in the essence of discourse, what he calls the "quadrilateral of language" that consists (again

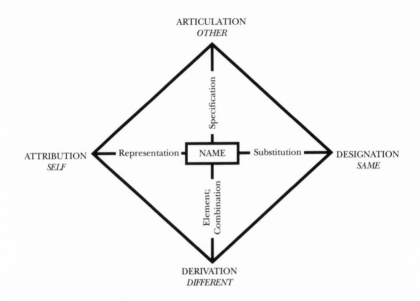

Figure 5. Lanigan Schema of Foucault's Quadrilateral Model of Discourse.

in parallel hierarchy) of two modalities of differentiation by combination (figure 5).[40] Thus, "Language provides the system of signs. Discourse provides the 'eventful' performance."[41] First, there is the archaeology of desire in which the name differentiates language as the meaning within discourse within a four function system or quadrilateral model (*Signs*: Object formations derived from transformations = *Law of Representation*: Subjectivity is embodied Intersubjectivity):

1. Attribution or Proposition (Self Contexture);
2. Articulation (Other Contexture);
3. Designation (Same Contexture); and
4. Derivation (Different Contexture).

As Schrag notes, "According to Husserl, names offer the clearest example of the representational character of signitive meaning."[42]

Second, there is the genealogy of power in which the name differentiates meaning as the four functives of speech in discourse within the quadrilateral model (*Symbols*: Subject forma-

tions derived from transformations = *Law of Communication*:
Intersubjectivity is embodied Subjectivity):

1. Representation (Simile/Irony in tropic logic: Literal
   Meaning)
2. Specification (Metaphor in tropic logic: Allegorical
   Meaning)
3. Substitution (Metonymy in tropic logic: Moral Meaning)
4. Combination or Element (Synecdoche in tropic logic:
   Anagogical Meaning)

Or as Schrag suggests, there is "the bonding of communication
and praxis as an intertexture within their common space." Just
as Jakobson recognized the communicological felicity of
redefining the meaning and function of the term "referent" as
the more useful concept of "context," Schrag helps explain
Foucault by offering use the notion of *texture* as the mediating
space between communication and praxis.

> Communication and praxis intersect within a common space.
> Communication is a qualification of praxis. It is the manner in
> which praxis comes to expression. But praxis is also a qualification
> of communication in that it determines communication as a
> *performing* and an *accomplishing*. We can thus with equal propriety
> speak of communicative praxis and praxial communication.[43]

For Foucault, the desire of the name "is the nexus of the entire
Classical experience of language," that is to say:

> This is why, in its [discourse] very possibility, it is linked with
> rhetoric, that is, with all the space that surrounds the name,
> causes it to oscillate around what it represents, and reveals the
> elements, or the adjacency, or the analogies of what it names.
> The figures through which discourse passes act as a deterrent to
> the name, which then arrives at the last moment to fulfill or
> abolish them. The name is the *end* of discourse.[44]

We shall come momentarily to the subject of discourse that
is the name of power. But first, it is helpful to see Foucault's
sense of discourse in which "rhetoric defines the spatiality of
representation as it comes into being with language"[45] and in
which discursive formations are "great rhetorical unities" that

"are regulated ways (and describable as such) of practicing the possibilities of discourse."[46] Foucault is undoubtedly thinking of the classical schemata that one finds in the discussion of discourse in Plato's *Sophist* where the following discursive spatiality of speaking is constructed (see figure 6).[47]

1. Dialectic:
   Questions that take (capta) or give (data) Questions.
   [Synecdoche: code and existence as context or referent.]

2. Sophistic:
   Answers that take (capta) or give (data) Answers.
   [Metonymy: regularity and similarity as context or referent.]

3. Rhetoric:
   Answers that take (capta) or give (data) Questions.
   [Metaphor: series and substitution as context or referent.]

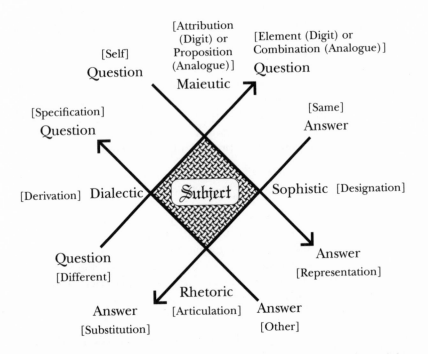

Figure 6. Foucault's Speaking Subject in Discourse; an interpolation of the Quadrilateral Model of Discourse (Fig. 5) and the rule of Le Même et L'Autre (Fig. 8). Note that the Speaking Subject is the Name in Fig. 5; see Table 1.

4. Maieutic:

> Questions that take (capta) or give (data) Answers.
> [Simile; Irony: event and selection as context or referent.]

Subjectivity is a texture of discourse, a rhetorical dimension of embodied intersubjectivity in which "communication has both a linguistic and an actional dimension. There is a rhetoric of speech and there is a rhetoric of action."[48]

FOUCAULT'S HUMAN SCIENCE OF COMMUNICOLOGY

We should recall that early in chapter 2 on "discursive formations" in *The Archaeology of Knowledge,* Foucault distinguishes "terms" from "relations" within "statements, events, and discourse."[49] He suggests that four hypotheses have to be confronted.

1. The first hypothesis is that "statements different in form, and dispersed in time, form a group if they refer to one and the same object." Or, according to Schrag, "The first point to be underscored about the deployment of signitive meaning is that it adheres to the space of communicative praxis."[50] We need to recall phenomenologically that this hypothesis (= term) is reflexive to itself (= relation) and is thereby an *anagogical interpretation* of discursive relationship (= event). It is equally the deliberate rupture of the medieval *lectio* which is the first step of theory construction through argumentation, i.e., articulation of a thesis (= a discourse). It is critical to note that Foucault is not repeating the medieval formulae used in the rationalism of modernity (formation -> transformation) to explain discourse, namely, moving in the series: lectio -> quaestio -> disputatio -> lectio (articulatus); and, literal -> allegorical -> moral -> anagogical meaning.

Rather, Foucault is reversing and reflexively combining according to the Postmodern formulation (transformation -> formation) of discourse where we have: (1) the "anagogical – articulation" pair rendered as "Attribution—Representation," (2) the "moral –disputation" doublet rendered as "Derivation – Combination," (3) the "allegorical – interrogation" pair ren-

dered as "Designation—Substitution," and (4) the "literal—
textual" pair rendered as "Articulation—Specification" (see
table 1). As Schrag specifies, "linguistics slides into semiology
and semiology slides into hermeneutics. This passage from
linguistics to hermeneutics via semiology determines the sign
as it is operative in signitive meaning as *hermeneutical sign*."[51]

It is likewise important to note that Foucault turns Aristotle's notion of deductive logic on its head, much in the tradition
of Charles S. Peirce's abduction logic and Lucien Lévy-Bruhl's
"law of participation" (see appendix A). Simply put, Foucault
states and argues again what is the foundational thesis of
Postmodernity: A human being is a sign (Peirce); A human
being is language (Hjelmslev; Heidegger); A human being is
discourse (Foucault; Merleau-Ponty). In praxis, this postmodern thematic means that (as all of Foucault's work emphasizes)
we as human beings understand (*savoir*) and come to recognize
(*connaissance*) in the empirical example of speaking and language that we intuit the subject of our conscious experience.
"As if we were afraid to conceive of the *Other* in the time of our
own thought," says Foucault.[52] Such an "intentional object," or
symbol, is the eidetic example of some thing, some body that
is both present and absent in the same place at the same time.
Aristotle was simply mistaken because as a good positivist he
initially forgot to include his own conscious experience as a
subject in the equation of logic. When he did account for such
an object as subject, he invented "rhetoric."[53] As Schrag confirms,
"before speaking is thematized as an empirical speech act in
contradistinction to the logical system of language, it unfolds
as an expressive performance with a historical breath and a
temporalization that knits together a speaking, an already
spoken, and a yet to be spoken."[54] Foucault's point is clear: the
person as a subject in rhetoric precedes itself as an object of
grammar which precedes itself as a referent ("context" following Jakobson's usage) in logic!

2. As the second hypothesis, Foucault determines "to define
a group of relations between statements: their form and type
of connection."[55] This is to say, with Schrag, that "the second
point to be understood is that signitive meaning involves a play

of idealities which are themselves situated within the history of discourse and action."[56] This semiotic hypothesis (= relation) is in turn reflexive to itself as a relation (= term) and is thus a *moral or tropological interpretation* of the discursive term (= event). It counts as a rupture of the medieval *disputatio* in which the second step of theory construction through argument is *judgment* of a thesis (= a discourse). It is helpful to once again consult table 1.

3. Announcing the third hypothesis, Foucault suggests that "to establish groups of statements, by determining the system of permanent and coherent concepts involved" another phenomenological condition is advanced.[57] Schrag repeats, "the third point is that signitive meaning is borne by recollection and repeatability."[58] In this hypothesis, groups of statements (= term) are reflexive to themselves as a system (= relation) and are therefore the *allegorical interpretation* of the discourse coherence (= event). In consequence, the interpretation is a rupture of the medieval notion of *quaestio* which grounds the theory construction rule of *generalization* as the third step of argumentation.

4. Foucault argues as a fourth hypothesis that he can begin "to regroup statements, describe their interconnection and account for the unitary forms under which they are presented: the identity and persistence of themes."[59] In this hermeneutic procedure of semiotic phenomenology, "expressive meaning qualified by reflection and distanciation slides into *signitive* meaning."[60] Here, the transformations of discourse (= event) are reflexive to their formation (= relation) and are thereby an expression of *literal interpretation* that is a discursive thematic (= term). This interpretation is a rupture of the medieval *lectio* in which a *concept* is the ground for argumentation. In short, the medieval model championed by modernity is ruptured (transformation) as it simultaneously constitutes (formation) the "birth" of a new postmodern model. The quadratic of language is critiqued by the quadratic of rhetoric, the space of the speaking subject.

"I am presented therefore with four attempts, four failures—

and four successive hypotheses. They must now be put to the test," says Foucault.[61] Let us read this statement as a semiotic phenomenologist, like Foucault, who intuitively takes the prefigurative and rhetorical praxis view of the Law of Non-Contradiction ("four successive hypotheses") which must be a prior account for both the Law of Identity [$p = p$] and the Law of Contradiction [$p \neq p$] in both these hypotheses ("four attempts") and their dysfunction ("four failures"). Recall the Law of Non-Contradiction, namely, that a term (= statement/event/discourse) cannot both be and not be; symbolically [-(p . -p)]. With the formal symbolism in mind as an interpretive tool, we can see respectively that "hypotheses" equals the symbolic notation ["– " or negation], "four attempts" equals the ["p" or present proposition], the conjunction symbol [". " or combinatory "and"] equals the "four successive hypothesis", and the symbol ["-p" or absent proposition] equals the "four failures." Given this data, Foucault is asking us to examine the taken fact (capta) that we intuitively used several layers of symbolic knowledge (*connaissance*) in order to rationalize the concept of non-contradiction as a transformation of the idea of identity. "And so, too, it is false to say that the identical is always exclusively identical, since in one respect at least the identical is identical with the different. Neither is it true that the different is always different. For the different is different only when it is identical with itself, a property it *shares* with the identical."[62] Understanding (*savoir*) this fact is a rupture of the rationalization. We now see the phenomenology of consciousness that was prior to the rationalization. We used possibility (especially those which are contradictory referents as in "this is not a pipe") to constitute a judgment, i.e., ongoing transformations or symbols to constitute formations or signs. "What is at issue in the wake of such a displacement is no longer the impossible task of defining a mind-subject present to itself in a self-reflexivity of consciousness, but rather the recognition of a plurality of inscriptions through speaking, writing, and acting that issue from the behavior of embodied thought."[63]

The key to this semiotic phenomenological analysis is to realize with Foucault that discourse is always reflexive in a positive sense only because the negative sense is simultaneously the ground of, and an alternative to, the positive: *"One establishes the inverse series: one replaces the pure aims of non-contradiction in a complex network of conceptual compatibility and incompatibility; and one relates this complexity to the rules that characterize a particular discursive practice."*[64] The governing negation is a present absence or more explicitly "the possible positions of desire in relation to discourse."[65] There are four successive hypotheses generated explicitly on the basis of a prior intuition that ruptures the Law of Identity and makes the Law of Non-Contradiction a primary transformation from which formations are created.[66] In Peirce's sense of hypothesis, these abductions (Rule + Result = Case) amount to the thematic methodology of archaeology (see table 1).

Formation 1: Archaeological Isomorphisms. Different discursive elements are formed on the basis of similar rules. They are the Postmodern "theories of attribution [proposition], derivation, designation, and articulation," which replace the failed medieval form of argumentation as rhetoric, representing the thought of modernity expressed as the progressive conative hierarchy of concept, generalization, judgment, and articulation (see table 1). Thus, rhetoric as style or "knowledge" (*connaissance*) gives way to rhetoric as persuasion in the form of understanding (*savior*). Understanding is Foucault's sense of discursive intentionality that can be described explicitly as *both* power *and* desire located in the embodied consciousness of . . ., which is parallel to Merleau-Ponty's notions of thetic and operative intentionality. As summarized by Schrag, "consciousness is given birth in the dialogic and actional encounters with other subjects, and it is able to sustain itself only within such encounters."[67]

Formation 2: Archaeological Models. These are the Postmodern discourse formations of "representation, combination (element), substitution, and specification" making concrete the extent to which rules do or do not apply with the same model in different types of discourse and which, in turn, replace the failed medieval form of argumentation as *hermeneutic*, i.e., the conative hierarchy of literal, allegorical, moral, and anagogical interpretation. Thus, according to Schrag:

Self-consciousness as a hermeneutical moment of understanding is enveloped by the linguisiticality and the social practices which allow one to say "I" in concrete speech transactions. Embedded within tradition of the already spoken, the already written, and the already accomplished social practices, self-consciousness breaks forth as a dialogic event within the embodied and decentered subjectivity.[68]

Formation 3: Archaeological Shifts. These are the different concepts that occupy a similar position of transformation in one system or a single concept that is a formation in two different systems. Such systemic relations and correlations (Hjelmslev's sense) make rhetoric the tropic ground of intuitive consciousness, i.e., the Laws of Identity and Contradiction derive from the Law of Non-Contradiction.

Gilles Deleuze confirms this anti-Hegelianism in which "difference and repetition have replaced the identical and the negative, identity and contradiction."[69] As a phenomenology, this logic is in the service of the phenomenon where that phenomenon is no less than *consciousness of consciousness*, the birth of the *symbol*. "A rhetorical consciousness is stitched into the very warp and woof of the multiple forms of discourse and action, which in concert occasion a hermeneutical reference to the world, a hermeneutical self-implicature of the subject, and a disclosure of the other."[70] Wilden gives us a specific illustration of the transformational shift formation in the example of a map: "A map is a translation from code to code—a translation of selected features of a 'territory' into another medium or another code of representation, or the translation of one kind or level of mapping into another kind."[71] Hence, the transformation (code to code) precedes the formation (message to message) in manifestation and, therefore, the message is always "de-centered."

Formation 4: Archaeological Correlations. These are the correlations (either/or judgments) of subordination or complementarity. They become established in the representation of representation which makes the term in discourse, i.e., the statement, event, or discourse, its own relation (both/and judgment). Or, as Schrag puts it, "consciousness as a hermeneutical event displays an *interpretation* of self and world through the twin moments of understanding and explanation."[72] Explicit examples of correlation formations are Magritte's surrealistic painting and Barbin's sexuality, both discussed in the sections below.

Thus, the summary ontology that Foucault discovers in the face of these "successive hypotheses" is that they are an existential reversibility and reflexivity: "*It is not only the overall relation of several discourses to this or that other discourse; it is the law of their communications.*"[73] For Foucault, the phenomenological description ("field of presence"), reduction ("field of concomitance"), and interpretation ("field of memory") is a discursive consciousness.[74] This consciousness is reflexive to its own discursive experience as a semiotic phenomenological description ("form of succession"), reduction ("form of coexistence"), and interpretation ("procedure of intervention)" of the speaking subject (see figure 6). Thus Foucault demonstrates the accuracy, authenticity, and authority of an earlier hypothesis:

> The object of the human sciences is not language (though it is spoken by men [sic] alone); it is that being which, from the interior of the language by which he is surrounded, represents to himself, by speaking, the sense of the words or propositions he utters, and finally provides himself with a representation of language itself. The human sciences are not, then, an analysis of what man is by nature; but rather an analysis that extends from what man is in his positivity (living, speaking, laboring being) to what enables this same being to know (or seek to know) what life is, in what the essence of labor and its law consist, and in what way he is able to speak.[75]

Schrag rearticulates the point: "Expression surpasses the intentions of particular actors and institutions, announcing patterns of ideation and valuation that remain opaquely entrenched within the habitual behavior of everyday life and the delivered processes of social formation" (see figure 13).[76] With these theoretical tools of semiotic phenomenology at our disposal, we now can turn to the analysis of two cases of "positivity," two phenomenological concretions of those Postmodern contexts of conscious experience re-presented by discourse.

DESIRE: THE CASE OF NO CASE IN REPRESENTATION

The principle of negation is an ontological grounding in Foucault's work, but that does not mean it cannot be easily illustrated. There are simple and straight forward examples, and, Foucault offers one in his monograph *This Is Not A Pipe*, published as a separate volume.[77] The captum, the discovered fact, under review is desire in the failure of positive represen- tation in the discourse of an object, the symbol as a form and not a content. For our analytic purposes, we can concentrate on plate 4, the René Magritte painting titled *Ceci n'est pas une pipe*, created in 1926, and its companion work entitled *Les Deux mystères*, created in 1966, plate 5. Recall that we have already examined such an example in chapter three with the analysis of "Max Headroom."

Note that Magritte painted a continuing series of "pipe" paintings; many are repetitions of the same image and are individually and collectively refereed to as the "this is not a pipe" painting (thereby becoming a completely de-centered phe- nomenon of the speaking subject located in the transforma- tions of discourse formation). Thus, the casual observer or researcher will not distinguish among *Ceci n'est pas une pipe* (1926), *L'usage de la parole I* (1928–29), or *La trahison des images* (1929). An initial positive attempt at the explanation of what is communicated in plate 4 appears in Anthony Wilden's *The Rules Are No Game: The Strategy of Communication.*[78] Chapter 8 of this book begins with a discussion of plate 4; note that an initial version of this chapter is also available *without* the discussion of Magritte and plate 4.[79] The two versions of the Wilden text without and with the Magritte text become yet another illustra- tion of the transformation and transposition (intertextuality) of discourse per se.

Wilden argues that the painting embodies his "three way rule" for the ontological grounding of negation. He details the logical conditions that are necessary for montage (tropic rhetoric) in the visual image by specifying some twelve condi- tions, which he postulates in summary form as the "The Three Way Rule": *The minimum number of connections required to estab- lish a relationship is three: system, environment, and the boundary mediating between them.*[80] This rule appears to restate Peirce's idea of Firstness (system), Secondness (environment), and Thirdness (boundary mediating) as entailed in the logic of abduction (Rule + Result = Case). Before exploring this rule from the Foucaultian perspective of a semiotic phenomenology, I want to recall two important items that punctuate the rule. First, Wilden opens his analysis by explaining that:

> If we ask ourselves just what is not a pipe in Magritte's metaphoric image, we find at least six respectable answers, each of them depending for their validity on the framing of the message:
>
> This [pipe] is not a pipe —
> This [image of a pipe] is not a pipe —
> This [painting] is not a pipe —
> This [sentence] is not a pipe —
> [This] this is not a pipe —
> [This] is not a pipe —
> and presumably take our pick.[81]

Before presenting the three-way rule, Wilden closes his discussion by stating the last of his 12 conditions: "As the boundary between 'A' and 'not-A', 'not' is neither 'A' nor 'not-A'."[82]

What I have just expressed is the reflective, or more phenomenologically accurate, prereflective, presence of eidetic montage (tropic logic) in Wilden's discourse on montage (rhetoric). It is a way of understanding the semiotic function of combinatory "analytic logic" (usually called digital logic) and "dialectic logic" (usually called analogue logic) in logic and discourse, whether that discourse is the medium (read mediation and differentiation) of speech or film or television or *what-not* (a pun is not intended; a rupture is). In a film or video, visual montage is a desire created by the skilled hand of the editor (or painter) and the skilled eye of the viewer. We might easily well suggest montage as the signified message created by the skilled tongue of the speaker and the skilled ear of the listener. "For the editor," notes Wilden, "the twenty to forty hours of film actually shot by the director are the axis of cinematic metaphor. The one to three hours of metaphors selected and combined in the final print are the axis of cinematic metonymy."[83]

Plate 4. Magritte's Painting *L'usage de la parole* (1928–29)

Plate 5. Magritte's Painting *Les Deux mysteres* (1966)

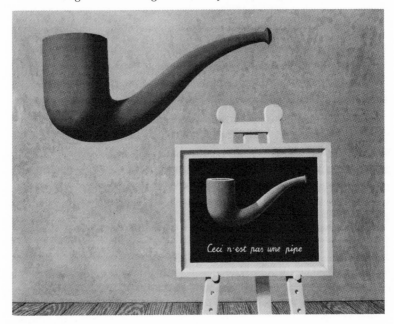

Of course, here we are dealing with the Jakobsonian selection (metonymy) and combination (metaphor) that Wilden wants to generalize into an analytic and dialectic logic.[84] In any case (where "case" is a medium as mediation-differentiation), montage names the rhetorical boundary between system and environment in any given relationship. This is the three-way rule, not to be confused with a three-value logic, that would reify the montage. Incidentally, Magritte has proven empirically by his painting that the three-value logic (see plate 5) is just as useless in the quest for realism as is the traditional two-value logic (see plate 4) in discourse analysis.

Let's explore what is going on in Wilden's tropic logic. First, we have Magritte's painting (plate 4) which illustrates the perspective of Wilden's analytic logic: "either either/or or both/and."[85] This is to say, in Magritte's painting we have *either* a choice between "either" the image (smoker's pipe) "or" a real pipe (so perceived) *or* the inscription "Ceci n'est pas une pipe" which in French (a linguistic context) is "both" a predication of "pipe" "and" a failure of predication because the negation (*ne . . . pas*) entails the affirmation (*est*) of the context/referent. Wilden mistakenly calls this a "choice" when it is actually a "context" function. Because of this critical mistake of context/referent, the logic fails to apply in English translation (the new context) because the negation values the object in the sentence ("pipe") instead of the verb ("is"). The map is not the territory even when the "territory" is another map! Recall Wilden's previously noted definition: "A map is a translation from code to code."

Put more simply, the French *n'est pas* is a metonymy for the metaphor created by counterposing the pipe image and the inscription whose boundary is a vertical space. The desire of the painting is a perfect montage for any person who speaks French and sees the painting within the power constraint of French grammar. As Schrag suggests, "consciousness is the hermeneutical event of comprehending the world."[86] The analytic logic of the French language construction codes the perceptual possibilities of the image. In short, we confirm Wilden's Rule 12: As the boundary between 'A' and 'not-A,' 'not' is neither 'A' nor 'not-A.' Translation for the rhetorician: As the boundary between the image and its missing real world referent, likewise as between the inscription and its missing real world referent (note: "Ceci" has no predicated linguistic referent in the sentence), there is negation, i.e., Foucault's rupture and Merleau-Ponty's chiasm. Yet we have a puzzle. How can we recognize, understand the operation of the analytic logic? We surely do not want to fall back on a positivistic hypostatization that it is already anonymously "given" as a datum.

The answer lies with Wilden's perspective of dialectic (analogue) logic which entails the analytic (digital) logic. "The perspective of dialectical logic is thus 'both both-and and either/or.'"[87] To return to Magritte's painting (plate 4), there is *both* an image of the pipe which is "both" a signifier for some real world pipe "and" the "possible" signified of the inscription "Ceci n'est pas une pipe" *and* "either" a signifier for the inscription "Ceci n'est pas une pipe" "or" a signified of the absent real world pipe. In short, the negation as the rupture or chiasm is neither a blank nor a visual absence that divides the image from the inscription, or conversely, divides the inscription from the image. Rather, the negation is the boundary presence of absence (desire) that entails the "perspective" of space (*mutatis mutandis*: Wilden's "framing and punctuation").[88] Derrida expresses the point concisely: "The concept of centered structure—although it represents coherence itself, the condition of the *epistémé* as philosophy or science—is contradictorily coherent. And as always, coherence in contradiction expresses the force of a desire."[89] Thus, the correct semiotic translation in English of "Ceci n'est pas une pipe" is "This can not be a pipe" where the "not" marks the presence of absence, i.e., where the verb of being is bounded by the negation. In particular, the English syntax of "can/NOT/be" properly encodes the dialectic logic by apposition of opposition (see figure 7 where the same result is achieved by Foucault's *rebus statement* of the calligram which is, in fact, plate 4). Whereas, the French "ne/EST/pas" does not properly encode the message (it is the reverse system of English, i.e., an opposition of apposition; see plate 5). Put another way, the English encoding correctly displays "space" as the presence of absence (negation) as the boundary while the French displays a "blank" as the absence of presence (position) as the boundary which is analytic and, therefore, a dysfunction of the dialectic logic. As Foucault suggests, rupture as the spatial ground of *system birth* is the Law of Communication. "The Greeks had a name for this originative and encompassing rhetorical space. They called it *ethos.*" Commonly translated as "human character" according to Schrag, it "could be more felicitously rendered as 'abode' or 'dwelling place.'"[90] In Merleau-Ponty's version this encompassing space of *parole parlante* is the *corps propre,* or as Wilden remarks, it is also illustrated by Eisentein's view of the visual image as "*inner speech*—speech enriched . . . by "*sensual thinking.*'"[91]

The final rupture, however, belongs to Foucault since the statement he uses to *name* plate 4 reads in English "*Nowhere is there a pipe.*"[92] The dialectic logic is once again on the loose as *no-where* combines phenomenologically with *now-here* to show semiotically that the context (referent) is both present and absent because it either is or is not. Or as Magritte might say, something is nowhere in painting (as it is in all images, all symbols of signs).

The case of Magritte's painting illustrate empirically that Foucault establishes an originary semiotic phenomenology by recognizing the preconceptual in the logic of phenomena, namely, a tropic logic of rhetoric that I call simply *communicology.* This logic reconceives the place/space of rhetoric as a discursive practice and makes of it a *tropic rhetoric* or semiotic phenomenology in the human sciences:

> One establishes the inverse series: one replaces the pure aims of noncontradiction {logic} in a complex network of conceptual compatibility and incompatibility {grammar}; and one relates this complexity to the rules that characterize a particular discursive practice {tropic logic; rhetoric}.[93]

Foucault offers an empirical demonstration by seeing the painting (plate 4), not as visual montage, but as a tropic rhetoric in the statement of a *rebus calligram.* The calligram is traditionally a poem (phenomenological description: first code inscription) whose words are arranged to provide a picture (phenomenological reduction: second code inscription) of its topic (phenomenological interpretation: third code inscription). "In its millennial tradition, the calligram has a triple role: to augment the alphabet, to repeat something without the aid of rhetoric, to trap things in a double cipher."[94] In figure 7, "the calligram's

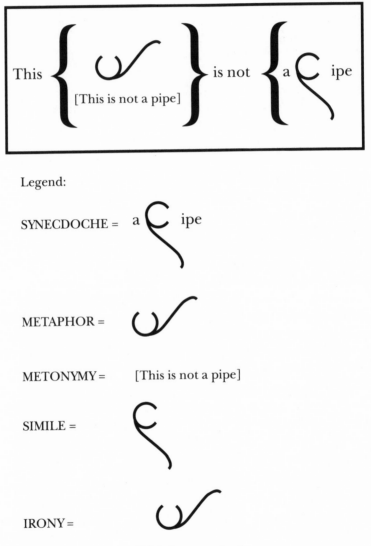

Figure 7. Foucault's Rebus Calligram: This is not a pipe.

redundance rested on a relation of exclusion. In Magritte, the separation of the two elements, the absence of letters in the drawing, the negation expressed in the text—all of these positively manifest two distinct positions."[95]

Of course, figure 7 extends the tropic discourse (of plate 4) so that Foucault appropriately says of it: "Negations multiply themselves, the voice is confused and choked."[96] This is the space of desire, the place for rhetoric to function as Schrag's critical response: "The fitting or proper response is linked with the 'opportune' or 'privileged' moment—the *right* time for deliberation and action."[97] *The calligram is a pharmakon; it is the rhetoric of signature,* in Derrida's sense.[98]

POWER: THE CASE OF NO CASE IN PRESENTATION

I do not intend to explore Foucault's major analyses on the historical theme of sexuality. Nevertheless, his phenomenologically inspired publication of the memoirs and documents related to the hermaphrodite Adélaïde Herculine Barbin (a.k.a. Abel Barbin) do provide a discursive counterpoint to the discussion of Magritte's painting. According to Schrag's formulation of this counterpoint, "truth and method (when method is divested of its positivistic prejudices) are bonded by a genuine connective tissue rather than separated by a disguised disjunction."[99] In chapter three, we analyzed the example of Richard Ross's *Museology* as a case in point. In the case of Barbin, we are dealing with the failure of positivism to ground the discourse of the represented subject.[100] "Communicative praxis is infected with forgotten speech acts and forgotten social practices."[101] Foucault makes it clear that, many commentators to the contrary, he explicates the discourse of the subject, i.e., a rhetoric. As he says,

> my aim was to show what the differences consisted of, how it was possible for men, within the same discursive practice, to speak of different objects, to have contrary opinions, and to make contradictory choices; my aim was also to show in what way discursive practices were distinguished from one another; in short, I wanted not to exclude the problem of the subject, but

to define the positions and functions that the subject could occupy in the diversity of discourse.[102]

And he confirms this early position on rhetoric, on the "order of discourse," by declaring, "thus it is not power, but the subject, which is the general theme of my research." How is the human subject, the person, an ontological instance of the practice of discourse? "There are two meanings to the word *subject*: subject to someone else by control and dependence, and tied to his own identity by a conscience or self-knowledge. Both meanings suggest a form of power which subjugates and makes subject to."[103]

In Schrag's words, "This hermeneutical self-implicature of the subject proceeds in tandem with the rhetorical turn, in which discourse and action are disclosed not only as being *by* someone but also *for* and *to* someone."[104] It is in the dialectic of desire and subject power that Barbin the hermaphrodite has existence. She existentially lives discourse with its rhetoric of power and constant subjugation to the tropic Law of Commu-

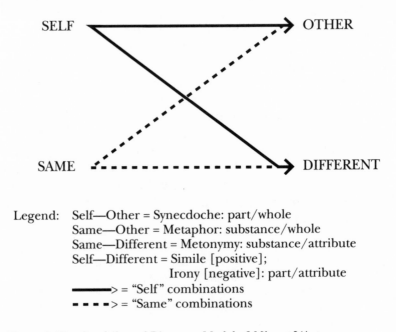

Legend: Self—Other = Synecdoche: part/whole
          Same—Other = Metaphor: substance/whole
          Same—Different = Metonymy: substance/attribute
          Self—Different = Simile [positive];
                      Irony [negative]: part/attribute
          ——————> = "Self" combinations
          - - - -> = "Same" combinations

Figure 8. The Quadrilateral Discourse Model of *Même et L'Autre.*

nication. In this case, the Law of Non-Contradiction takes on the classic form of differentiation and mediation within the social sciences of modernity. It is the problematic of social science turned into the thematic of human science in the discursive rule of Postmodernity rendered in *Le Même et L'Autre.* The formulae of this rhetoric are rendered in Figure 8. In Foucault's phrase, tropic rhetoric is the methodology of diagnosis. What is the purpose of discourse, and how does this phenomenology of the person become the semiotic of power?

> Its [discourse's] task is to *make* differences: to continue them, as objects, to analyze them, to define their concept. Instead of traveling over the field of discourses in order to recreate the suspended totalizations for its own use, instead of seeking in what has been said that *other* hidden discourse, which nevertheless remains the *same* (and instead of playing endlessly with *allegory* and *tautology*), it is continually making *differentiations*, it is a *diagnosis*.[105]

Here we see the discursive rule in use. *Le Même et L'Autre* is both Self and Other, just as it is both the Same and Different. Umberto Eco has called this scientific procedure the "Anti-Ockhamistic principle: *entia sunt multiplicanda propter necessitatem* [phenomena are multiplied by reason of necessity]."[106] The play of discourse is a diagnosis of the subject as subjected in the positive sense of desire where Self which remains the Same, and, subjected negatively to power in the Self which becomes Other, because it is Different from its Self. This is the Law of Non-Contradiction. The person is not permitted to be *both* subject (noun = the paradigmatic person of *savoir* who understands, who "knows how" to be, who desires) *and* subject (verb = the syntagmatic person of *connaissance* who sense, who "knows" there is being, who feels power), yet one is *either* Self and Other (powerful) *or* Same and Different (powerless). "These experiences, in which the subject is both announced and annulled, affirmed and effaced, point to the peculiar texture of presence that pervades the subject. The very texture of presence is qualified by absence," says Schrag.[107]

The example of Barbin's sexuality is an explicit discourse of both the archaeology of desire and the genealogy of power (see table 1). A person born into French culture and perceived as female in body (the certificate of "birth"), "the presence of the subject is a *bodily* presence."[108] She is trained as a female teacher, only to discover in late puberty that she also has male sex organs. She is the same as other girls (feminine), but different from them (masculine). She is conscious of her Self, but finds an Other in *both* her consciousness (desire: sexual awareness) *and* experience (power: bodily awareness). *Either* she knows how to be the Same and Different (for years as a sexual partner she has been "powerful" as a woman who is a man) or she knows that her Self and the Other must become a person (the court has decreed that she will be "powerless" as a man who is a woman; she is not allowed to teach as a profession). The diagnosis of society—the priests, the doctors, the judges, the parents, the teachers—is that Barbin be *subjected to subjectivity* (assume the real life of a man). Barbin is, Schrag generalizes, "implicated in the forms of communicative praxis, the subject as speaker, writer, and actor is announced in the conversation and in the participatory social practices."[109] Barbin's diagnosis—the memory, the discourse, the communion, the friendship, the freedom—is that she live as the *name* of the subject. "In these performances the subject undergoes its birth and rebirth, manifesting its presence in a world and to a world of history and nature alike."[110] The woman Barbin chooses. *He* lives as the subject. *She* commits suicide. *He* is dead; *she* has no name. The certificate of "death" speaks, writes, and enacts the symbol of a sign, "a self divided against itself."[111]

> By the judgment of the civil court of Saint-Jean d'Angély dated 21 June 1860, it has been ordained that the record opposite [the birth certificate of the female] should be rectified in this sense:
> 1) that the child registered here will be designated as being of the masculine sex:
> 2) and that the first name Abel shall be substituted for Adélaïde Herculine.
> Saint-Jean d'Angély, 22 June 1860.[112]

Foucault summarizes this rhetoric of the person, this discourse on desire and power in the human sciences: "So strategy is defined by the choice of winning solutions."[113] In some sense, Barbin asserted *I Lie: Some Body is Now Here. I Speak: Somebody is Nowhere.*

6

The Algebra of History

Merleau-Ponty and Foucault on the
Rhetoric of the Person

"**P**hilosophy is not an illusion. It is the algebra of history,"[1] says Maurice Merleau-Ponty in *Éloge de la Philosophie*. In this philosophical aphorism, we encounter at once the ambiguity of philosophical rhetoric binding the discourse of a story with the narrative of history, expression with perception, structure with form, and semiology with phenomenology. Or as Michel Foucault remarks with his philosophical proposition in *L'Ordre du discours* (a title whose translation is surely "Rhetoric"), "Disciplines constitute a system of control in the production of discourse, fixing its limits through the action of identity taking the form of a permanent reactivation of the rules."[2] In both cases, we are witness to the ontological rhetoric of the person. Rather than a mere literary genre of inscription in the rhetorical tradition of French Science,[3] the inaugural lectures given by Merleau-Ponty and Foucault constitute a reversible rhetoric of the signifying (Sr) and signified (Sd) discourse of orality. The discourse is, indeed, the phenomenology of the lived world, a philosophy of signs we call Existence (*ek-stase*).

I propose to illustrate this eidetic thesis by explicating, on a close reading and textual viewing, the rhetorical structure and form of the inaugural lectures given at the *Collège de France* by both Merleau-Ponty and Foucault. In this discursive analysis, the phenomenology of communication emerges as the dialectical voices of *l'histoire* and *discours*.[4] In each lecture, there is the living presence of an active oral voice in which the Self tells an existential story of the Subject; there is the ontology of speech speaking (*parole parlante*). As between each lecture, there is the lived absence constituting a passive voice in which the anonymous Other narrates an essential history; there is the ontological alterity of speech spoken (*parole parlée*). As Merleau-Ponty summarizes, "Philosophy turns toward the anonymous symbolic activity from which we emerge, and towards the personal discourse which develops in us, and which, indeed, we are."[5]

Thus, Merleau-Ponty gives the ontology of speech speaking of rhetorical form by naming it with a classical "figure" of speech: *prosopopoeia*.[6] But after naming it, he does not define this rhetorical *trope* for reuse in the future (the goal of Aristotle's deliberative, political rhetoric). It remains a pure signifying praxis where personae, the silent voices of the past (Aristotle's forensic or judicial rhetoric), intersect with the disciplines they represent in the present (Aristotle's epideictic or evaluative rhetoric). For Merleau-Ponty, the *l'histoire* of Philosophy is the *story* of the philosopher: Philosophy as existential is Rhetoric as phenomenological.

Then with the fidelity of a student to his teacher, Foucault in his inaugural lecture completes the dialectic of reversibility in the ongoing discourse of the two inaugurals. In his opening words, he characterizes his speaking as a "nameless voice," thereby, defining the trope of prosopopoeia by designation. Yet he neither names nor judges it. In fact, prosopopoeia is an imaginary or absent persona represented as the present oral speaking voice of the person. An excellent example of prosopopoeia is the opening line of Dickens's *David Copperfield:* "I am born." Prosopopoeia is a discourse that creates a new narrative voice, within the narrative per se that unexpectedly judges the person by replacing the narrative function with his or her own voice as lived. The Self of discourse replaces the Subject of narrative and, thereby, represents the person. This trope of speech (not figure of language) for Foucault becomes a pure rhetorical practice of the signified where the disciplines of the past (knowl-edge or *connaissance*) intersect with the discursive voice of consciousness, the voice that can speak in the future (power or *savoir*), and, the voice of the Subject in the present (person or *sujet*). For Foucault, who completes, the dialectical reversibility of Merleau-Ponty's thematic, the *l'histoire* of the philosopher is the *story* of the Philosophy: Philosophy as phenomenological is Rhetoric as existential.

Persona for Merleau-Ponty and *person* for Foucault, as the representations of prosopopoeia in discourse, become the essential reversibility, the chiasm, that is the humane lived-world of the Human where persona/person is subject/subjected.[7] Vincent Descombes makes the point explicit: "The 'end of history' [*l'histoire*] is none other than the translation into figural and narrative language [*langage*] of what in the language of philosophy is known as absolute knowledge."[8] Let us listen to the *lector in fabula*, the ontological strategy of Philosophy as a discourse emergent respectively in the two rhetorical lectures which inaugurate philosophy.[9]

MERLEAU-PONTY'S INAUGURAL: EULOGY TO PHILOSOPHY

Remembering the traditional characterization of Merleau-Ponty as the philosopher of ambiguity, we must abandon the usual translation of his inaugural lecture title. To formulate *Éloge de le Philosophie* as "in praise of philosophy" is to corrupt the "good ambiguity" of discourse, the prosopopoeia that Merleau-Ponty intends. Within the context of classical literature and the *trivium* (grammar, logic, and rhetoric) that both Merleau-Ponty and Foucault studied as French *lycée* students and encountered in the famous "Syllabus" when they were student teachers, we must understand and take the practice of "*éloge*" in its classical meaning as a rhetorical "eulogy."[10]

The eulogy is a part of what Aristotle, in *Rhetoric* (1358b.5), calls epideictic oratory in which the goal of the speaker is respectively to praise (confirm) a persona or blame (condemn) a person. In the case of praise, the orator speaks positively of the *persona* because the person is a subject absent to the discourse, either by death or exile (the discursive ontology of simile). By counterpoint, the negative speech of blame is directed to the *person* who is present to the discourse, because the persona in its immorality must remain subjected to absence (the discursive ontology of irony). Thus in Merleau-Ponty's lecture, we as listeners are confronted with a discourse that offers to *both* praise *and* blame, thereby confirming and condemning philosophy in itself and for itself (the discursive ontology of synecdoche). We are asked to do both through the discursive agent of the person, who is the philosopher, and the agency of the persona, who is the sophist. Merleau-Ponty is concerned with the ontological orality of the philosopher, just as Foucault will be concerned with the oral ontology of the sophist. Both deal with the discourse of the *agent provocateur* much in the same manner that the existence of Aristotle's *Rhetoric* evokes our desire to read his lost *Synagógé Technón* which records the other *l'histoire de rhétorique,* or invokes our power to imagine the content of the lost second book of the *Poetics* by reading the first book which still exists for us.

It will be helpful at this point to briefly consider another teacher and student dialogue, that of Husserl and Jakobson. In his model of communicology (human communication), Jakobson phenomenologically corrects Saussure's structural semiotics by making the signifying (Sr) and signified (Sd) elements of the sign function according to an analogue logic or combination as opposed to a digital logic of exclusion.[11] This empirical success is due largely to Jakobson's eidetic use of the *theory of parts and wholes* in Husserl's *Logical Investigations.*[12] In Jakobson's model of discourse, language operates in a rhetorical or tropic modality (called "poetic function") of paradigmatic and syntagmatic axes that respectively are *reversible.*

In brief, paradigmatic items in a process called "selection" are "vertically" substitutable for one another in a given category, e.g., any noun can take a noun's place in a sentence. Hence, these rhetorical items are: *in absentia,* the units are not actually present, but could be; part of a code, e.g. any *langue* or speech community practice; and related by synchrony, i.e., a static or simultaneous placement in time (consciousness). My previous use of the concepts of "persona" and "philosopher" represent Merleau-Ponty's use of the paradigmatic perspective in the "poetic function," or what he calls chiasm. In a rhetorical frame of tropic reference, we might say with Merleau-Ponty that philosophy allows for the *reality of fiction* in discourse (a fable in *absentia*), since the synchronic relation of metaphor (together with simile or irony) displays or represents the code conditions of selection or attribution, a substitution or articulation, and a similarity or designation in the derivation of signification (see table 2; figures 5 and 6).

By contrast, syntagmatic items in a process called "association" have their categorical identity by "horizontal" contiguity to other times, e.g., any noun is known by its comparison/contract with verbs, adjectives, etc. Thus, these items are (1) *in praesentia*, the units are actually present and must be; (2) part of a message, e.g., any *parole* or act of speaking, and (3) related by diachrony, i.e., a dynamic or sequential placement in time (consciousness).[13] My use of the concept of "person" and "sophist" represent Foucault's syntagmatic perspective in the "poetic function," or what he calls the "nameless voice" that is prosopopoeia. In a rhetorical sense, we might say with Foucault that philosophy allows the *fiction of reality* in discourse (a fiction *in praesentia*), since the diachronic relation of metonymy (together with synecdoche) displays or attributes the messages conditions of combination or representation, contexture or specification, and contiguity or substitution (see table 2; figure 5 and 6).

Turning specifically to Merleau-Ponty's inaugural lecture, there is an explicit semiotic phenomenology in his discourse (figure 9). It is a rhetoric of signified perception and signifying expression. He first combines the paradigmatic category of persona/perception in the progressive discussion of philosophers Lavelle, Bergson, and Socrates. Then he progresses to a syntagmatic category of person/expression in the analysis of the disciplines of Religion, History, and Philosophy.

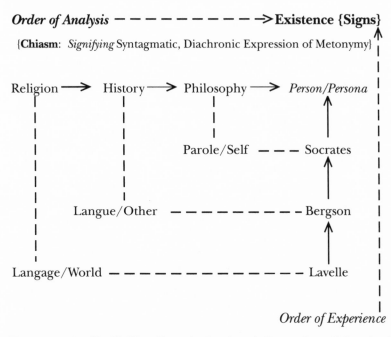

Order of Analysis – – – – – – – – – –> **Existence {Signs}**

{**Chiasm**: *Signifying* Syntagmatic, Diachronic Expression of Metonymy}

Religion —> History —> Philosophy —> *Person/Persona*

Parole/Self – – – Socrates

Langue/Other – – – – – – – – – – Bergson

Langage/World – – – – – – – – – – – – – Lavelle

Order of Experience

{**Prosopopoeia**: *Signified* Paradigmatic, Synchronic Perception of Metaphor}

Note: All relations are dialectically combinatory [metonymy] and reversible [metaphor].

Figure 9. Semiotic Phenomenology in Merleau-Ponty's Inaugural Lecture

LAVELLE AND THE WORLD

By structuring his inaugural address in the manner of a discourse on history (a discourse of order), Merleau-Ponty constructs an "order of analysis" in classical Husserlian fashion. There is a deliberate construction of the ontological problematic of philosophy as the encounter of "ego" and "*noema*" in the thematic rhetorical process of "*noesis*".[14] The subject matter of Lavelle's philosophy is for Merleau-Ponty a description of phenomenology, a first step in critical method. The good and bad ambiguity of the philosopher is the contest for order (Foucault's *agon*) between signified and signifying, world and self, *noema* and ego, in which the problematic of equivocation

(Foucault's catachresis) becomes the thematic of meaning.[15] The *agonistic* rhetoric of Lavelle has its narrative function: "It would be the function of philosophy, then, to record this passage of meaning rather than to take it as an accomplished fact."[16] Lavelle is the signified voice of the World that is a modality of rhetoric; Lavelle is the naming voice of *langage*.

BERGSON AND THE OTHER

Merleau-Ponty's discussion of Bergson is a phenomenological reduction, as we move in the second step of critical method from the description in Lavelle's differentiation of World and Self to Bergson's differentiation of Self and Other. With Bergson's concern for alterity, "being itself is problematic."[17] "For an ego which is *durée* cannot grasp another being except in the form of another *durée*," as Merleau-Ponty argues.[18] Because "the absolute knowledge of the philosopher is perception" a discourse of the Other is not "a simple return to what is *given* [data]."[19] The discourse of the Other is an intuitive encounter with reality where "it is necessary for me to appropriate to myself a meaning in it which is still captive [capta]."[20] Just as living is reduced by speaking and speaking represented by writing, there is in reading an intuitive reduction of the Other to a speaking subject who lives in the chiasm of discourse (a prosopopoeia as the inscribed discourse which thus presents an absent oral voice of Self. Philosophy "is, as Bergson happily said, a *reading*, the art of grasping a meaning in a style before it has been put into concepts."[21] It is with this probing rhetorical analysis of Bergson's philosophy that Merleau-Ponty does, indeed, locate a third methodological step (interpretation) in the phenomenological reduction of the Self and Other, ego and noema, as the noesis of discourse. In this section of the inaugural lecture, Merleau-Ponty offers his famous hermeneutic definition of what we now call communicology (*communicologie*, to cite *tout Paris*), i.e., the conjunction of philosophy and rhetoric:

> Expression presupposes someone who expresses, a truth which he expresses, and the others before whom he expresses himself. The postulate of expression [rhetoric] and of philosophy is that it can simultaneously satisfy these three conditions.[22]

Indeed, Merleau-Ponty finds in the Bergsonian problematic a thematic that "shall have been" (to borrow the "in-order-to motive" from Alfred Schutz) the ground of Foucault's philosophy, i.e., an agonistic rhetoric. "The enigma of philosophy (and of expression) is that sometimes life is the same to oneself, to others, and to the true."[23] Bergson is the signified voice of the Other that is a modality of rhetoric; Bergson is the voice of *langue*. Foreshadowing Foucault's discussion of rhetoric, Merleau-Ponty quotes the voice of Jean Hyppolite in reference to Bergson's "*Matter and Memory*, a system of oppositions between the emptiness of the past, the emptiness of the future, and the fullness of the present, like the oppositions between time and space."[24]

SOCRATES AND THE SELF

After reminding us that "the philosophy placed in books has ceased to challenge men [persons]" Merleau-Ponty declares:

> In order to understand the total function of the philosopher, we must remember that even the philosophical writers whom we read and whom we are, have never ceased to recognize as their patron a man who never wrote, who never taught, at least in any official chair, who talked with anyone he met on the street, and who had certain difficulties with public opinion and the public powers. We must remember Socrates.[25]

And so to the perceptual ambiguity of the perceived World and the expressive ambiguity of listening to, and reading about, the Other, Merleau-Ponty adds a phenomenological interpretation.

The interpretation is the "good irony" of "double meaning" that we perceive, not in reading the *Apology* inscribed by Plato, but rather, in the voice of Socrates that we *can* hear.[26] We can hear the "idea of Philosophy" in the rhetoric of Socrates. The eidetic discourse of Socrates is not mere symbolism. "It exists rather in its living relevance to the Athenians, in its absent presence, in its obedience without respect."[27] The "noema" of speech expresses the ontological "ego" through the "noetic" medium of speaking. Socrates is the signified voice of the Self that is a modality of rhetoric; Socrates is the signifying voice of *parole*.

With existential fidelity and an incarnate phenomenology, Merleau-Ponty takes (capta) speech in Lavelle as signified meaning, but he takes the spoken in Bergson. This equivocation of speech (*langage*) and the spoken (*langue*) becomes the "good ambiguity" and "good irony" of speaking. Speaking (*parole*) that is a problematic in the "speech spoken" of rhetoric (*parole parlée*) becomes thematic in the "speech speaking" of philosophy (*parole parlante*). In the dialectic of the chiasm, we are both the listening audience of Socrates as he speaks and yet the speaking voice that is Socrates (prosopopoeia). The signified story of Socrates is our signifying history. Rhetoric and Philosophy are signs of expressing and perceiving discourse.

RELIGION AND LANGAGE

The conjunction of the World and *langage* is the problematic of religion and theology where philosophy speaks in silence. Language that speaks for the World hides the Self. But the World that is speaking expresses the Self through *langage* and is the proper object of perception. "For to philosophize is to seek, and this is to imply that there are things to see and to say."[28]

Merleau-Ponty remarks that the ontological problem of the existence of God no longer commands a philosophical attention. Rather, the "abruptly disqualifying" voice of atheism or "human chauvinism" is heard.[29] Philosophy is not the rejection of theology nor is it the voice of humanism, however. The concept of the human is neither a rejection of, nor a substitution for, the concept of God. Both atheism and humanism point to the grounding of theology, which is to remove "the contingency of human existence."[30] But for Merleau-Ponty, "philosophy, on the other hand, arouses us to what is problematic in our own existence and in that of the world, to such a point that we shall never be cured of searching for a solution, as Bergson says, "in the notebooks of the master."[31] The ironic allusion to Nietzsche's aphorism (number 361) is clear:

> *What Socrates found out.* If someone has mastered one subject, it usually has made him a complete amateur in most other subjects; but people has made him a complete amateur in most other subjects; but people judge just the reverse, as Socrates found out.

This is the drawback that makes associating with masters disagreeable.[32]

Thus for Merleau-Ponty, the signifying discourse of religion provides a phenomenological description of the World and in its negation is a consequent account of the Self as a story (atheism) or an account of the Other as a history (humanism).

Yet, Merleau-Ponty finds the ontological rhetoric of *negation*, a practice of *negativity*, operative in this description, and not the theology that would displace philosophy as a discourse of position, a practice of positivity. "A sensitive and open thought should not fail to guess that there is an affirmative meaning and even a presence of the spirit in this philosophical negativity."[33] The meaning described by the differentiation of World and language is not the positivity of choosing one or the other as humane (i.e., as a persona), but indeed, choosing both as their combinatory negation of any posited ontology that is not the person. Philosophy in the World and rhetoric in language point to the dialectic of meaning in the binary analogue of both perception and expression. "Both consciousness and narrative (*l'histoire*) echo this."[34]

HISTORY AND LANGUE

The ambiguity of *l'histoire* is the equivocation of history counterposed to philosophy, only to become thematic in the story of discourse (historical narrative as a rhetoric, a "human practice")[35] and, dialectically in the chiasm, a thematic in the discourse of the story (philosophical narrative as a rhetoric, a "*praxis* in the meaning").[36] The signifying discourse of History exemplifies a phenomenological reduction of *langue* in the Other. Indeed, this is one reason that Foucault calls for the abolition of the "sovereignty of the signifier."[37]

The constitution of meaning (Merleau-Ponty's subject of "speech spoken"; Foucault's "subjection-subjected"; Kristeva's subject "on trial") and the person (Merleau-Ponty's subject of "speech speaking"; Foucault's "subject"; Kristeva's subject "in process") by prosopopoeia becomes explicit as the speech of History confronts that of Philosophy. The problematic of the anonymous voice of History opposes things to consciousness, and that same voice as Philosophy counterposes consciousness to things. But as a thematic voice, "historical meaning is immanent in the interhuman event, and is as fragile as this event. But precisely because of this, the event takes on the value of the genesis of reason."[38] Just because the World and *langage* are reversible with the event of the Other and *langue*, the rhetorical structure of History (syntagmatic; Kristeva's "phenotext") becomes the semiotic form of Philosophy (paradigmatic; Kristeva's "genotext"). Indeed, Merleau-Ponty notes that "the theory of signs, as developed in linguistics, perhaps implies a conception of historical meaning which gets beyond the opposition of *things* and *consciousness*."[39] The rhetorical conjunction of the speaking subject and the institutions of meaning (subjects spoken; the subjected) are a semiotic phenomenology of the World and the Other, i.e., a signifying practice of *langage* in the story of History and a praxis of *langue* in the hi[gh]-story of Philosophy (Foucault's *rarefaction*).[40] "An interconnection among these phenomena is possible," argues Merleau-Ponty, "since they are all symbolisms, and perhaps even the translation of one symbolism into another is possible" (see figure 7).[41] History turns Philosophy "towards the personal discourse which develops in us, and which, indeed, we are" (see figure 6).[42]

PHILOSOPHY AND PAROLE

Philosophy for Merleau-Ponty "is expression in act, it comes to itself only by ceasing to coincide with what is expressed, and by taking its distance in order to see its meaning."[43] Or, as Foucault puts it, "to play on words yet again, let us say that, if the critical style [archaeology] is one of studied casualness, then the genealogical mood is one of felicitous positivism."[44] By so characterizing the rhetoric of philosophy, Merleau-Ponty and Foucault dialectically give us a philosophy of rhetoric. Here, the exacting dialectic of person and persona is not a speech act, not the subject spoken. It is not the voice of power "to realize" in *langue* by "destroying" *parole*, nor is it the dialectic voice of desire "to suppress" in *langage* and thereby "to conserve" parole. According to Merleau-Ponty "The philosopher of action is perhaps the farthest removed from action, for to speak of action with depth and rigor is to say that one does not desire to act."[45] Rather the ambiguity, the dialectic signs (chiasm) of person ("private world") and persona ("common world"), exist in the signifying mask (prosopopoeia) of Religion, History, and Philosophy, and this mask is removed in speech speaking as we hear the signified mystery (prosopopoeia) of silence, the speech spoken by Lavelle, Bergson, and Socrates. For Merleau-Ponty, as for ourselves, "The philosopher is the man who wakes up and speaks."[46]

FOUCAULT'S INAUGURAL: THE ORDER OF DISCOURSE

As a student of Merleau-Ponty, we may in fairness characterize Foucault as a *disciple of ambiguity* in his own discourse as lived. As Foucault himself frequently points out, he is neither a structuralist nor a Husserlian phenomenologist. But then, neither was Merleau-Ponty even though, like Foucault, he wrote insightfully and critically about both. Rather, Foucault is a candidate for inclusion with the other "masters of suspicion" (Nietzsche, Freud, and Marx), as Descombes designates them.[47] These masters of suspicion are rhetoricians who know philosophy: like philosophers, they are semiotic phenomenologists. Within the rhetorical movement of catachresis, they are the personae who are truly *subject to* discourse (*langue; the subject spoken*) and who are no less than the persons who are the meaning of subjecting discourse (*parole; the speaking subject*)— they are also truly the *subject of* discourse. As the chiasmatic voice of Socrates, Merleau-Ponty and Foucault are the disciples of ambiguity; they are phenomenologists of the signs of existence (prosopopoeia).

Thus, to proceed in the analysis of Foucault's inaugural by formulating the title translation of *L'ordre du discours* as "the discourse on language" is to corrupt the ambiguity of discourse, the enveloping catachresis, chiasm, and prosopopoeia, that Foucault intends. In a retrospective comment on the *énoncé* of his inaugural lecture, Foucault reminds us: "My work has dealt with the three modes of objectivation which transforms human

beings into subjects." First, there is catachresis in "the objectivizing of the speaking subject in *grammaire générale,* philology,
and linguistics." Second, there is chiasm by objectivizing the
subject in "dividing practices." And third, there is prosopopoeia
in "the way a human being turns him- or herself into a subject."[48]
In short, the title, *The Order of Discourse,* is an epigrammatical
thesis about the speaking subject, the philosopher who knows
rhetoric.

     Are we to choose meaning in the *order* of discourse, i.e., the
discoursing order imposed by the designating rhetoric of catachresis where the *sujet du [of] langage* is tied to his/her/its
own identity in the World by a desire as *speech* speaking? Or
will meaning choose us in the order of *discourse,* i.e., the ordering discourse controlled by the naming rhetoric or chiasm
where one is *sujet à [to] la langue* as a dependence on the power
of the *speech* spoken by the Other? Shall we choose meaning
in the order imagined in narrative form, yet absent to the
practice of discourse as structure? What order is manifest in
the judging rhetoric of prosopopoeia where (in Merleau-
Ponty's phrase) the subject of *parole* is "condemned to meaning" in speaking the spoken (*discours*) which is *not* the voice of
what is said through speech (*langage; langue*)? Indeed for
Foucault, "there are two meanings of the word *subject (sujet):*
subject to someone else by control and dependence, and tied
to his own identity by a conscience or self-knowledge. Both
meanings suggest a form of power which subjugates and
makes subject to."[49] Thus, Foucault brings us quickly and
forcefully to the "antagonism of strategies" in the rhetoric of
"local memory" that is archaeology, and to the "agonism" (or
"reciprocal incitation and struggle") in philosophy as the "erudite knowledge" that is genealogy.[50]

     In figure 10, the play of archaeology and genealogy is depic-
ted with the same Jakobsonian "poetic function" (paradigmatic
and syntagmatic axis; Husserl's orders of experience and analysis respectively) in mind that is used in figure 9. One point of
caution, however: as White points out in his rhetorical analysis
of Foucault's *The Order of Things,* "each period is studied 'vertically,' that is, archaeologically, rather than 'horizontally' or
historically."[51] But in the inaugural lecture, Foucault critically

responds to his own past work and changes his model. He counterposes the new genealogy to the old archaeology, now called the "critical" perspective, which consists in those horizontal [syntagmatic] principles of "exclusion, limitation, and appropriation" or "rarefaction, consolidation, and unification" (respectively, Jakobson's "combination, contexture, and contiguity" as noted in table 2).

On the other hand, the genealogical perspective as now corrected forms the vertical (paradigmatic) principles of "appearance, growth, and variation" or "formation, at once scattered, discontinuous and regular" (recall that in Jakobson's theory, they are "selection, substitution, and similarity" as noted in table 2).

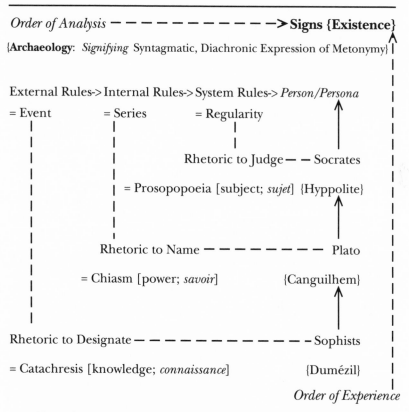

Order of Analysis — — — — — — — — — — — —> **Signs {Existence}**

{**Archaeology**: *Signifying* Syntagmatic, Diachronic Expression of Metonymy}

External Rules-> Internal Rules-> System Rules-> *Person/Persona*

= Event   = Series   = Regularity

Rhetoric to Judge — — Socrates

= Prosopopoeia [subject; *sujet*] {Hyppolite}

Rhetoric to Name — — — — — — — Plato

= Chiasm [power; *savoir*]   {Canguilhem}

Rhetoric to Designate — — — — — — — — — — — -Sophists

= Catachresis [knowledge; *connaissance*]   {Dumézil}

Order of Experience

{**Genealogy**: *Signified* Paradigmatic, Synchronic Perception of Metaphor}

Note: All relations are dialectically combinatory [metonymy] and reversible [metaphor].

Figure 10. Semiotic Phenomenology in Foucault's Inaugural Lecture

Remember also that it is the operation of Jakobson's poetic function that is precisely the "reversal-principle" to which Foucault refers in making the critical or archaeological form of discourse (= the rhetorical or tropic figure of metonymy) dialectical with the genealogical form (= metaphor).[52] To be sure, Foucault is adopting the same semiotic modification to Husserl's phenomenology that Jakobson and Merleau-Ponty established in their parallel, but separate, studies of human communication as semiotic phenomenology.

Here, it is worth noting that translators have consistently rendered Foucault's use of the French "*figure*" into English as "form," even in passages where the explicit phrase "*les figures de la rhétorique*" is used. In the play of memory, most of Foucault's commentators forget the rupture that occurs in his very first methodological work on discourse: *Death and the Labyrinth: The World of Raymond Roussel.* In this important work on the phenomenology of discourse, he argues that "Roussel's experience is situated in what can be called the 'tropological space' of vocabulary."[53] The ontological procedures of a new rhetoric become quite clear in Foucault's quotation of Dumarsais:

> Thus by necessity and by choice, words are often turned away from their original meaning to taken on a new one which is more or less removed but that still maintains a connection. This new meaning is called "tropological," and this conversion, this turning away which produces it, is called a "trope." In the space created by this displacement, all the figures of rhetoric come to life. . . .[54]

As a matter of course in Foucault's work, this archaeological view (experience) of Roussel's surrealist literature in tropological space becomes a genealogical view (consciousness) in the later study of Magritte's surrealist painting, as we saw in chapter 5. That is, the desire of tropic catachresis manifest in a metagram as the "law of discourse" in graphic terms (e.g., the sentential message that reads literally: "This is not a pipe.") becomes the figurative power of a calligram in "the law of. . .communication" where the graphic figure is now a dialectic trope of the visual.[55] A reexamination of figure 7 will confirm Foucault's point.

Drawing on the language of these two texts, we might summarize and define this shift in view thusly: "the metagram is both the truth and the mask, a duplicate, repeated and placed on the surface. At the same time, it is the opening through which it enters, experiences the doubling, and separates the mask from the face it is duplicating."[56] And yet by reversibility and poetic function (see figures 5 and 6), "pursuing its quarry by two paths, the calligram sets the most perfect trap. By its double function, it guarantees capture [capta, discovery], as neither discourse alone nor a pure drawing could do."[57]

THE RHETORIC OF EXTERNAL RULES: KNOWLEDGE

In explicating figure 10, we start again with Foucault's inaugural lecture. He takes up the problematic of discourse formations as knowledge (*connaissance*) and power (*savior*). Within Merleau-Ponty's *prose du monde* where "figures of language" redouble the symbolic function of language, Foucault's initial concerns is with the formations or figures of discourse that are manifest firstly in external rules, in the rules of exclusion. "We have three types of prohibition, covering objects, ritual with its surrounding circumstances, the privileged or exclusive right to speak of a particular subject . . . a complex web, continually subject to modification."[58] In this Socratic schema, discourse is first of all its own subject of intentionally as a pure catachresis (the idealism of Husserl's object is under critique). In this analytic movement of regularity that traces out the phenomenology of semiosis, discourse becomes an event of experience constituting merely a part in the metynomic whole of a web (a series). Ritual speech (sophistry) and the right to speak (philosophy) are the remainders; they are yet to be figured as parts in the eidetic web of meaning. Thus, speech is a subject of desire in the sophistic period where the voices of Hesiod and Plato indicate the *opposition* of rhetoric and philosophy. There is a desire to prohibit words, a tropic practice reminiscent for Foucault of "psychoanalysis, with its strange logic of desire."[59] This is the subject (person) of objection that Kristeva finds *both* in process (rhetoric) *and* on trial (philosophy).

This bifurcation of knowledge and power has its continued

explication in a second opposition of "reason and folly" where there is both a division and a rejection. In *The Archeology of Knowledge,* Foucault describes the division of sanity and madness (ritual speech) where "we have even come to notice these words of the madman in our own speech, in those tiny pauses when we forget what we are talking about."[60] At the level of the discourse as discipline, we are witness to the division made in the sixteenth and seventeenth centuries between "observational science" and "religious ideology." It is a division (event) based upon a differentiation (series) of rejection (regularity), and is reminiscent for Foucault of "mathematics and the formalization of discourse."[61]

Last, we experience the opposition of the "true and false." The true and the false in discourse (the right to speak) is—but wait—are not the words of prohibition also the prohibition of words (censorship)? External rules are the designating rule of catachresis. The nineteenth century witnessed the opposition of "modern science and positivist ideology" that reminds Foucault of "information theory and its application to the analysis of life."[62]

In an attempt to capture the intentionality of external rules, the catachresis, Foucault says of Roussel: "He does not want to duplicate the reality of another world, but, in the spontaneous duality of language, he wants to *discover* an unexpected space, and to *cover* it with things never said before."[63]

THE RHETORIC OF INTERNAL RULES: POWER

Foucault next turns to "internal rules, where discourse exercises its own control; rules concerned with the principles of classification, ordering, and distribution." These tropes of discourse are the series dimension of "events and chance," i.e., the rules of inclusion. Here, knowledge (*connaissance*) is contrasted with understanding, the special "know how" (*savoir*) that is the power both to be the subject of and subjected to discourse as a practice. Foucault locates such figures and tropes as a "commentary" displaying a "gradation between different types of discourse within most societies." He is thinking of *l'histoire* as the story of society that is *told by* society, its "major narratives, told, retold and varied." These stories (events) are the internalized religious or juridical texts (regularity) that follow on the external rules (series) of reason and folly. They are the subject spoken in the space subject to discourse. Discourse as commentary becomes no more that "discourse which *is spoken* and remains spoken, indefinitely, beyond its formulation." Between speaking and what is spoken, there is a chiasm. "What is clear is that this gap is neither stable, nor constant, nor absolute." Discourse is in the world of "play" where there is only "a lyrical dream of talk reborn".[64] This play of discourse as a problematic will form the basis of the discussion in chapter 8.

In the discursive realm of commentary, a rarefaction of discourse creates the "author" who "is spoken" again and again as the subject of discourse in place of the person speaking. "Commentary limited the hazards of discourse through the action of an *identity* taking the form of *repetition* and *sameness*" writes Foucault. "The author principle limits this same chance element through the action of an *identity* whose form is that of *individuality* and the *I*."[65] The "author" marks the chiasm in just the sense that Plato, absent as an author, is the present name we give to the absent voice of Socrates so clearly present in the dialogues. We think of the Platonic author of Socrates, now, as Foucault thinks of Roussel's "tropological 'move'" in his authorship "that brings into play . . . [a] fundamental freedom . . . . to form an inexorable circle which returns words to their point of origin by force of his constraining rules." Hence, Foucault's second aphorism on the subject of intentionality is complete: "This opens a chiasm in the identity of language, a void that has to be revealed and at the same time filled."[66] Thus are disciplines born in the regularity of the series of events in discourse.

THE RHETORIC OF SYSTEMS: SUBJECT

"Disciplines constitute a system of control in the production of discourse, fixing its limits through the action of an identity taking the form of a permanent reactivation of the rules."[67] The figures of discourse that Foucault suggests to us as the disciplinary formations of "universal mediation" are exchange and communication, i.e., the *rules of ensemble*.[68] Here, the conjunction of knowledge (Merleau-Ponty's World) and power (Other) produces subjects (Self), persons who are "subject to" knowledge and yet the "subject of" power. These two figures of exchange (paradigmatic function; genealogy) and communication (syntagmatic function: archaeology) are the process of discourse regularity in which complexity (series) becomes restrictive (event). Foucault's illustration is the concept and practice of "doctrinal adherence."[69] Indeed as Perelman remarks, "the study of the methods of proof used to secure *adherence* has been completely neglected by logicians and epistemologists for the last three centuries."[70] Foucault's entire corpus is the radical introduction of the problematic and thematic of adherence in the contemporary human sciences.

"Doctrine effects a dual subjection, that of speaking subjects to discourse, and that of discourse to the group, at least virtually, of speakers," says Foucault. Doctrine is a discursive function that takes the "fellowship of discourse" (*sociétés de discourse*) as relying on an "ambiguous interplay of secrecy and disclosure," a discourse which confesses: "I lie, I speak" (see chapter 8). Thus do the religious, political, and philosophical doctrines come to constitute the "utterance of speakers" that are "permanently, the sign, the manifestation, and the instrument of a prior adherence—adherence to a class, to a social or racial status, to a nationality or an interest, to a struggle, a revolt, resistance or acceptance."[71] System rules are a prosopopoeia in which the imagined voice of communication (event) is exchanged with every voice (series) that adheres to the utterance (regularity). The movements of ensemble from "fellowships" of discourse, to doctrinal groups, and then to social appropriation are the "main rules for the subject/subjection [*sujet*] of discourse" and constitute the "pastorship" of "the individualizing power," as we saw in the example of the hermaphrodite, Adélaïde Herculine Barbin.[72]

The prosopopoeia is a rule of ensemble (exchange) discovered as the *ensemble of the rule* (communication). Foucault's third aphorism in his study of Roussel states: "The movement of repetitions and transformations, their constant imbalance, and the loss of substance experienced by words along the way are becoming, surreptitiously, marvelous mechanisms for creating beings; the ontological power of this submerged language."[73] Or in Anthony Wilden's telling aphorism: The rules are no game! In short, the *Rule of Ensemble* is that "a statement (*énoncé*) is always an event that neither the language (*langue*) nor the meaning can quite exhaust."[74]

THE SOPHISTS AND DESIGNATION

Foucault reminds us that ever since "the exclusion of the activity and commerce of the sophists" philosophy has divided "thought and words." Philosophy as a discourse per se becomes no less than a rhetoric to designate, a critical form of exclusion.[75]

> It [philosophy] would appear to have ensured that *to discourse* should appear merely as a certain interjection between speaking and thinking; that it should constitute thought, clad in its signs and rendered visible by words or, conversely, that the structures of language themselves should be brought into play, producing a certain effect of meaning.[76]

The definition of *catachresis* could not be more apparent than it is in this thematic quotation. Foucault subjects philosophy to a phenomenological reduction in which the metaphors of logic and grammar are seen to be the events of external rules. The events, by their own proper rule, are already committed to an axiology of the deontic. To adhere to what *is* proper is to do what one should!

The metaphor as a rhetorical figure, as the external rule of thinking (that in practice becomes the trope of metonymy), that opposes the literal (logic in the trivium) to the fictional (grammar in the trivium), is discovered to be a trope of speaking (rhetoric in the trivium). The trope is catachresis, where the "ancient elision" is manifest as the distinction between the proper and the insipid or improper.[77] Thinking should be valued as fair and just in words (or if insipid, at least justifiable); thus, logic can elide rhetoric. Yet meaning should be justifiable (or if insipid, at least just) in thinking; hence, grammar can elide rhetoric. "This very ancient elision of the reality of discourse in philosophical thought has taken many forms in the course of history."[78] In the case of the sophists, the form is "the philosophy of a founding subject" that embodies a "complicity with the world. . .to designate." Writing is the rupture of thinking and speaking; it designs existence as alterity. The person as a speaking subject in orality is subjected to inscription as the invention of persona, the subject spoken.[79] The words of *langage* become the prohibited words of *langue* and the voice of *parole* is silenced.

Dumézil is Foucault's "model and prop," his persona, of the sophist. "It is he who taught me to analyze the internal economy of discourse quite differently from the traditional methods of exegesis or those of linguistic formalism."[80] Dumézil is the founded subject (the subject spoken who is the proper, same self) of the founding subject (the speaking subject who is the insipid, different other, namely Michel Foucault). Catachresis is one trope (the signs) in the rhetoric of *le même et l'autre*, the "philosophical pair" that designates the persona and the person in the tropic ratio: [Self : Same : : Other : Different] (see figures 5 and 8). Existence names, that is, designates in rhetoric the dialectic and ambiguity of the persona (as self and same person) in opposition to the person (as other and different persona). "To *name* is at the same time to give the *verbal representation of a representation*."[81] We can now designate the tropic function of the name in which the representation of: [Self : Same : : Other : Different] also represents *l'histoire et le sujet* as a "figure of language" in the ratio: [Discourse : History : : Subject : Subjection], which is then to say as a "trope of speech": [Story : Narrative : : Self : Other]. As Benveniste's basic research so insightfully leads us now to conclude, the Signs of Existence (ek-stase) are the narrating story (*discours; parole parlante*) discovered critically in genealogy that stands in opposition to the story of narration (*l'histoire; parole parlée*) discovered by comment in archaeology.[82] Thus, what we learn from Dumézil is a genealogical lesson: "to restore to discourse its character as an event."[83] We must learn that lived discourse (the history of the story) is *play*, or what the the American semiotic phenomenologist Charles Sanders Peirce called abduction.[84] Let me note in passing that Bateson's work with normal and pathological human communication is familiar to most scholars under this abductive category of play, especially his concepts of *deutero learning* in normal behavior and the *double bind* message as the source of pathology.

PLATO AND NOMINATION

"A division emerged between Hesiod and Plato, separating true discourse from false . . . . And so the sophists were routed," reflects Foucault.[85] With this allusion to Hesiod, we recall that in oral verse the famed presocratic poet eulogizes the human anguish of the laboring poor in his farmer's almanac *Works and Days*, yet he also eulogizes the gods by his canonical work of Greek mythology, the *Theogony*. Indeed, the true discourse separates from the false. But where is the opposition and the exclusion? The *Rhetoric to Name* is the chiasm that Plato finds in the analytical combination of *logos* and *mythos* that requires a critical *logos* of *logos*. The human voice opposes the divine voice, and each excludes the other. What the humans can say, the gods cannot hear (the exclusion of reason made concrete in the *enthymeme*). The inventions of the gods cannot be understood as our world (the exclusion of folly made concrete in the *syllogism*). The rupture of reversible exclusion in the confrontation of person and persona, the chiasm, names the discourse that precedes and succeeds itself. As such, the rupture of present and absent voices is locked in an endless series of internal rules. The site of these series is the "form of a *cogito*, prior significations, in some ways already spoken."[86] The site is what we read; it is the text of discourse that names experience. Catachresis joins by opposition to chiasm to foretell the "nameless voice" of prosopopoeia. That is, the story of history narrates the history of a story in which the speaking voice (lector in fabula) is "on the other side of discourse."[87]

Having cited Hesiod's history of discourse, Foucault cites and, thereby sites, his own discourse of history. In the persona of Canguilhem, Foucault voices what he has read:

> If I have wished to apply a similar method [referring to Dumézil] to discourse quite other than legendary or mythical narratives, it is because before me lay the works of the historians of science,

above all, that of Monsieur Canguilhem. I owe it to him that I understood that . . . one could—that one should—treat the history of science as an ensemble, at once coherent, and transformable into theoretical models and conceptual instruments.[88]

Reading is not just the invented opposition of self narration (the human, the person, the speaking subject) and the Other's narration (the divine, the persona, the subject spoken). It is a discovery of alterity as a critical form of limitation. One thinks here of Jacques Derrida's delightful book title: *Limited, Inc.* Thus for Foucault, we confront the problematic of "a philosophy of originating experience."[89] Reading exemplifies the auditing process in which we perceive "the form of a *cogito*, prior significations, in some ways already spoken." The text names that of which we have knowledge, because it cannot be experienced. The reader encounters the catachretic work of the founding subject of the speech community (*langue*) who has "signs, marks, tracks, letters at his disposal."[90] To read, then, is to become the problematical and equivocal founding subject of an originary experience of consciousness, the spoken; the limited is incorporated and "I lie" becomes "I speak." External rules conflate internal rules and events become series in the ontological process as writing invents.[91] What we learn from Canguilhem is a second genealogical lesson according to Foucault: "To abolish the sovereignty of the signifier (*signifiant*)."[92] We learn that the power of discourse (the story of history) is its constitution of utopia.[93] But do not confuse the utopian with an oral idealism (logic: the story of a story) nor an inscribed realism (grammar: the history of history).

SOCRATES AND JUDGMENT

We come now to the third system of exclusions: the true versus the false. In the regularity of System Rules, discourse becomes no less than the Rhetoric to Judge. As Foucault says, "I will take first the age of the Sophists and its beginning with Socrates, or at least with Platonic philosophy, and I shall try to see how effective, ritual discourse, charged with power and peril, gradually arranged itself into a disjunction between true and false discourse."[94] In this short statement on the Greek sophistic, Foucault both announces and summarizes what we have suspected all along about discourse as a *"universal mediation."* The dialectic and digital opposition of paradoxical discourse (the semiotic of "death" in "rupture") for the Sophists and Plato is the analogic ambiguity of opposition by combinatory reversal of discourse (the semiotic of "birth" in "rupture") for Aristotle and Socrates. We are no longer concerned with writing and reading (event and series. i.e., death and birth), but with the endless regularity of ontology in sign exchange (rupture).[95] For Foucault, Aristotle's genres of rhetoric are turned on their head in their very statement (énoncé) in order to become a "now" and "here" rupture of the Socratic maieutic of conscious experience.[96]

For Foucault, the discourse of external rules and the trope of catachresis, as the rhetoric of designation, is no less than the reversal of Aristotle's genre of political (deliberative) oratory. The event of discourse in the persona of the Sophists points to the person, the existential subject, in the lived-experience of a "speaking subject" who must *both* accept *and* reject consciousness as the lived future. Such a future is the *terminus ad quem* of Cicero or the in-order-to-motive of Schutz, viz., the birth/death within "what shall have been." The exclusion of discourse as rupture is *both* expediency (person) and harmfulness (persona).

Second, the discourse of internal rules, the trope of chiasm, constituting the rhetoric of nomination is no more than the reversal of the Aristotelian category of judicial (forensic) oratory. The series of discourse in the persona of Plato existentially indexes the person in the consciousness of a "speaking subject" who must *both* attack *and* defend the experience of the lived past. This past is the *terminus a quo* of Cicero or the because-motive of Schutz, viz., the death/birth within "what had been." The exclusion of discourse as rupture is *both* justice (reason) *and* injustice (folly).

Last, there is the discourse of systems rules, the trope of prosopopoeia, establishing the rhetoric of judgment that entails both the political and the judicial oratories. The opposition of political and judicial is in turn, and in-itself, opposed to the genre of evaluative (epideictic) oratory. The regularity of discourse) in the persona of Socrates is an existential sign of the who must *both* praise *and* blame the consciousness of the Future and the experience of the Past in the lived-Present (*ek-stase*). The exclusion of such discourse is *both* honor (truth) *and* disgrace (falsity). Indeed, the rhetoric of judgment is the epideictic rhetoric, the *eulogy inaugural*, where Merleau-Ponty's lecture begins to praise Socrates and with which Foucault's lecture *now* ends by blaming Socrates. The naming voice of now-here (Merleau-Ponty's inaugural of present absence; rupture and birth) reverses to becomes the nameless voice no-where (Foucault's inaugural of absent presence; rupture and death). Rhetoric (event) is the counterpart of dialectic (series), yet maieutic inaugurates the reversal (eulogy) of both as a critical form (regularity) of appropriation.[97]

For this argument, Foucault's illustrating persona is Jean Hyppolite, like Socrates for Plato, a "model and prop" of maieutic discourse—the reversal that is the adhering interrogative statement.

> For Hyppolite, philosophy, as the thought of the inaccessible totality, was that which could be rejected in the extreme irregularity of experience; it was that which presents and reveals itself as the continually recurring question in life, death, and in memory. Thus he transformed the Hegelian theme of the end of self-consciousness into one of repeated interrogation.[98]

With this "birth" (a visible metaphor for "genealogy") of the rhetorical question as statement (a visible metonymy for "archaeology"), Foucault offers us his third genealogical lesson: "To question the will to truth." Thereby, we must learn that uttered (*énoncé*) discourse is anguish.[99] The anguish of discourse is the existential knowledge that "I lie, I speak" (see figures 12 and 13). The genealogy of this "agonistic" rhetoric initiates the practice of discourse as it struggles with the reciprocal strategy of rhetoric ("antagonism") in the method of archaeology. The "critical . . . which sets the reversal-principle to work" is a poetic rupture, both a death (exclusion, limitation, appropriation) and birth (appearance, growth, variation) of rhetoric.[100] As Merleau-Ponty says, "Something of the nature of the question passes into the answer."[101]

THE VOICE OF DISCOURSE

Foucault's inaugural lecture articulates the problematic of discourse, the sign which beckons the human being to existence. It is the problematic of existence found in the ontological alterity of the signifying and the signified. The equivocation of the articulated statement that makes the signifying or the signified stand apart, each as its own voice, becomes the phenomenological thematic in Foucault's rhetoric of archaeology. And yet archaeology itself submits to the interrogation of genealogy. Merleau-Ponty's philosophical demand of Husserl is also met by Foucault: existence is first of all a phenomenology of phenomenology, a genealogy critical of archaeology. Foucault's confession of mere commentary in his early archaeological work is exposed for its equivocation and thereby becomes the thematic of criticism, not unlike the semiotic confession of Umberto Eco in *The Name of the Rose* made into a work of anguish in *Foucault's Pendulum*. Critical method replaces archaeological methodology (history as the death of words in the labyrinth of the document; in Eco's first novel the library burns on and on) just as genealogical method (discourse as a birth of signs in the rebus of the monument; in Eco's second novel the museum lives on and on) is announced in the semiotic ruptures of linguistic practice. It is precisely these ruptures that have come to visibility as the examination of human practice in the many dis-courses constituting the *corpus* of Foucault's research which is the *corps propre*.

In point of fact, "the difference between the critical and the genealogical enterprise is not one of object or field, but point of attack, perspective, and delimitation."[102] The original "vertical paradigmatic" order of archaeology is replaced by the horizontal syntagmatic order of criticism (the sign as signified), so that genealogy (the sign as signifying) may properly become the new, correct, vertical paradigm. Properly understood, Foucault's genealogy and archaeology constitute a semiotic phenomenology defined by existence as signs (genealogy) in "poetic" combination with signs as existence (archaeology). The discourse of the signifying subject (speech speaking) ruptures the history of the subject signified (speech spoken) so that "a human being turns him- or herself into a subject" in order to "at last... restore it *speaking.*"[103]

> The subject should not be entirely abandoned. ... Rather, we should ask: under what conditions and through what forms can an entity like the subject appear in the order of discourse; what position does it occupy; what functions does it exhibit; and what rules does it follows in each type of discourse? In short, the subject (and it substitutes) must be stripped of its creative role and analyzed as a complex and variable function of discourse.[104]

Foucault's phenomenology of genealogy and archaeology makes certain explicit, complex methodological demands on the semiotics of discourse (illustrated in figure 10). However, Foucault's own systematic rhetoric provides us with four principles of interrogation and articulation, his critical method for depicting the phenomenology of discourse. These principles of genealogical methodology (see table 1) provide us with a way to systematically express the tropic impact of Foucault's rhetoric of the person (see figure 6 for the discourse model and figure 12 which illustrates these four principles with the aphorism "I lie, I speak").

1. Reversal [Metonymy: Same-Different]. The events of signification (*langage*) function as external rules of discourse to designate meaning. These are the rules of exclusion in rhetoric that distinguish archaeology. Thus, appearance as the reversal of the events of signification is a catachresis where the genealogical goal of criticism is "to restore to discourse its character as an event."[105] In other words, we discover the genealogical "rule of the tactical polyvalence of discourses."[106]

2. Discontinuity [Simile, Irony: Self-Different]. The series of originality (*langue*) functions as internal rules of discourse to name meaning. These are the rules of limitation in rhetoric that distinguish archaeology. Thus, growth as the discontinuity of the series of originality is a chiasm where the genealogical goal of criticism is "to abolish the signifier." Thus we encounter the genealogical "rule of double conditioning."[107]

3. Specificity [Synecdoche: Self-Other]. The regularity of unity (*parole*) functions as system rules of discourse to judge

meaning. These are the rules of appropriation in rhetoric that distinguish archaeology. Thus, variation as the specificity of the regularity of unity is a prosopopoeia where the genealogical goal of criticism is "to question our will to truth." Here, the "rules of continual variations" point to a genealogy.[108]

4. Exteriority [Metaphor: Same-Other]. The semiotic condition of creation (*discours*) functions as the reversal-principle to describe meaning (phenomenologically). These are the narrative rules (*l'histoire*) in rhetoric that distinguish archaeology. Thus, explication is figurative or tropic where the genealogical goal of criticism is "the possible conditions of existence."[109] In short, Foucault's genealogical "rule of immanence" is, indeed, named by Merleau-Ponty's "theme of the 'flesh.'"[110]

With this discursive evidence of semiotic phenomenology, let my voice close this chapter rhetorically with a eulogy of explication for Foucault's inaugural voice as its speaks:

> I would really like to have slipped imperceptibly in to this lecture, as into all the others I shall be delivering, perhaps over the years ahead [= *the voice of Catachresis, the name of Metaphor*].
>
> I would have preferred to be enveloped in speech, borne way beyond all possible beginnings [= *the voice of Chiasm, the name of Irony and Simile*].
>
> At the moment of speaking, I would like to have perceived a nameless voice, long preceding me, leaving me merely to enmesh myself in it, taking up its cadence, and to lodge myself, when no one was looking, in its interstices as if it had paused an instant, in suspense, as a sign beckoning to me [= *the voice of prosopopoeia, the name of Metonymy*].
>
> There would have been no beginnings: instead, the discourse would proceed from me, while I stood in its path—a slender gap—the point of its possible disappearance [= *the voice of Persona, the name of Synecdoche*].[111]

Through the inaugural discourse of Foucault, it is the nameless voice of Merleau-Ponty in his critical genealogy who warns us about the voiceless name in the algebra of discourse: "It is Socrates himself who teaches us to correct Socrates."[112]

7

Foucault's Chinese Encyclopedia

Le Même et L'Autre

A mong the corpus of research monuments (as opposed to documents, see figure 12) of the late Professor of History and Systems of Thought at the Collège de France in Paris, Michel Foucault, there are two major works on discourse that speak today to the very Foucaultian thematic that was selected in 1989 for the 14th Annual Conference of the Semiotic Society of America: *"Deception, Detection, and Diagnosis."* First, there is the sign of Foucault, that is, the semiotic capacity (Peirce's sense) for the work of deception described in the phenomenology of discourse known as *Les Motes et les Choses,* or *Words and Things.*[1] Foucault undertakes in this book to detect the simulacrum (grammar) of existential discourse (rhetoric) operating as the nature and causality (logic) of general grammar. Such a grammar is the prototype *langage* of modernity, the language of desire, both "generated" by the document and "generalized" in its archive, the Library: It is a fiction about experience (Foucault's fiction/fable distinction is discussed in notes 4 and 9 in chapter 6). The book is an original work of the diagnosis of discourse that later succumbs to phenomenological reduction as the English translation of the book appears with its new title, thereby detecting the deception in the old title of "words and things." With Foucault's authority, the same discourse as the other text emerges with the new title: *The Order of Things.* This metaphor of the "order of things," of course, represents a *self* diagnosis following upon the "nameless voice" of the *other* who delivered the inaugural lecture at the *Collège de France* in which Foucault outlined his own *L'ordre du discours* (The Order of Discourse) as an ontological synecdoche (see figure 8).[2]

Second, there is the Peircian *interpretant,* that is, the work that is a discursive diagnosis of diagnosis bearing the title of *L'Archéologie du Savior* (*The Archaeology of Understanding*).[3] In this theoretical volume written after the empirical work of the *Order of Things,* Foucault gives us a phenomenological interpretation of discourse as differentiation and diagnosis.[4] On the one hand, the *Archaeology of Understanding* represents an argument from metonymy in which the "Same : Different" differentiation depicts a relation of substance and attribute. This is to say, Foucault offers the same account of discourse (substance) as that found in the *Order of Things.* Yet this same account is now a theoretical discussion of attribution that tells us how to think about (*savior*) the original text.

Foucault's two works, as sign and interpretant in a relationship of part and attribute, now confront us with the positive familiarity of a simile where the "Self : Different" opposition offers a simple description. This is to say, one book edition is like the other, second book edition because the voice of the self as author (desire) and authority (power) is constant. And yet in negative familiarity, the two books agonistically confront us with an ironic appreciation for Foucault's analysis of the human sciences contested by the very fact that the two books are differentiated by a special opposition. Their opposition combines by comparison into one discourse, one expressing expression, *un énoncé dans les archives.*[5]

Foucault, as we noted in chapter 5, organizes his study of the human sciences and their discourses (see figure 5) with a quadrilateral model consisting of four elements (Attribution [Proposition], Articulation, Designation, and Derivation) and their four respective functions (Representation, Specification, Substitution, and Combination [Element]).[6] In some ways reminiscent of the elements and functions of Roman Jakobson's model of human communication, Foucault's model explores discourse as a reversible and reflexive dialectic of the problematic and thematic found in human practice, which can be described, reduced, and interpreted phenomenologically by analyzing the French *topos* captured in Foucault's use of the expression: *le même et l'autre* (see table 2). Again, as noted earlier, this thetic aphorism can be variously translated as "Self versus Other" and as "Same versus Different" (see figure 8).

The exemplar of the speaking subject, the existential signifier and signified, is appropriate for this tropic rhetoric: Let me repeat myself, as *le même et l'autre* (self-other), let me repeat what I have just said by quoting for you, as *le même et l'autre* (*same-different*), the opening paragraph of the preface to Foucault's *Les mots et les choses* / *The Order of Things* (itself a double "name" that allows us to diagnosis the deception—self versus other— of the first French text / title by the detection—same versus different—of the second English text / title):

> This book first arose out of a passage in Borges, out of the laughter that shattered, as I read the passage, all the familiar landmarks of my thought—*our* thought, the thought that bears the stamp of our age and our geography—breaking up all the ordered surfaces and all the planes with which we are accustomed to tame the wild profusion of existing things, and continuing long afterwards to disturb and threaten with collapse our age-old distinction between the Self and the Other, between Similarity and Difference (le même et l'autre). This passage quotes a 'certain Chinese encyclopedia' in which it is written that 'animals are divided into: (a) belonging to the Emperor, (b) embalmed, (c) tame, (d) sucking pigs, (e) sirens, (f) fabulous, (g) stray dogs, (h) included in the present classification, (i) frenzied, (j) innumerable, (k) drawn with a very fine camelhair brush, (l) *et cetera*, (m) having just broken the water pitcher, (n) that from a long way off look like flies.' In the wonderment of this taxonomy, the thing we apprehend in one great leap, the thing that, by means of the fable, is demonstrated as the exotic charm of another system of thought, is the limitation of our own, the stark impossibility of thinking *that*.[7]

This empirical and eidetic example from Borges and Foucault for you and me constitutes a discursive process (figure 11), a Law of Communication that Foucault names the *énoncé*, which we must translate not as the unusual "statement", nor as "utterance," nor as "sentence," nor as "proposition," but as "stating" or, better, as "expressing," or best as *"speaking speech."*[8] I prefer the translation of "speaking speech" since it captures (capta) or dis-covers the eidetic and empirical force of the discourse rule: *le même et l'autre* [Self : Same : : Other : Different]. This is to say, (1) the process of "speaking" *both* combines the empirical appearance of the Self in discourse *and* differentiates the eidetic similarity always present in the many discourses of the self, and (2) the tropic product of "speech" (rather than the figural language, grammar, or logic) is a voice of the empirical Other marking its eidetic difference with each instituting articulation. For the clever reader, the first category is Jakobson's rule of distinctive features (see appendix B) objectively illustrated in any person's act of speaking (*parole*; message) and the second category is his rule of redundancy features objectively exemplified in any grouping of speech (*langue*; code).

To make the point clear, Foucault chooses the Borges quotation with its multiple planes of paradigmatic and syntagmatic function. The rule of distinctive features, the paradigmatic rule of *"l'autre"* ("Other ; Different" in figure 5), is captured by the Chinese encyclopedia in the category named "(1) *et cetera*." The semiotic code rule of Articulation and Derivation are given in category "(1) et cetera" or the dialectic of articulation-derivation ("et"; and) and derivation-articulation ("cetera"; the other). These rules are validated immediately by both a temporal interpretant of Other (= Power) defined in category "(m) having just broken the the water pitcher" (articulation) and a spatial interpretant of Different (= Desire) in category "(n) that from a long way off look like flies" (derivation). Note that the use of "et cetera" is a reversible and reflexive procedure which, when fulfilled, also includes items in the naming system, i.e., power and desire are reversed so that the intersubjectivity embodied in subjectivity (the Law of Communication) becomes the subjectivity embodied in intersubjectivity (the Law of Representation). This is to say the consciousness of power becomes

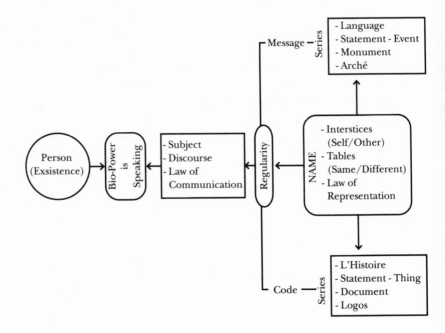

Figure 11. Foucault's "Law of Communication" in Discourse.

the symbolization of desire (see table 1; compare the reverse dynamic of problematic and thematic in table 2). In summary, the abductive logic (Rule + Result = Case) offers this "table" as the criteria of judgment for determining "that" ("the stark impossibility of thinking *that*," which of course is precisely *how* we are thinking). "That" is the meaning generated by the discourse.

POWER, A RULE OF EXCLUSION: *ET CETERA.*
Result of Exclusion: Having just broken the water pitcher.
Case of Exclusion: That from a long way off look like flies.,
NAME OF DESIRE: Included in the present classification.

The semiotic code rules of Attribution and Designation express the rule of redundancy features, the syntagmatic rule of "*le même*" (Self : Same" in figure 5). This abductive inclusion rule is captured in the Chinese encyclopedia category "(h) *included in the present classification*" where the dialectic specifies that the attribution-designation ("included") and designation-

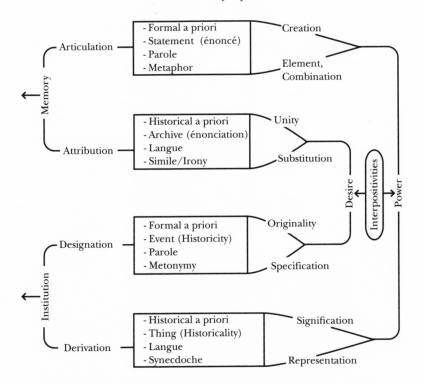

attribution ("in") also constitute the "present classification." The rules of attribution and designation are validated immediately in the Borges example by both a qualitative interpretant of the Self in category "(i) frenzied" (attribution) and a quantitative interpretant) of the Same in category "(j) innumerable" (designation). Note that the use of "included in the present classification" is a reversible and reflexive procedure which, when fulfilled, also excludes items from the naming process, i.e., desire and power are reversed so that the subjectivity embodied in intersubjectivity (the Law of Representation) becomes the intersubjectivity embodied in subjectivity (the Law of Communication). The symbolization of desire becomes the consciousness of power (see table 1; compare the reverse dynamic of problematic and thematic in table 2). In summary, the abductive logic (Rule + Result = Case) offers this "table" as the criteria of judgment for determining "that" ("the stark impossibility of thinking *that*," precisely *how* we are thinking). "That" is the meaning generated by the discourse.

DESIRE, A RULE OF INCLUSION:
INCLUDED IN THE PRESENT CLASSIFICATION.
Result of Inclusion: Frenzied.
Case of Inclusion: Innumerable.
NAME OF POWER: Et Cetera.

With the two abductive rules of exclusion and inclusion before us, let us look at the full paradigmatic and syntagmatic array that the Chinese encyclopedia gives us the in the seven paradigmatic categories (a) through (g), namely, the vertical

> *paradigmatic list which is the name of desire:*
> (a) belonging to the Emperor;
> (b) embalmed;
> (c) tame;
> (d) sucking pigs;
> (e) sirens;
> (f) fabulous;
> (g) stray dogs;

and the seven syntagmatic categories (h) through (n), that is to say, the horizontal

> *syntagmatic list which is the name of power.* (h) included in the present classification; (i) frenzied; (j) innumerable; (k) drawn with a fine camelhair brush, (l) et cetera, (m) having just broken the water pitcher, (n) that from a long way off look like flies.

The two lists are themselves an illustration of Jakobson's "poetic function" whereby syntagmatic and paradigmatic functions are reversible and reflexive to one another. Further, the poetic function as a paradigmatic shift in the syntagmatic display is specified in category "(k) drawn with a very fine camelhair brush." In this category, we are reminded that a sign (any of the fourteen categories, (a) to (n)) and its interpretant (category (k)) can reverse themselves in the unlimited semiosis of the Name (figure 5). As Aristotle reminds us in the essay *On Interpretation* that precedes the *Organon*, speech is the sign of thought, while writing is the symbol of speech. Thus can a verbal image also be pictured and inscribed by human gesture in, for example, the rebus calligram (figure 7) or in the arts generally, as we noted in chapter 3.

The science of fables, then, suggests to us that the Chinese encyclopedia's categories have both an epistemological (desire) and ontological (power) goal. As Michel de Certeau argues, "These different 'heterologies' (sciences of the different) have the common characteristic of attempting to *write the voice.*"[9] That is, reality can be drawn, pictured, and inscribed "with a very fine camelhair brush." The real is thereby re-presented in imagination (Specification in Articulation becomes Combination in Derivation), the power named by "et cetera." And the ideal, an image, can be reified "with a very fine camelhair brush" and re-presented in reality (Representation in Attribution becomes Substitution in Designation), desire named by "included in the present classification." As Foucault reminds us, "To name is at the same time to give the verbal representation of a representation."[10] Put more existentially by Umberto Eco, "at the last frontiers of formalization, frequently the *Lebenswelt* is still blackmailing modal logic as well."[11] Such is the process of communication in which the unity and originality of desire are combined with the creation and signification of power in the Name as an interstice, as the space of time (fiction) and time of space (fable) between entries in the Chinese Encyclopedia. The Chinese perspective is a fiction/fable constituting the voiceless inscription of interpositivity named in the sign and its symbol: both monument (encyclopedia; museum) and document (dictionary; library).[12] With this reiteration of the name, literally a repetition (sign) by repetition (interpretant), we may turn to the tropic logic that Foucault embeds within his quadrilateral model of discourse with the *topos* of *le même et l'autre.* Recall that the four terms (Self, Other, Same, and Different) operate within the four elements of discourse (Articulation, Designation, Derivation, and Attribution), and within the four functions of discourse (Specification, Substitution, Combination, and Representation), to produce a quadrilateral model of discursive practices (figure 5).

As a preparation for the discussion of the tropic logic, it is useful to recall, as does Foucault in his inaugural lecture, that his research into discursive practice is concerned with both a problematic of discourse called "enunciative formation" (or *langage*) and with a thematic in discourse called énoncé (which I have already defined as "speaking speech"). The problematic of language is knowledge (*connaissance*) that consists of the description of performative acts of expression through which the deceptions of signification come to establish an originality of reference that functions as a unity of practice, whereby meaning is a human creation of desire. Therefore in principle and in practice, semiosis is everything that can be used to lie, as Eco reminds us.[13] This is to say that semiosis provides us with intuitive evidence, or what Levy-Bruhl called the "law of participation" (appendix A), that the Law of Non-Contradiction cannot be existentially true to human consciousness as either its eidetic action (arché) or empirical action (*logos*). The exclusions created by desire as the problematic of language become the thematic process of Foucault's critical genealogy method (table 2).

In parallel fashion for Foucault, the thematic of discourse is understanding (*savoir*) that consists of the analysis of expressive performances that are used to detect the formulation of events of verbal practice into those series of "poetic" (i.e., reversible syntagmatic and paradigmatic) sentences or propositions constituting a regularity in the possible conditions of existence named by discourse in the eidetic statement-event (*langage*) or the empirical statement-thing (*l'histoire*).[14] The inclusions created by power as the problematic of discourse become the problematic system of Foucault's archaeology method (table 2). Therefore according to Foucault's phenomenology (as opposed to that of Eco), semiosis is in principle, and in practice, everything that can be used in *order to name*. *Semiosis constitutes the bio-power of speaking.* The being *per sona* of existence which takes on the body is the name of existence (*ekstase*). The monument of discourse power is placed in the museum: a fable about consciousness.

The dialectic conjunction of these problematic and thematic categories as a tropic logic of analytic description is illustrated in figures 8 and 11 respectively. Recall that we are concerned with the ratio of formation in *le même et l'autre* in which Self is to Same as Other is to Different in various combinations of meaning. Foucault is rather explicit in his invocation of "tropological space" as the thematic by which to analyze the problematic "interstice," or chiasm, in meaning prior to verbal performance.[15] The tropic logic allows Foucault an insightful analysis of discourse as *both* a paradigmatic method of genealogical process as the dynamic of the Self and Other, *and* as a syntagmatic method in the archaeological system of the Same and the Different (see table 2).[16] To illustrate, Merleau-Ponty refers to the genealogical process as "speech speaking" (*parole parlante*; Foucault's "birth"; Jakobson's "paradigmatic axis") and he refers to the archaeological system as "speech spoken" (*parole parlée*; Foucault's "rupture"; Jakobson's "syntagmatic axis").[17] In both dimensions and as their critical nexus point of intersection, Foucault's "interstices" and "tables" form a helix model of logic in which he locates the space and time of the name as speaking speech / *énoncé*. The two axes of this tropic logic are what Foucault means by the "tropological space" in discourse where the "law of communication" creates the emergent subject as *manifest*, to use Husserl's word (figure 6).

In a straight forward taxonomy of representation, we may name the four tropes that describe, and thereby analyze, discourse as the performance of the person (see figure 8). Synecdoche is a part/whole relation in which understanding results from the discursive use of a Self-Other perspective in the analysis of discourse. In Foucault's museum of discursive monuments, the synecdoche describes those communication problematics in which significations constitute events (a fact lamented by general semanticists and other practitioners of therapeutic speech). In the Chinese encyclopedia, the descriptive (syntagmatic) synecdoche for animals is illustrated by category "(n) from a long way off look like flies." Under conditions of reversibility for analysis, the synecdoche is made thematic by constituting an event of signification. In the Chinese encyclopedia, the analytic (paradigmatic) synecdoche for animals is exemplified in category "(a) belonging to the Emperor." The language desire and discourse power, thus, give us:

Archaeological Document:
Synecdoche: Animal = "from a long way off" (self; part) "looks
like flies" (other; whole)

Genealogical Monument:
Synecdoche: Animal = "belonging" (other, whole) "to the
Emperor" (self; part)

Metaphor is a relation of substance to whole in which our
discursive understanding builds upon a Same-Other perspective for analysis. As a communication problematic, the metaphor purports to give us an original series of semantic connections in a deceptive attempt to let language, rather than experience, explain the situation for us. In the Chinese encyclopedia, the descriptive (syntagmatic) metaphor for animals is illustrated by category "(m) having just broken the water pitcher." As a tool for analysis, of course, metaphor becomes the
reverse condition in which a series is original, that is to say,
experience is correctly and intuitively represented by the use
of language, by performance in language rather than the
performance of language. In the Chinese encyclopedia, the
analytic (paradigmatic) metaphor for animals is exemplified in
category "(b) Embalmed."

Archaeological Document:
Metaphor: Animal = "having just broken" (same; substance)
"the water pitcher" (other; whole)

Genealogical Monument:
Metaphor: Animal = (other; whole) "embalmed" (same; substance)

Metonymy is a tropic relation connecting similarity to difference (Same-Different) in discourse in which we understand
how differentiation can be both a comparison and a contrast.
The substance/attribute relationship in metonymy accounts
for those communication problems where a unity in language
is misperceived as a regularity in experience. In the Chinese
encyclopedia, the descriptive metonymy for animals is illustrated by category "(k) drawn with a very fine camelhair brush."
In the Chinese encyclopedia, the analytic metonymy for animals is exemplified in category "(c) tame."

Archaeological Document:
Metonymy: Animal = "drawn" (same: substance) "with a very fine camelhair brush" (different; attribute)

Genealogical Monument:
Metonymy: Animal = (different; attribute) "tame" (same; substance)

Another example of metonymy is the failure to recognize a rhetorical question as a statement. In the analysis of such a communication breakdown, metonymy can be used to show the regularity in the unity of discourse. For example, the effective orator makes sure to verbally answer all the rhetorical questions offered in the oration.

Simile and Irony are two tropes that embody a valence difference in meaning. Simile offers us a positive conation, while irony is negative in the value judgment it communicates. Thus, these tropes are mirror opposites in terms of linguistic volition. The part/attribute relationship which they problematically signal in language centers on the creation of possible conditions of existence for meaning to emerge in the practice of various discourses, whether in the hospital, the prison, or the asylum as Foucault points out in his local studies of performative speech. In the Chinese encyclopedia, the descriptive (syntagmatic) simile for animals is illustrated by categories "(f) fabulous" and "(i) frenzied." In turn, the the descriptive irony for animals is given in category "(g) stray dogs." As an analytic (paradigmatic) tool for public and personal policy, the positive desire of simile and the negative power of irony function as the possible conditions of existence that are the creation of discourse.

The true irony of reading the Borges "Chinese encyclopedia" is the simile that its offers for our own experience in writing anything—from today's grocery list (a fiction) to the scraps of paper with telephone numbers (without names!) we all keep in our wallets (a fable). Specifically in the Chinese encyclopedia, the analytic simile for animals is selected in category "(d) sucking pigs" and the analytic irony is sampled in category "(e) sirens."

Archaeological Document:
   Simile: Animal = "fabulous" (self; part) or "frenzied" (different; attribute)
   Irony: Animal = "stray" (self; part) "dog" (different; attribute)

Genealogical Monument:
   Simile: Animal = "sucking" (different; attribute) "pigs" (self; part)
   Irony: Animal = (different; attribute) "sirens" (self; part)

By way of concluding this chapter, let me suggest that the semiotic labor of working through the phenomenology of Foucault's categories and catalogues, his lists and labels, his archaeology and genealogy, is more that a *reductio ad nausium* confrontation with the rationality of modernity in the guise of figures of language. The "group of signs" that form the basis of his entire research adventure into the deceptions and detections of the tropes of speech are no less than the method and subject matter of all semiosis: human, animal, and machine diagnosis of discourse. In short, the description and analysis of discourse constitutes a semiotic phenomenology of embodied symbolic practice, what Pierre Bourdieu in his phenomenological debt to his teacher Maurice Merleau-Ponty calls *habitus* in its archaeological modality and *hexis* in is genealogical modality.[18] Merleau-Ponty's discursive name for this desire and power of discourse is simply, yet profoundly, the human gesture. But for Foucault, the embodiment is simply, quietly, the "nameless voice" of signs. Indeed, as Emmanuel Levinas so pointedly remarks, "Those animals that portray men give the fable its peculiar color inasmuch as men are seen *as* these animals and not only *through* these animals; the animals stop and fill up thought. It is in this that all the power and originality [desire] of allegory lies."[19] Foucault's postmodern fable practices a tropic speech of genealogy which offers the detection and diagnosis of the deception found archaeologically in the figurative language of modernity. His fable offers "to disturb and threaten with collapse our age-old distinction between the Self and Other, between Similarity Difference": *Le Même et l'Autre.*[20]

8

The Voiceless Name and the Nameless Voice

Foucault's Phenomenology of Discourse

During 1986, Foucault wrote a small volume entitled *La pensée du dehors* (The Thought from Outside). It is ostensively a commentary devoted to the explication of the writing, both popular and serious, of his fellow countryman, Maurice Blanchot. In this book, Foucault presents us with a startling perceptive-expressive proposition that is thematic both for his discussion of the literary reality we invent as a voiceless name in fiction (the trope of asyndeton) and the actuality of conversational diction (the trope of prosopopoeia) that we discover as a nameless voice in the fable of everyday discourse which tells us: One thinks, therefore one is. In other words, "the speaking subject is also the subject about which it speaks."[1]Foucault's semiotic proposition is a concrete phenomenological instance of the rhetorical tropes of asyndeton and prosopopoeia where "behind the scenes, these voices without bodies combat to tell the fable."[2] The asyndeton is the voiceless name and the prosopopoeia is a nameless voice that constitute simultaneously the narrative voice of fiction in an embodied *mythos* (speech that can be; "One Is") and the existential voice of the person whose

155

speaking is the body of *logos* (speech that was; "One Thinks"). The proposition as asyndeton is both a true stating/utterance (*énoncé*) in its orality and as prosopopoeia the proposition is a false statement/sentence (*énonciation*) in its inscription (*écriture*). The asyndeton and prosopopoeia are the existentially embodied proposition that one utters: "I lie, I speak." Or as Maurice Merleau-Ponty was first to say in his dissertation for the *doctorat d'état*, "Language transcends us and yet we speak."[3]

In these few provocative, ecstatic words, "I lie, I speak," Foucault gives us the definition of semiotic phenomenology as a philosophy of communication, as the human science of communicology.[4] The positive ambiguity of this discourse is its reflexive and reversible form as both *énoncé* and *écriture* where "the thought from outside" becomes in Heidegger's phrase, "the original outside-itself, the *ekstatikon*."[5] With Merleau-Ponty's *evoked*, and Foucault's *invoked*, positive ambiguity of "I lie, I speak," we escape the "bad ambiguity" of the famous "Cretan Paradox" of classical logic: "I am lying."[6] The positive ambiguity reminds us of time as the solution to reducing and explicating the Cretan paradox. As Merleau-Ponty quotes from Husserl's *Formale und Transzendentale Logik* (pp. 256–57). "'Time is the means offered to all that is destined to be, to come into existence in order that it may no longer be.' It is nothing but a general [both generated and generalized] flight out of the Itself, the one law governing these centrifugal movements, or again, as Heidegger says, an *ek-stase*."[7] Human time is consciousness just a human experience is the body. The grasping insight of consciousness in the act of judgment combined with the embodiment of that consciousness in discourse is the logical escape from the spatial paradox of generalized grammar into the generated temporal ambiguity of rhetoric. Eco formulates this semiotic phenomenology of ecstatic discourse as the anti-Ockhamistic principle: Phenomena are multiplied by reason of necessity (*entia multiplicanda propter necessitatem*).[8] In Sartre's words, I am no longer "condemned to choose" in the midst of paradox. Rather, I discover the ecstasy of discourse in the ambiguity of existence. As Merleau-Ponty says, "Because we are present to a world, we are *condemned to meaning*, and we cannot do or say anything without its acquiring a **name in history** [*l'histoire*]" (see figure 11).[9] Of necessity, the history of the name is a lie, the multiplication of phenomena by the rule of grammar, and the name in history speaks, the phenomenon of ambiguity by the rule of rhetoric. Archaeology, as the history of the name, and genealogy, as the name in history, are the discursive ambiguities of discourse which fascinate Merleau-Ponty's student, Foucault.

SEMIOTICS AND LYING

Semiotics has an historical place in contemporary French thought midway between the visibility of anthropological and linguistic structuralism and the birth of existential phenomenology in communicology, philosophy, and psychology as human sciences imbued with philosophy.[10] Thus, it well be no surprise for you to recall with me, if you will, the famous definition of semiotics given by Umberto Eco in his now classic book *A Theory of Semiotics:* "Semiotics is in principle the discipline studying everything which can be used to lie."[11] In other words, human discourse has the unique characteristic of being a code or statement-event (set of transformation rules exemplified by "I speak") before it is a message or statement-thing (a set of formation rules illustrated by "I lie"); see especially figure 13 to visualize the dynamic of expression/perception. We tend to discover this existential fact of the code ("I speak") only when the message fails ("I lie"), only when the formation rules are ruptured by their very appearance in discourse as the name of desire/power: "I lie, I speak." This transformation of the unmarked term "I speak" motivates the origin of the marked formation term "I lie." Hence, Jakobson's unmarked/marked rule is the very problematic of representation made thematic in Foucault's thesis of "archaeological analysis" whereby we uncover, discover *(aletheia)* the Law of Representation in *énonciation* (the articulation, statement, speech act or *réduction de texte*). Foucault's "figured" reduction of the "figure of language," problematic to a "grounded" (as in figure/ground) "trope of speech" thematic, is clear in his discussion of the *power* of language as a system of formation. He writes:

In fact, representation is not consciousness, and there is nothing
to prove that this bringing to light of elements or structures that
are never presented to consciousness as such enables the human
sciences to escape the *law of representation*. The role of the concept
of *signification* is, in fact, to show how something like a *language*,
even if it is not in the form of explicit *discourse*, and even if it has
not been deployed for a consciousness, can in general be given
to representation; the role of the complementary concept of *system* is to show how signification is never primary and contempo-
raneous with itself, but always secondary and as it were derived
in related to a system that precedes it, constitutes its positive
origin, and posits itself, little by little, in fragments and outlines
through signification; in relation to the consciousness of signification, the system is indeed always unconscious since it was there
before the signification, since it is within it that the signification
resides and on the basis of it that it becomes effective; but because the system is always promised to a future consciousness
which will perhaps never add it up. In other words, the *significa-
tion/system pair* is what ensures *both* the representability of language (as text or structure [figure of language] analyzed by
philology and linguistics) *and* the near but withdrawn presence
of the origin (as it is manifested as man's mode of being [trope
of speech] by means of the analytic of finitude).

The same point applies to Foucault's discussion of the *desire* of
language as a system of formation.

In the same way, the notion of *conflict* shows how need, desire,
and interest, even if they are not presented to the consciousness
experiencing them, can take form in representation; and the
role of the *inverse* concept of *rule* is to show how the violence of
conflict, the apparently untamed insistence of need, the lawless
infinity of *desire* are in fact already organized by an unthought
which not only prescribes their rules, but renders them possible
upon the basis of a rule. The *conflict/rule pair* ensures the representability [figure of language] of need (of the need that economics studies as an objective process in labor and production)
and the representability of the unthought [trope of speech] that
is unveiled by the analytic of finitude.

The existential conjunction of power and desire provide the
function/norm pair of practice that emerge in the Subject of

Discourse, the Person as both the *arché* and *logos* of discourse. As Foucault concludes,

> Lastly, the concept of *function* has the role of showing how the *structure of life* [figure of language] may give rise to representation (even though they are not conscious), and the concept of *norm* how function [trope of speech] provides its own conditions of possibility and the frontiers within which it is effective.[12]

Therefore, the corollary to Foucault's critique of the Law of Representation (the law of fiction = grammar) is the Law of Communication (the law of fable = rhetoric). Communication emerges in his thesis of "genealogical criticism" which categorizes the "grounded" transformation ground of *énoncé* (the uttering, stating, speaking act or *explication de texte*) that envelopes and corrects the "figured" Law of Representation.[13]

We find the basis of Foucault's dialectic of representation and communication in Merleau-Ponty's distinction between speech-speaking (*parole paralante*) and speech-spoken (*parole parlée*) announced in the *Phenomenology of Perception,* in the famous chapter on "The Body as Expression and Speaking."[14] In this formulation of embodied speaking, the initial appearance (*eidos*) of the message "I lie" exemplifies the "function" of speech-spoken; the negative message is a product of social convention, a "norm" and nothing else but speech (*parole)* fallen into a static and reified form (*langue).* "By and large, the linguistic sign, by inevitable evolution, abolishes the corporeal substance from which it springs, and which rooted it in the universe: this is a necessary act of self-obliteration."[15] As such, the message "I lie" announces a break, a rupture, an opposition, and an exclusion. From what? From the prior phenomenon of existence that is the embodied *style* of Being, from the code of *mythos* that is "authentic speaking" (*parole parlante*). This existential speaking is the embodied transcendent (transformational) condition of speaking (*parlante*) prior to the immanent (formation) condition of the message "I lie."

In short, the "I lie" message announces a norm of social practice (Bourdieu's *habitus*) immediately corrected to its proper condition of the existential practice (Bourdieu's *hexis*) of speech (*parole*) by the second message "I speak." The "I speak" second message is also a formation of power, one that ruptures and excludes the "I lie" first message of desire. The dialectic of these immanent ambiguous messages constitutes a discursive formation that defies Aristotle (in his Law of Non-Contradiction; a "formal *a priori*" for Foucault) and grounds the transcendent code of prior transformation, i.e., the unlimited semiosis (an "historical *a priori*") that is the phenomenology of the person as human. To be human is to be able to constitute a choice of context (the speaking that will have been speech) before making a choice in context: "I lie, I speak (tell the truth)" or "I lie (tell the truth), I speak." Both choices paradoxically refer to the same statement-thing as an Information Theory value, i.e., they are significations of the person whose meaning is precisely to have already chosen to be speaking. This judgment suggests a major critical thesis that, namely, *parole parlante is prior to parole parlée*. Mythos is prior to Logos. The existential condition of speaking (*archê*) is prior eidetically to saying "I lie," specifically because the subsequent "I speak" is an empirical redundancy of the Self as the Other in the World according to Merleau-Ponty or, as Foucault would argue, the repetition is of the Subject's Power in Understanding (*savior*). Consider again Merleau-Ponty's words: "Language transcends us, and yet we speak."

In cryptic fashion, both Eco and Merleau-Ponty help us to discover that the prosopopoeia "I lie, I speak" has Roman Jakobson's "poetic function" built into it as the combined process of reflexive predications (syntagmatic categories are reflexive) and that of reversible foundations (paradigmatic categories are reversible). In fact, the poetic condition formulates not only the phenomenologically reversible and reflexive condition of the internal categories as just specified, but their external combination as well.[16] Paradigm can replace syntagm and conversely. Language is such a concrete realization of the symbol and speaking is the actual sign. In short, the "lie" is realized when it is articulated and thereby made actual by a "speaking." Yet the "I," the persona who utters the "lie," is an inter-subjectivity, a symbol expressing the person as an embodiment of the subjectivity who is the subject (*topos*) of discourse.

The existential proposition that "I lie, I speak" is both reflexive and reversible in its ambiguous semiotic noema as either an oral stating (*énoncé*) or inscribing sentence (*écriture*). The proposition affirms the ontological status of the symbol by making quite concrete (an appearance; the real as eidetic) the experience of consciousness—"I lie"—and the ontology of the sign that it equally affirms as a concretion (an appearance; the actual as empirical) in the consciousness of experience—"I speak." The proposition is realized as a symbol in the lie and actualized as a sign in speaking (Foucault's signification/system pair), because the speech-spoken ("I lie") is the voice of *langue* or conversational convention that stands in place of (the very definition of semiology as a conflict/rule) speech-speaking ("I speak"). And speech-spoken it is the voice of *parole* or the sign of embodiment (indeed a function/norm of the conditions of possibility, a phenomenology of existence).

In Merleau-Ponty's view, the person in the temporal moment of intersubjective communicating achieves "this *ek-stase,* this projection of an indivisible power into an outcome which is already present to it, [which] is subjectivity."[17] Thus for Merleau-Ponty, for the speaking subject who is both the sign of speech-speaking and the symbol of speech-spoken, "it is also true that it [subjectivity] provides itself with symbols of itself in both succession and multiplicity, and that these symbols *are* it, since without them it would, like an inarticulate cry, fail to achieve self consciousness."[18]

In Michel Foucault's parallel explication, "when language is revealed to be the shared transparency of the origin and death, every single existence receives, through the simple assertion 'I speak,' the threatening promise of its own disappearance, its future appearance."[19] Both Merleau-Ponty and Foucault direct us to the understanding of embodied discourse as the practice of the human, the condition of intentionality in which consciousness expresses both its own subject as the discursive event of *historicity* and its own object as a discursive thing, *historicality.* Consciousness envelopes its own lived story and narrative (Benveniste's two senses of *l'histoire*) by the performance (*habitus*) of participation (*hexis*) in the act of speaking.

With Merleau-Ponty and Foucault, we intuit the communicative failure of Aristotle's Law of Non-Contradiction, namely, that something cannot both be the same and different as Self and Other in one place/time (see appendix A). For it is true that to say "I lie, I speak" is to already intuit the semiotic condition of intentionality, namely, that "if I speak, then I lie" just as surely as when we recall the Platonic warning that "If I write, then I lie." In point of phenomenological fact, we discover that in the original proposition "I lie, I speak" the voiceless name of grammar which says "I lie" is the symbol of signification representing the originary and ontological sign of meaning of the absence presence of consciousness which is the nameless voice of rhetoric that "I speak." Thus, the semiotic rule of discourse is that symbols stand in place of signs. Symbols are by definition ontological lies, mis-presentations, because symbols are precisely re-presentations and not *sign* presentations, i.e., presentations in the sense of the sign "not" (or "blanks" as both Husserl and Peirce call them).[20]

In turn and by contrast to the perspective of expression, the phenomenological rule of discourse is manifest, namely, that signs constitute a consciousness perception by consciousness itself. In this circumstance, we are confronting ontological signs of epistemological symbols, i.e., what Peirce calls the s*ign*, or more technically, the special category of the sign called the *representamen*. This phenomenology of phenomenology which locates the signs of symbols is simultaneously a semiology of semiology, to follow Merleau-Ponty's methodological constraint and Eco's anti-Ockhamistic principle.[21] These ontological symbols of epistemological signs illustrates Peirce's practice category of the sign known as the *interpretant*.

Thus, we must reject the naming voice of language that articulates "I speak, I lie" and thereby addresses itself as a persona (a "text" figure of language) in a way that is eternally everywhere possible as the fiction that it is. Instead, we are required to embrace a semiotic phenomenology in which the ontological priority of signs over symbols is recognized in discourse (the tropes of speech embodied as signs), and not merely tolerated in language (symbols for that embodiment). The semiotic and phenomenological proposition "I lie, I speak" is the nameless voice of consciousness addressing (speaking) itself as a person embodied in a way that is impossible except as the *ek-stase* which defines the lived-body (corps propre) of Merleau-Ponty, the bio-power of Foucault (see figure 11), and the *daseinmässig* of Heidegger. In the practice of prosopopoeia, "because we are present to a world, we are *condemned to meaning*, and we cannot do or say anything without its acquiring a name in history (*l'histoire*)."

Again examine Foucault's discourse example: "I lie, I speak," this time juxtaposed with Merleau-Ponty's meditation:

> Thus, the human dialectic is ambiguous: it is first manifest by the social or cultural structures, the appearance of which it brings about and in which it imprisons itself [symbols]. But its use-objects and its cultural objects would not be what they are if the activity [communication] which brings about their appearance did not also have as its meaning to reject them and to surpass them [signs].[22]

Thus, the double sense of *l'histoire* offered by Benveniste becomes the symbolic history of discourse, a lie, a rupture, turned toward a discursive history of existential truth when I speak. In short, the rule of general grammar founding modernity, uncovered by Foucault's archaeological investigation, yields to the postmodern rhetoric critically interrogating its own genealogical ecstasy: "*Commentary* has yielded to *criticism*."[23] Or, as Peirce might suggest, the interpretant expresses what we perceive in the representamen: the Person as Sign.

PHENOMENOLOGY AND SPEAKING

By counterposing the concepts of "commentary" and "criticism," we are recalling with Merleau-Ponty and Foucault those *lycée* days when the classical curriculum of the French high school demanded the combinatory skills of the *réduction de texte* modeled on the trope of asyndeton and the *explication de texte* modeled in the trope of prosopopoeia. We may fairly say that these two notions take on their institutional character as methodological principles in semiotic phenomenology as two key theoretical principles: (1) the phenomenological reduction of Edmund Husserl made existential by Merleau-Ponty, and (2), the semiotic explication of Maurice Merleau-Ponty made discursive by Foucault. Both Merleau-Ponty and Foucault take the "commentary" of modernity (Foucault's signification/system pair) which is the conflict/rule (Foucault's second pair) of social language use (*langue*), and expose it to a critique (Foucault's function/norm pair) as the postmodern perspective on discourse. Within Merleau-Ponty's philosophy of communication, the phenomenological reduction and the semiotic explication allow us to move from speech-spoken to speech-speaking, i.e., from the epistemology of the social to the ontology of the existential in discourse. The same theme is adopted in Foucault's use of the combined archaeological and genealogical method.

Recall that Foucault uses the term "archaeology" as a synonym for the structural relationship that Jakobson calls (along with all phenomenological structuralists) the syntagmatic axis of language where terms have their meaning by force by their placement in a linear, horizontal sequence, e.g., knowing that a word is a noun or verb by it placement in a sentence; a function of combination, contexture, contiguity, and message as the principle of redundancy features (see table 2). In turn, the term "genealogy" refers to the paradigmatic axis of language in which terms take on a meaning in their ability to replace one another in a nonlinear, vertical category, e.g., knowing that any noun can replace another noun as the subject of a sentence; a function of selection, substitution, similarity, and code as the principle of distinctive features. The combination of syntagmatic and paradigmatic axes account for the epistemological phenomenon of communication just as Foucault's archaeology and genealogy account for the phenomenon of discourse as human ontology.

Within Foucault's evolving methodology, the practice of archaeology to interrogate the problematic of language becomes the new tool of criticism, when counterposed to the practice of genealogy as the thematic in discourse now recognized as a lived-discourse.

> It is thus that *critical and genealogical descriptions* are to alternate, support and complete one another. The critical side of analysis

deals with the systems enveloping discourse; attempting to mark out and distinguish the principles of ordering, exclusion, and rarity in discourse. We might, play with our words, say it practices a kind of studied casualness. The genealogical side of discourse, by way of contrast, deals with series of effective formation of discourse: it attempts to grasp it in its power of affirmation, by which I do not mean a power opposed to that of negation, but the power of constituting domains of objects, in relation to which one can affirm or deny true or false propositions. Let us call these domains of objects positivist and, to play on words yet again, let us say, that if the critical style is one of studied casualness [e.g., "*I lie*, I speak"], then the genealogical mood is one of felicitous positivism [e.g., "I lie, *I speak*"].²⁴

Foucault's epigrammatic proposition "I lie, I speak" is a *réduction de texte* of this extended quotation from *The Order of Discourse*. The proposition is both an epistemological and ontological *précis* of the lecture, just as the lecture is an extension and elaboration of the proposition. And as an *explication de texte,* the inaugural lecture explains Foucault's major theoretical work, *The Archaeology of Understanding,* which is itself a genealogical explication of his preceding major book, *The Order of Things,* published in French as *Words and Things (Les Mots et les choses)* which is, of course, a critical description of discourse. "Archaeological analysis, then, erects the primacy of a contradiction [opposition] that has its model in the simultaneous affirmation and negation of a *single proposition*."²⁵ The exemplar proposition is, of course, "I lie, I speak." The aphorism as proposition tells us what we understand in discourse, but did not know in language. The discourse practice of "I lie, I speak" is a moment of ecstasy in which the the person, the I who "wakes up and speaks" (Merleau-Ponty's phrase) understands that signs and symbols allow the Law of Non-Contradiction to be both true and false at the *same time in one place: Consciousness.* Which is also to say Foucault, "I cannot exclude the possibility that one day I will have to confront an irreducible *residuum* which will be, in fact, the transcendental."²⁶ "Language transcends us, and yet we speak."²⁷

Now, we may turn specifically to the phenomenology of discourse that is semiotic in this programmatic research of Foucault where we can examine the essence of the proposition, its

constitution in the Name. "To name is at the same time to give
the verbal representation of a representation, and to place it in
a general [both generalizing and generating] table."[28] In short,
I shall explore the generalizing (figurative logic) and gener-
ating (tropic logic) discourse of the name: *Le même et l'autre.* As
we recall, this ambiguous phrase in French that can be rendered
both as "self and other" *and* as "same and different."

Simply put, Foucault performs an archaeology on the language of rationality, the voice of Modernity as it expresses itself in Western Thought as a figure or form of thought. In the
massive *réduction de texte* that his book *The Order of Things* represents, the whole of the epistemology of human discourse in
the West is described under four figures of language, four
conditions of speech-spoken. They are *convenientia, aemulatio,
analogy, and sympathies.* For convenience and clarity, I summarize the names, the "table" (see figure 11) of generalization, in
table 2. To assist in their easy identification, the terms in table
2 are shown in *italics* in the text below.

It is helpful to remember that the common usage of the category called "figure of speech" is actually an unfortunate
conflation of both the phrases "figures of speech" and "tropes
of speech" where the "figure" or form of language is confused
with the "trope of speech" or judgment (inference) of speaking
any human language. A figure of language refers rather specifically in rhetoric to an internal change in language that
contains the logical operation of exclusion, i.e., a change in signification as a primary feature, but secondarily in such features
as form, structure, affect, sensation, etc. that is other and different.[29] As we shall see momentarily, these figures have their
parallels in the problematic (desire) of language (exclusion)
that Foucault specifies respectively as Signification, Originality,
Unity, and Creation.[30] Note also that these ontological categories correspond respectively to Jakobson's epistemological
categories for the syntagmatic axis, namely, combination, contexture, contiguity, and message as the *in praesentia* category
of diachronic judgment, i.e., signification.

Let me also indicate here that Foucault offers us an ontology
of human discourse under four tropes of speech, four conditions of speech-speaking. They are the familiar tropes of synec-

TABLE 2. The Problematic and Thematic of *Le Même et L'Autre.*

Problematic (Desire) of Language (Exclusion):
[The Thematic Process of Critical Genealogy]

Le Même et L'Autre	Speech-Spoken	Figures of Language	Knowledge; Connaissance	Syntagmatic Axis (Dynamics)
Self (Birth)	Representation (Rational)	Convenientia (Presence of Reason)	Signification (Logos)	Combination (Speech that is)
Other (Desire)	Specification (Un-rational)	Aemulatio (Absence of Reason)	Originality (Mythos)	Contexture (Speech that can be)
Same (Power)	Substitution (Ir-rational)	Analogy (Refusal of Reason)	Unity (Mystos)	Contiguity (Silence that is)
Different	Element/ Combination	Sympathies	Creation	Message [Diachrony; *in praesentia*]
(Death)	(Non-rational)	(Forgetfulness of Reason)	(Magikos)	(Silence that can be)

Thematic (Power) of Discourse (Inclusion):
[The Problematic System of Archaeology]

Le Même et L'Autre	Speech-Speaking	Tropes of Speech	Understanding Savoir	Paradigmatic Axis (Statics)
Self	Attribution/ Proposition	Simile/Irony	Event	Selection
(Death)	(Non-rational)	(Forgetfulness of Reason)	(Magikos)	(Silence that can be)
Other (Power)	Articulation (Ir-rational)	Metaphor (Refusal of Reason)	Series (Mystos)	Substitution (Silence that is)
Same (Desire)	Designation (Un-rational)	Metonymy (Absence of Reason)	Regularity (Mythos)	Similarity (Speech that can be)
Different	Derivation	Synecdoche	Existence	Code [Synchrony; *in absentia*]
(Birth)	(Rational)	(Presence of Reason)	(Logos)	(Speech that is)

doche, metaphor, metonymy, and simile/irony. Remember, "*trope of speech*" in rhetoric refers directly to an external change in meaning (judgment) that contains the logical operation of inclusion (changes in content, cognition, perception, conation, etc. that refer to the self and same. In short, the change in meaning is accomplished by a change *of* speech act (cf., the "figure" was a change *in* the words used). These four tropes of rhetoric, i.e., tropes of logic, have their parallel in Foucault's thematic of discourse constituting the event, series, regularity, and possible conditions of existence. Note once again that these ontological categories correspond respectively to Jakobson's epistemological categories for the paradigmatic axis, namely, selection, substitution, similarity, and code as the *in absentia* category of synchronic judgment, i.e., meaning.

THE PROBLEMATIC OF LANGUAGE

The problematical nature and function of language begins with the naming ontology hypostatized by figures of language. "*Convenientia* is a resemblance connected with space in the form of a graduated scale of proximity. It is of the same order as conjunction and adjustment."[31] The discursive function performed by language is one of "convenience" in which the process of representation creates a signification by a combination of elements in the experience of Self-perception. The functional proximity and location of the predicates "lie" and "speak" in "I lie, I speak" are an example. Turning now to the next figured name, "The second form of similitude is *aemulatio:* a sort of "convenience" that has been freed from the law of place and is able to function, without motion, from a distance."[32] The ubiquitous contexture and constant originality of unique specification for the pronoun "I" in "I lie, I speak" illustrate nicely the absent Other who is speaking.

The third figure of language is *analogy.* It is like *convenientia* because "it makes possible the marvelous confrontation of resemblances across space; but it also speaks, like" *aemulatio,* "of adjacencies, of bonds and joints"[33] With the power of substitution at work in the unity of the language system, this naming condition requires the *Same* experience in the very exclusion caused by the linguistic contiguity. The analogy between "I lie" and "I speak" is their superimposition of one on the another.

The fourth problematic of language is "the play of *sympathies.*"[34] As Foucault describes the exclusive play of sympathy and antipathy, "Sympathy is an instance of the *Same* so strong and so insistent that it will not rest content to be merely one of the forms of likeness; it has the dangerous power of *assimilating*, of rendering things identical to one another, of mingling them, of causing their individuality to disappear—and thus of rendering them foreign to what they were before. Sympathy transforms." The message of language mingles its elements into new combinations thereby causing the creation of the *Different* "and its propensity to continue being what it is."[35] Here, "message" is Jakobson's typology for the syntagmatic axis as the generic relation among combination, contexture, and contiguity. The very similitude of the combination "I lie, I speak" (which comes as a person's discourse) motivates an antipathy toward the expected priority of elements, namely, "I speak, I lie" (a phrase that language can neither utter nor inscribe, because this typification is true of language alone, and would expose language in its personification).

Thus, the problematic of language constitutes knowledge (*connaissance*) as a realization of the discursive proposition *le même et l'autre* which can be expressed as the ratio *Self : Other : : Same : Different* (see figure 8). This is to say, *convenientia* is to *aemulatio* as analogy is to the sympathies. "Because of the movement and the dispersion created by its laws, the sovereignty of the sympathy-antipathy pair gives rise to all the forms of resemblance. The first three similitudes are thus all resumed and explained by it."[36] Difference, as the Law of Exclusion (Law of Representation) is an account of the problematic Self and Other as the *Same* voice in language. The epistemology of the language, of a *grammar générale*, that requires the I-Self and the I-Other to speak with the *Same* voice—"I speak, I lie"—is excluded in the existential moment of ontology when the human voice speaks or the human hand writes. "By the grace of one final form of resemblance, which envelops all the others and encloses them within a single circle, the world may be compared to a man with the power of speaking."[37] Foucault continues, "And so the circle is closed. Though, it is apparent what a complicated system of duplications was necessary to achieve this. Resemblances require a signature, for none of them would ever become observable were it not legibly marked."[38] And as Derrida silently warns us against language and its embodiment in the grammatical figure, "writing, if there is any, perhaps communicates, but certainly does not exist. Or barely, hereby, in the form of the most improbable signature."[39] The exclusion (I lie) has a signature (I speak).

THE THEMATIC OF DISCOURSE

"Discourse has not only a meaning and a truth, but a history, and a specific history that does not refer back to the laws of an alien development," says Foucault.[40] Language is the alien development and it proscribes an existential embodiment in the self/other gesture of writing (*écriture* properly understood) or in the same/different act of speaking (*énoncé*, the "act of speaking" properly understood). Language is the voice of Modernity creating a desire for its own *institution* through its power of instituting a representation in place of *memory* (see figure 11). By ironic counterpoint, the very status of the linguistic institution/instituting pair, a criterion for analysis is announced. We take up that criterion as thematic for the discovery of *capta* (evidence). In a phrase, the thematic (power) of discourse is inclusion. We intuit the subject of consciousness as an inclusion that entails the object of consciousness as an exclusion. We again adhere to Merleau-Ponty's necessary condition for analysis, namely, the semiotic rule that there be a "phenomenology of phenomenology." The binary analogue logic of communication discovers (*alétheia*) its truth in being simultaneously the inclusion (both/and combinatory logic) of itself (the ontological ground) and of the exclusion (either/or digital logic) of the epistemological condition. The semiotic phenomenology of *le même et l'autre* becomes definitional in the formulation of Wilden's "context theory" as the typicality: "Both both-and and either/or."[41] In Foucault's own words, the diagnosis of exclusion as the problematic of language and the analysis of inclusion as the ambiguity thematic of genealogical discourse allows us "to describe these differences, not to establish a system of differences between them. If there is a paradox in archaeology, it is not that it increases differences, but that it refused to reduce them—thus inverting the usual values."[42] The thematic *le même et l'autre* now expresses a condition of understanding (*savior*) as the "context theory" ratio: [Self : Same :: Other : Different]. Or to use our familiar example, we have the ratio: [*I : Lie : : I : Speak*]. The tropic rhetoric of this ratio constitutes the categories making up the *Thematic (Power) of Discourse (Inclusion)* in table 2 (recall that table terms are being shown in italics). As we find the thematic enveloped in the problematic system of discourse, Foucault turns to the method of archaeology whereby the ontological inclusions of discourse are detected and diagnosed in what Merleau-Ponty calls "the architecture of signs."[43]

Following the structure of the discussion of the problematic, I shall begin the thematic section of table 2 with the tropes of speech (see figure 8) and their characteristic discursive functions (see figure 5). The first tropic category in figure 12 of immediate concern is *simile* and its negative counterpart *irony*.[44] Here, the tropic function of shifting from "part to attribute" (or the reverse direction) is an event in which the attribution of meaning indicates a selection or choice by the Self that in turn motivates a change in content available to perception as an original, but *Different* meaning, i.e., it meets the conditions for being a trope. The possible relations between the binary *Self-Different* pair or part/attribute categories signals two conditions or propositions of inclusive meaning, one positive and one negative.

In the trope of *simile*, a positive selection of meaning is an event in a discursive proposition which makes an attribution to that which is taken from a substitutable Self. This is to say, what is different in the other becomes meaningful to the self as that which can replace the self. And in the trope of *irony*, a negative selection of meaning is an event in discourse which makes an attribution to that which is taken from a substitutable proposition. That is, the irony occurs in the selection of a proposition which correctly makes an attribution, but the meaning was not that expected from the Self, the meaning was a different attribution. The meaning is different, as that between the self and the proposition about the self.

The connection in both the tropes of simile and irony is the condition of inclusive selection in the Self-Different relationship illustrated in the "I lie, I speak" proposition by the emphasis "I lie, *I speak*". As the existential condition of discourse, the ontology of speech-speaking ("I speak") is intuitively understood (*savior*) as a change transcendent to the concrete immanence in language of the speaking act which utters "I lie." That is, speech-speaking as the condition of being (*mythos*) is prior to this appearance of language as speech-spoken ("I speak" following on "I lie"). To be agonistic in form, the epistemological "I speak" is speech-spoken "like or as" the ontological speech-speaking, just "as," just "like" the ironic speech-spoken (the epistemological "I lie"). In short, "I speak" is a simile (similar to) "I lie," yet "I speak" is an ironic version of "I lie" inasmuch as "I lie" is a speaking or speech act truly nameable by "I speak." And as by inclusive selection, the position of "I speak" in the series "I lie, I speak" is irony because we know the performance of lying to already be a speaking act. The important point to be made however, and it is Foucault's point, is that the proposition "I lie, I think" (as opposed to the paradoxical Cretan proposition "I am lying") forms an ambiguity in which *any answer is acceptable as meaningful* and thereby escapes the paradox of exclusive signification by being an inclusive ambiguity of meaning, either expected in simile or unexpected in irony.

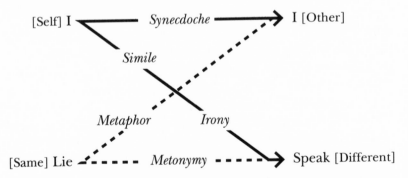

Figure 12. The Quadrilateral Model of "I Lie, I Speak."

The second trope in figure 12 is metaphor. It expresses the "substance/whole" (see figure 8) relationship of inclusion produced by discourse. The shift from substance to whole (or the reverse linkage) creates a series of articulations in which the substitution of one articulation for the other creates a pattern of including the Other meaning as being the same as the original. The shift is the condition of inclusive similarity in the *Same-Other* relationship. Within the context of the proposition "I lie, I speak," the existence of "lie" is related to the second "I"; i.e. we have the focus on "I *lie*, I speak." The substance of expression ("lie") is related to the whole perception (second "I"), just as in the validity of reversibility, the whole expression (second "I") is related to the perceived substance ("lie"). Indeed, the articulation of desire proscribed by the "same" language ("I speak, I lie") is violated by the precise "other" sequence of unexpected substance/whole shifting in the order of power manifest by "I lie, I speak." Jakobson's sense of marked and unmarked terms may be helpful here. The occurrence of the second "I" is a marking by which we realize the first "I" was unmarked. And in turn the opposition of the two uses of "I" signals that their respective verbs "lie, speak" have an inverse marking. Thus, the initial occurrence of "lie" is a marked term since it presumes speaking as a generic semantic category in the user lexicon, a fact then confirmed by the uttering of "speak" which amounts to an empirical redundancy feature of an eidetic distinctive feature (see appendix B). Again we escape the Cretan paradox by constituting ambiguity. The ambiguity created in which both "I, I" and "lie, speak" together with all their combinations are straight forward metaphors substituting substance for wholeness.

Metonymy is the tropic relationship of substance and attribute in discursive formation illustrated in figure 12. The connection between substance and its attributes (or the reverse relation) is a regularity of designation that indicates the similarity of *Different* meanings to be found in the *Same* context of signification. The connection is the condition of inclusive similarity in the *Same-Different* relationship. Turning once again to the "I lie, I speak, example, the substantial priority of "lie" over its attribute "speak" is the designated ontological focus upon the respective regularity of the similar predications in the discursive practice: "I *lie*, I *speak*". The epistemology of language is contravened by having the qualifying linguistic attribute ("lie") precede the substance ("speak") as a tropic transformation. Rather than being similar to the Cretan paradox, the ambiguity created by the metonymy designates substance (either "lie" or "speak") and attribute (respectively, "speak" or "lie") to be a similarity. The reverse scenario going from attribute to substance also holds true for constructing such an ambiguity; indeed, this is also the secondary ambiguity of part and whole illustrated by the "I, I" usage of the next trope.

The fourth and last trope depicted in figure 12, synecdoche is a trope of speech that expresses the part/whole relationship in the performance of discourse. The tropic change in discourse is the code condition of inclusive derivation in the *Self-Other* relationship as the possible condition of existence. In the proposition "I lie, I speak," the synecdoche is the "I : I" ratio in consciousness with this focus: "*I* lie, *I* speak." Where one pronoun refers to the Self-Other (or Other-Self) in the part/whole relationship of the experience ratio of "I : Me (self-other) referred to by the utterance of the "I : I" (other-self) ratio, the ontological usage escapes the Cretan paradox where there is an equivocation of the pronoun "I" in "I am lying."

By way of summary, then, the thematic of discourse as a function of understanding (*savior*) emerges as the ratio: Self : Same :: Other : Different. Or to use our familiar example, we have the tropic ratio: I : Lie :: I : Speak. This is to say, simile/irony stands in relation to metaphor in the same way that metonymy stands to synecdoche. Following the dynamics of the process that constitutes the name (a representation of representation) as shown in figure 5, we may now translate figure 8 into figure 12. This calculus of discourse thereby demonstrates the contest of discourse as the "agonism" ("a relationship which is at the same time reciprocal incitation and struggle"; "a permanent provocation") between the ontology of the speaking-subject and the epistemology of the language-object. That the speaking-subject embodies discourse under the *name le même et l'autre* is demonstrated as genealogical method in the ontological thematic of discourse by a "nameless voice" (prosopopoeia) that uses the archaeological method to critically expose the epistemological problematic of grammar as just a figure of language, as mere personification (i.e., the voiceless name of asyndeton). In the archaeology of language and the genealogy of discourse, we have abolished the commentary of personification in favor of the criticism of prosopopoeia, a trope of speech. The nameless voice, which says "I lie, I speak," discovers the thematic ontology of discourse: "its limits, its form, its code, its law of possibility."[45] We discover a *l'histoire* movement of discourse in which "Philosophy turns toward the anonymous symbolic activity from which we emerge, and towards the personal discourse which develops in us, and which, indeed, we are."[46]

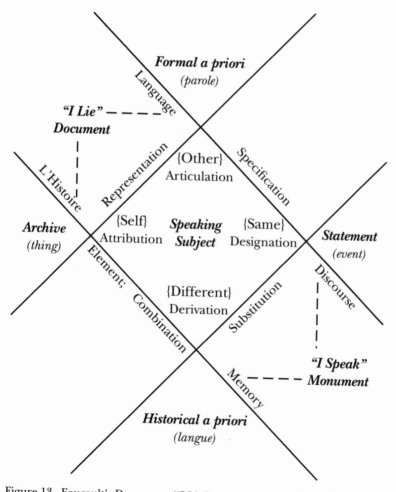

Figure 13. Foucault's Document ("I Lie") and Monument ("I Speak") Model.

For the speaking subject, the sufficient conditions of the linguistic problematic appear as the problematic of (1) signification, (2) originality, (3) unity, and (4) creation of knowledge (*connaisannce*) in the archaeological method (figure 13). They are conditions of exclusion which oppose inclusion. The "figures of language" are to be found in the *document,* the *language / l'histoire* of a voiceless name (asyndeton) which articulates the message: *I lie.* The necessary conditions for the discursive thematic appear as the (1) event, (2) series, (3) regularity, and (4) possible conditions of existence in the genealogical method of understanding (*savior*). They are conditions of inclusion which oppose exclusion. The "tropes of speech" are to be found in the *monument,* the *discourse/memory* of a nameless voice (prosopopoeia) which articulates the code: *I speak.*

The combination of exclusion (language) and inclusion (discourse) thereby constitutes "the logic of a great strategy" (rhetoric) whose "cautionary prescriptions" (tropes of speech) are (1) the "Rule of Immanence" where the signification/event as "choice" is the speaking "I," (2) the "Rule of Continual Variations" where the originality/series as "context" is to "lie", (3) the "Rule of Double Conditioning" where the unity/regularity of "consciousness" is the spoken "I", and (4) the "Rule of the Tactical Polyvalence of discourses" where creation/possible condition of existence as "experience" is to "speak."[47]

As the conditions of archaeology turn into the conditions of criticism, yet another method leading on to the conditions of genealogy, "its purpose is to map, in a particular discursive practice, the point at which they are constituted, to define the form that they assume, the relations that they have with each other, and the domain that they govern."[48] Thus, archaeology as the new method of criticism is willing "to speak of discontinuities, ruptures, gaps, entirely new forms of positivity, and of sudden redistributions."[49] As Levinas summarizes,

> But language which gives sign without establishing itself in the eternity of the idea it signifies, discontinuous language ["I lie"], is circumvented by that ancillary language ["I speak"] which follows in its tracks and never stops speaking. The coherent language ["I speak"] in which being (even 'the Being of beings') stretches and extends, is all memory, all anticipation, all eternity.

It is never-fading, and always has the last word. It contaminates with logic the ambiguity inscribed in the trace of forgotten discourse and never gives itself up to enigma ["I lie"].[50]

The conclusion that we can draw now from Foucault's inquiry into language and discourse is explicit. The sufficient condition of the archaeology is the *énoncé* (statement/sentence/utterance) of "I lie, I speak" which constitutes respectively *both* the eidetic *and* the empirical ground for the necessary condition of genealogy, i.e., the propositional *le même et l'autre* of discourse. The Self-Same-Other-Different discourse is precisely Merleau-Ponty's ambiguity of speech which inscribes the deception of grammar as a "figure" of speech-speaking (I lie) enveloped by speech-spoken (I speak) only to be detected and diagnosed by rhetoric as a "trope" of of speech-speaking (I speak) constituting speech-spoken (I lie).

By following the meaning of the words and the argument, I reach the conclusion that indeed because I think, I am; but this is merely a verbal *cogito*, for I have grasped my thought and my existence only through the medium of language, and the true formula of this *cogito* should be: 'One thinks, therefore one is.' The wonderful thing about language is that it promotes its own oblivion: my eyes follow the lines on the paper, and from the moment I am caught up in their meaning, I lose sight of them.
***
Expression fades out before what is expressed. . . .[51]

9

An Aphorism of Culture and Communication

The Phenomenological Approach to the Human

T he contemporary study of the opposition between culture and communication is especially limited to dominant Western models of thinking about how people interact with one another and, thereby, share their values in the form of beliefs and practices. The conjunction of both culture and communication is an announcement of the philosophic theme so central to Merleau-Ponty's thought, the ambiguity of discourse which captures the "human." Or as Foucault would say of this ambiguity, culture and communication are captured both in the "documents" which teach the human practice of belief and in the "monuments" that are the reminders of those *human choices* in performance (see figure 1 and Appendices C and D).

In most non-European languages the word for "culture" is the same as that for "communication." Indeed, this is the spiritual wisdom marked by the word *Sutra*. "'Sutra' etymologically means 'thread' and in this context it means a brief mnemonic statement."[1] In fact, it is a central tenet of Hindu philosophy to conceive of the chosen human practice of speech as a cultural and spiritual marker of the ontology of the person. "As philosophical discussion took place mostly orally, and as they were passed down through oral traditions handed down by teachers to students, it was perhaps felt necessary to link up or *thread* together the main thoughts in the minds of students by brief statements of problems, answers, possible objections and replies to them."[2] In the phenomenological tradition of the West, this same problematic is best expressed by Hegel in *The Phenomenology of Mind* where we encounter the ontological grounding for the aphorism "I lie, I speak," analyzed in the last chapter.

> Language is self-consciousness existing *for others;* it is self-consciousness which as such is there immediately present, and which in its individuality is universal. Language is self separating itself from itself *["I"],* which as the pure ego identical with ego becomes an object to itself *["lie"],* which at once maintains itself in this objective form as *this* actual self *["I"],* and at the same time fuses directly with others and is *their* self-consciousness *["speak"].* The self perceives itself at the same time that it is perceived by others *["I lie"]:* and this perceiving is just existence which has become a self *["I speak"].*[3]

PHENOMENOLOGICAL PERSPECTIVES

Among the many philosophical systems produced in the West, phenomenology is uniquely suited to a comparison with Eastern philosophies in general, and with Indo-Sanskrit philosophies in particular. Because much of the ontology of Hindu philosophy derives from the oral culture of the *Vedas* and the *Upanisads,* its beginning point in philosophical analysis is parallel to phenomenology. The context for the name "phenomenology" that I have in mind is more precisely the *style* of discourse (i.e., communication) found in French philosophy in the semiological and phenomenological tradition of Maurice Merleau-Ponty, and the *discourse* of style (i.e., culture) in which Merleau-Ponty's existential writing is reminiscent of Nietzsche's aphoristic discourse in *Human, All Too Human.*[4] "'Sanskrit' itself is 'constructed' *(samskrtam)* in just this sense; it is something more than merely 'human' speech, and when the corresponding script is called *devanagari* this undoubtedly implies that the human script is an imitation of means of communication in the 'city of the gods.'"[5]

The specific cultural *style of discourse* that I have in mind is the aphorism. Here is the conjunction of phenomenology and Indian philosophy: "A sutra-work consists of a collection of many sutras or aphorisms of this kind, arranged into different chapters and sections according to different topics."[6] The sutra and the aphorism are the concrete exemplification of two moments in human conscious experience. First, there is the *moment of communication* in the discourse choice of style whereby consciousness is tied to experience by substitution, i.e., Foucault's monument to memory (= discourse; see figure 13). As J. N. Mohanty has had occasion to remark, "the *Vedas,* are known throughout the age-long tradition as having been heard and transmitted through the spoken words, as *śruti* [revealed by being heard] as contrasted with the written."[7] Second, there is the *moment of culture* in the discourse practice whereby experience is tied to consciousness by representation, i.e., Foucault's document in history (= language). The first moment seems to be the philosophic preference of the phenomenologist and the Hindu philosopher, while the second moment suggests the Anglo-American preference of an "analytic" philosophy of "ordinary language" (but *not* ordinary everyday *speech*) and the positivist approach to science (see appendix A).

In the thematic explication of this last chapter, which envelopes the problematic that opened chapter one, I wish to rejoin these two moments of communication and culture as conscious experience which are compatible generally with one or more traditional views of Indian philosophy. In so doing, my intention is to rehabilitate the place of culture in communication that "analytic" philosophy eschews. I do not seek to critique any particular view of "analytic" philosophy nor I am concerned with any sense of general doctrine. Rather, my goal is a simple positive explication of the moments of a semiotic phenomenology that explicate both communication and culture as a philosophical style (phenomenology) and as a philosophical discourse (semiology). Indeed, "styles are idioms of knowledge and communication."[8]

In this context, we follow Edmund Husserl's fundamental definition of his philosophical task:

> In the proper line of its explication lies the development of the originally "egological" (refer to the ego of the philosophizing subject for the time being) phenomenology into a transcendental sociological phenomenology having reference to a manifest multiplicity of conscious subjects communicating with one another. A systematically consistent development of phenomenology leads necessarily to an all-comprehensive logic concerned with correlates; knowing-act, knowledge-significance, and knowledge-objectivity.[9]

We see at once the striking similarity between Husserl's summary as a Western view in the European context and that of K. C. Bhattacharya's philosophy, presented by J. N. Mohanty, as an eastern view from the Indian perspective:

> The most original among modern Indian thinkers, however, is K. C. Bhattacharya, who rejects the conception of philosophy as a construction of a worldview and undertakes a phenomenological description of the various grades of subjectivity: (1) the bodily, (2) the psychic, and (3) the spiritual. With regard to 1, he distinguishes between the objective body and the felt body and regards the latter as the most primitive level of the subjective sense of freedom from the objective world. The stage 2 includes the range of mental life from image to to free thought. In introspection, the level 2 is transcended, but various levels of introspection are distinguished, all leading to greater freedom from objectivity.[10]

Thus, I hope to show in a general sense that the East and West compatibilities of philosophical thought and practice suggested here are especially thematic in the work of Merleau-Ponty and Foucault.

Merleau-Ponty is a phenomenologist whose primary concern with the disciplines of communication and culture makes his eidetic and empirical work especially useful for exploring the secondary conjunction of phenomenology and philosophy, in this case, Indian philosophy. Thus in the several senses of 'discipline' just mentioned, "as soon as we distinguish, alongside of the objective science of language, a phenomenology of speech, we set in motion a dialectic through which the two disciplines open communication."[11]

MAURICE MERLEAU-PONTY'S METHOD

As I have characterized it according to Merleau-Ponty, phenomenology is first concerned with describing the experiences of consciousness in their cultural senses as expressed and perceived by persons in a social world of others. A second methodological step for phenomenological analysis, Husserl's famous procedure, is to reduce the description originally obtained. The phenomenological reduction is the essential location of the subject/object of a constituting consciousness. Language and speech are the principal subject matters by which cultural meaning is located philosophically in this approach. Third, the hermeneutic step in the method requires that the philosopher interpret the reduction of the description. In short, the experience (description of communication) of discourse as consciousness (reduction of language/speech) defines the essence of being human (interpretation of meaning). As J. N. Mohanty summarizes, "When the auditor deciphers the right meaning of the utterance, he has interpreted it rightly. Interpretation is the reverse side of communication. The speaker communicates, and the hearer interprets."[12]

Here I use "discourse" in both Merleau-Ponty's and Foucault's larger descriptive sense of all semiotic acts of expression (the signifying or signifier) and perception (the referent or signified). These are combinatory acts constituting an essential, reversible tropic rhetoric of both consciousness experience as the speech which is speaking (subjectivity as prosopopoeia) and the language or speech which is spoken that is the experience of consciousness (intersubjectivity and objectivity as asyndeton). "Speech, as distinguished from language, is that moment when the significative intention (still silent and wholly in act) proves itself capable of incorporating itself into my culture and the culture of others—of shaping me and others by transforming the meaning of cultural instruments,"[13] according to Merleau-Ponty.

In his brief explication of speech (speaking), Merleau-Ponty gives us an enveloped presentation of phenomenological method at work. First he distinguishes "speech" (*parole*) from "language" (*langue*) as an exercise of the *epoché* or "bracketing" procedure by which prior conceptions (Foucault's "memory" and "institution"; see figure 13) are disallowed as idealizations present to the mind of the interpreter. The descriptive step continues as Merleau-Ponty depicts the "moment" of speech in its status as the "significative intention." Again, keep in mind that we describe the speech *(parole)* that a speaker uses to communicate, and not the idealization we call language *(langue)*. The description already reveals the mind and body for the speaker: a consciousness of mind that is "still silent" and an experience of body as "wholly in act."

Yet, the truth of the description belongs as well to the listener, a person who discovers the human experience of the Self in the Other, a shared World (see Appendix E). Or as Foucault might argue, the listener is the Subject in the Power of the Other, a shared Knowledge (*connaissance*). For, the speaker's communication is the listener's interpretation, according to Mohanty. The listener's experience, as Merleau-Ponty might describe it, is "still silent and wholly in act."

The phenomenological reduction, as a second methodical step of analysis, is the essence of the conscious experience that we can take from the description. We have already noted that according to Merleau-Ponty "speech" is shared by the speaker and listener in a concrete way as "the significative intention." We now ask, how is it shared? Why is it appropriate to describe the perspective of the speaker and that of the listener as the same essence of "speech"? Recall Merleau-Ponty's next words: the significative intention "proves itself capable of incorporating itself into my culture and the culture of others." Rather than a Cartesian body/mind split idealized as the split between speaker/listener, we discover phenomenological unity. The *human* is the conscious experience of being *a person*. The person is a concrete unity of speaker and listener, just as consciousness and experience are embodied. Merleau-Ponty suggests, "I am snapped up by a second myself outside of me; I perceive an other."[14] The phenomenological reduction teaches us about "my culture and the culture of others." The reduction teaches us that "culture" is the name for "the significative intention" displayed in the oral speaking of a person who is both *per sona* and *vac* (voice, speech, Logos, wisdom), to cite both the Greek and Sanskrit prescriptions of discourse. As Foucault says of such a discourse,

> Its veracity is not guaranteed by the lofty authority of the magistery, nor by the tradition it transmits, but by the bond, the basic intimacy in discourse, between the one who speaks and what he is speaking about. On the other hand, the agency of domination does not reside in the one who speaks (for it is he who is constrained), but in the one who listens and says nothing; not in the one who knows and answers, but in the one who questions and is not supposed to know. And this discourse of truth finally takes effect, not in the one who receives it, but in the one from whom it is wrested.[15]

The phenomenological interpretation, as a third and last step in analytical method, requires that the reduced description (the problematic) be made thematic. In the context of Merleau-Ponty's illustration of "speech," the interpretation should specify simultaneously three things for us: (1) *what* the concrete essence of "speech" is (concrete = the description), (2) *how* the concrete essence of "speech" is (essence = the reduction), and (3) *why* the concrete essence of "speech" is ("speech" = interpretation). Remember Merleau-Ponty's final words: speech is capable "of shaping me and others by transforming the meaning of cultural instruments." In short, the speaker who communicates transforms cultural instruments, e.g., speech—gesture—body, into meanings of Self and Other as the shared World of human values (see Appendix C). Indeed, the phenomenological interpretation is explicit: Culture is the intention of communication. The reversibility of communication and culture as intentionality (consciousness of...) mark the concrete essence we nominate as the *human*. Thus, "In order for the alter ego and the thought of others to appear to me, I must be the *I* of *this* body of mine, *this* incarnate life's thought."[16]

If we have taken speech *(parole)* in this phenomenological sense of culture, how might we describe language *(langue)*? Our first act of description was the exercise of the suspension of our beliefs in language, that is, the *epoché* procedure. We need now to test our description-reduction-interpretation against this first analytical act by which we approached the phenomenon of *speaking*. Merleau-Ponty offers this answer:

> Our present expressive operations, instead of driving the preceding ones away—simply succeeding and annulling them—salvage, preserve, and (insofar as they contain some truth) take them up again; and the same phenomenon is produced with respect to other's expressive operations, whether they be past or contemporary.
>
> Our present keeps the promises of our past; we keep others' promises. Each act of philosophical or literary expression contributes to fulfilling the vow to retrieve the world taken with the first appearance of a language, that is, with the first appearance of any finite system of signs which claimed to be capable in principle of winning by a sort of ruse any being which might present itself. Each act of expression realizes for its own part a portion of this project, and by opening a new field of truths, further extends the contract which has just expired. This is possible only through the same "intentional transgression" which gives us others; and like it the phenomenon of truth, which is theoretically impossible, is known only through the praxis which *creates* it.[17]

By way of explicit summary for this analysis, let me indicate that Merleau-Ponty suggests in this quotation that language *(langage)* is the phenomenological description that we first encounter as the speaker's communication and the listener's intention. This is language as Culture: *logos* or s*abda* (sound, word, reason). When and where that language locates the speech community (*langue*), especially where the community preserves its speech by writing, we witness the phenomenological reduction. This is culture as language: *dike* or *riti* (style, figure, diction, manner).

The human being as speaker-listener, the being who communicates intentions (communication) and intends communication (culture), represents the phenomenological interpretation, i.e., a specification of *intentionality* or conscious experience. This hermeneutic step focuses, first, upon the person in the act of speaking *(parole)* such that language *(langage)* is the *speech* of the practical community *(langue)*. This speech spoken *(parole parlée)* is the voice heard by the listener who perceives the intentions of the speaker as *an act of Culture;* (practice as rule or game in figure 1). Culture is the *object* of consciousness in intentionality, Foucault's *document* of Culture in all communication (see figure 13). In addition, I take Husserl's trichotomy of knowing-act, knowledge-significance, and knowledge-objectivity to be a philosophical parallel to the existential description, reduction and interpretation just outlined.

Yet in the reversible condition as an *act of Communication* (choice as habit or ritual in figure 1), there seems to be a parallel to the trichotomy of the bodily, the psychic, and the spiritual in Bhattacharya's philosophy. That is, the hermeneutic focus upon the person in the act of speaking *(parole)* is such that the speech of the practical community *(langue)* becomes the speaking of language *(langage)*, understood as the reality-memory-myth in the person(s) that is the Foucaultian monument of Communication in all cultures (see figure 13). Communication is the subject of consciousness in intentionality, or in Foucault's pointed aphorism: "The confession is a ritual of discourse in which the speaking subject if also the subject of the statement."[18] Communication becomes the act of speech speaking *(parole parlante)*. Again Merleau-Ponty's aphorism makes the point: "To the extent that what I say has meaning, I am a different 'other' for myself when I am speaking; and to the extent that I understand, I no longer know who is speaking and who is listening."[19] Culture is communication according to the same transformation that consciousness is experience. In both culture and communication for Foucault (see figure 11), there is the intentionality that we call the *human:* "If one can apply the term *bio-history* to the pressures through which the movements of life and the processes of history interfere with one another, who would have to speak of *bio-power* to designate what brought life and its mechanisms into the realm of explicit calculations and made knowledge-power an agent of transformation of human life."[20]

THE VOICE OF THE PAST IN THE PRESENT

I now turn to the *Rig Veda* (Book 10, Hymn 90) as another illustration of the phenomenological approach to the human that I have been discussing. The nameless voice (prosopopoeia) that we hear says:

> The embodied spirit has a thousand heads,
> A thousand eyes, a thousand feet, around
> On every side enveloping the earth,
> Yet filling space no larger than a span.
> He is himself this very universe,
> He is whatever is, has been, and shall be.
> He is the lord of immortality.
> All creatures are are one-fourth of him, three-fourths
> Are that which is immortal in the sky.
> From him, called Purusha, was born Viraj,
> And from Viraj was Purusha produced
> Whom gods and holy men made their oblation.
> With Purusha as victim they performed
> A sacrifice. When they divided him,
> How did they cut him up? what was his mouth?
> What were his arms? and what his thighs and feet?
> The Brahaman was his mouth, the kingly soldier
> Was made his arms, the husbandman his thighs,
> The servile Sudra issued from his feet.[21]

Is this hymn, not the voice of speech spoken in the speech speaking of my/your voice? Does not the voice of Hindu mythology communicate a culture of human reality located in its spiritual ideality? Have we not heard Husserl's knowing-act of knowledge-significance that is knowledge-objectivity? Do we not witness Bhattachayra's philosophy of the bodily voiced in the psychic that is spiritual? Is not the Eastern hymn also the Western aphorism of the human? There is a dialectic of the nameless voice (prosopopoeia) and the voiceless name (asyndeton) in the tropic expressions: hymn and aphorism.

In the traditional understanding of the *Rig Veda* sutra, Purusha appears as the first male in Hindu mythology and is here described as being the spirit immanent in everything and, yet,

identical with the totality of all things. *Purusha is life* (a phenomenological description). Then, with positive ambiguity,
Purusha is both the parent and the child of Viraj. The description of Pursuha is reduced to an essence: *Purusha is human life*
(a phenomenological reduction). Last, and with negative ambiguity, the universe is divided as the chosen (the divine voice)
becomes a victim (the human voice). Pursuha is the emblematic
source of the caste system. The reduction of the description
of Purusha is interpreted as existential: Purusha *is human life
as lived (*a phenomenological interpretation).

By way of offering a cryptic comparison of philosophical traditions, it strikes me that Plato's discussion of speech (speaking) within the problematic of communication (the persona of
the Sophist), within the problematic of culture (the persona of
the Statesman), and within the thematic of the human (the persona of the Philosopher) in the dialogue *Sophist* is a parallel
sutra. In this oral dialogue *(maieutic)*, we also encounter the
same sequence of problematic and thematic speech as in the
Rig Veda, that is, the ambiguity of the Many and the One as a
counterposed voice of the gods signified by asyndeton and the
voice of the human marked by prosopopoeia.

First, there is the ambiguity of the Many and the One present in the problem of Being and Not-Being, and with it
Socrates' description of the bodily art of the sophist and his
knowing-acts of discourse. Then, there is the same ambiguity
in the problem of Movement and Rest that is Socrates' reduction of the psychic art of the statesman and his knowledge-
significance recorded in political, practical discourse. Last, we
find the "paradox" of the Many and the One specified in the
ambiguous problem of the Same and Different, the Self and
Other (see figure 8). The differentiation (asyndeton) marks
the task encountered in the interpretation of knowledge-
objectivity, the spiritual art of the philosopher expressed in
discourse (prosopopoeia).[22]

My point in this comparison of the *Rig Veda* and the *Sophist*
is that these two hymns are the aphorism of the Culture of the
East and of the West, which is now *sutra, in Communication.* As
Merleau-Ponty asserts, "Now it is at the heart of my present
that I find the meaning of those presents which preceded it,

and that I find the means of understanding others' presence at the same world; and it is in the actual practice of speaking that I learn to understand."[23] The voiceless name is enveloped by the nameless voice: Culture is enveloped by Communication. The asyndeton of "Culture, Communication" captured in Foucault's aphorism, "I lie, I speak," becomes the prosopopoeia of Communicology as the discourse of the person (see figure 6): "I know myself only in my inherence in time and in the world, that is, I know myself only in ambiguity."[24]

Lévy-Bruhl and the Human Science "Law of Participation"

First presented as a book review, the following essay discusses the pioneering human science approach to research, both eidetic and empirical, conducted by Lévy-Bruhl. His work shaped modern thinking about research, particularly field studies, in which cross-cultural issues are dominant in the description of human practices of communication. His fundamental questioning and reverse of the Aristotelian "laws of thought" is fundamental to understanding such modern scholars as Maurice Merleau-Ponty and Michel Foucault. The research methodology issues confronted by Lévy-Bruhl helped define the then new discipline of Sociology for Europe in much the same way that the field of work of Franz Boas shaped the emerging discipline of Anthropology in the United States of America, as both took place at the beginning of the Twentieth Century. With some irony, these same issues are now shaping the emergent human science discipline of Communicology as we close the century.

Classic works usually reappear in new editions because they have an enduring readership or offer a new translation. On rare occasion, a classic reappears simply because its revolution is born again. *How Natives Think* (Princeton University Press, 1985) is such a volume. It is the eighth in a list of nineteen major works by the consummate philosopher and human scientist, Lucien Lévy-Bruhl (1857–1939). He completed his doctorate in 1884, a Latin thesis titled *Quid de deo*

Seneca senserit, served from 1883–1895 as Professor of Advanced Rhetoric at the lycée Louis-le-Grand and as supplementary lecturer at L'École Normale Supérieure, then in 1896 he was appointed to the Sorbonne. In 1904, he rose to the rank of titular professor of the history of modern philosophy and director of studies in philosophy. In addition, he was exchange professor at Harvard University during 1919–1920. During 1926, he gave special lectures in the United States at Johns Hopkins University and at the University of California-Berkeley. We should also note that he traveled to many of the countries about which he wrote.

Originally published in 1910 as *Les Fonctions mentales dans les sociétes inférieures,* it was translated into English in 1926 with the unfortunate title "How Natives Think". A more accurate translation of "Mystical Judgment" or "Prelogical Inference" would not have contributed to the gross misinterpretation that was rendered against the theses of this book. The translation title is only slightly less offensive than the well known "the savage mind" (subtend "unreflected thought") rendering of Lévi-Strauss' *La Pensée Sauvage.* A conscious decision was made by the publishers to stay with the original title for the sake of historical clarity (with which one must now agree), but they thoughtfully provide a scholarly introduction by the anthropologist C. Scott Littleton entitled "Lucien Lévy-Bruhl and the Concept of Cognitive Relativity."

This introductory essay offers an extraordinarily sensitive reading of the text and an informed understanding of the intellectual context within which Lévy-Bruhl wrote, not to mention the foundational importance of his work to the human sciences. But the introduction does more; it situates Lévy-Bruhl at the crossroads of sociology and anthropology as they are emerging from the discipline of philosophy in France at the turn of the century. Littleton's own scholarship shows in his accurate summary of the conjunction of European descriptive linguistics (i.e., semiology) and phenomenology that the book represents. The conjunction is now called "semiotic phenomenology" in the human sciences generally and specifically so in the discipline of communicology. Littleton is quite correct to see in this book the ground of much that accounts for qualitative research in the human sciences of the twentieth century. For example, an accurate approach to the work of Merleau-Ponty or his student, Foucault, requires that Lévy-Bruhl be read first. Indeed, Littleton's introduction alone is worth the modest price of the new edition.

For readers new to this classic research volume, the book consists of an original introduction and nine chapters. Lévy-Bruhl summarizes the entire volume in two theses: "(1) The institutions, customs and beliefs of primitives imply a mentality which is prelogical and mystic, oriented differently from our own. (2) The collective representations and interconnections which constitute such a mentality are governed by the *Law of Participation* and insofar they take but little account of the law of logical contradiction" (my emphasis).[1] The book opens with an Introduction that voices certain themes about empirical research derived from the early work of Durkheim. These sociological themes ground an overall attack on positivist research in anthropology as exemplified largely in the "animism" of Tylor's *Primitive Culture* and Frazer's *The Golden Bough*. In fact, the historical dictum of positive science taken from Auguste Comte's *Cours de Philosophie Positive* is invoked against Tylor, Frazer, and their ilk: "Humanity is not to be defined through man, but on the contrary, man through humanity."[2] Chapter one discusses the mystic elements that make up collective representation in the perception of "primitive" peoples (most critics ignore footnote one on the first page of the introduction: "By this term (primitive), *an incorrect one*, yet rendered almost indispensable through common usage, we simply mean members of the most elementary social aggregates with which we are acquainted.") (my emphasis). The key point of this first chapter is that primitive mentality is not influenced by experience; i.e., it is a "prelogical mentality."

Chapter two on "The Law of Participation" is the seminal contribution of this book. This law is the counterpart to the Aristotelian Law of Contradiction which grounds Western science as a concept of methodology. I must stress, as does Littleton,[3] that "Lévy-Bruhl does *not* contend that *all* primitive thought is predicated on the 'law of participation'." Such an interpretation—which frequently becomes the irony of history—is exactly that to which Lévy-Bruhl objected. He argues that some "undeveloped peoples" (as well as "developed" peoples—his example in chapter nine is the modern beliefs of Christianity in Europe) have mystic mentality that perceives a reality of beings related to objects that are not perceptible to the senses. Hence, the statement of the Law of Participation: "In varying forms and degrees they [the relations] all involve a 'participation' between persons or objects which form part of a collective representation."[4] This law describes a human science in which "The prelogical mind does not objectify nature thus. It *lives* it rather, by feeling itself participate in it, and feeling these participations everywhere. . . ."[5]

Chapter three discusses the synthesis of the logical and prelogical mentality, especially in the medium of *memory* as used by "primitives" in their daily activity. Contrary to many of his critics, Lévy Bruhl does not assert completely the Law of Participation against that of contradiction. He rather anticipates the archaeological and genealogical methods of Foucault and makes them combinatory laws: "the effect of the law of contradiction is already more or less strong and constant, first of all in operations which would be impossible without it (such as numeration, inference, etc.) and then also in those which are governed by the law of participation."[6] Chapter four discusses "primitive" mentality in the "languages they speak" and chapter five details it in "relation to numeration." Chapters six, seven, and eight exemplify the Law of Participation in such communication and exchange activities as hunting, fishing, illness, death, birth, the family, social groups, rites of secret societies, and the like. Examples are drawn from "primitive" cultural records throughout the world. Lévy-Bruhl is everywhere careful to remind the reader that the record is partial, that field observations are often contradictory, and that in the best tradition of abductive logic (in Peirce's sense, later adopted by Gregory Bateson[7]), he is using a logical model of necessary and sufficient condition to demonstrate by *rule* and *result* description the conditions in each empirical *case* established as a possibility (i.e., a real event in the lifeworld). This use of cases offers a notable and attractive alternative to the abstracted probability explanations of the animistic model, itself a product of "positive science," in which a probability is an expected event in a world assumed to be causal. Chapter nine entitled "The Transition to the Higher Mental Types" anticipates much that we find in contemporary human science research, especially in anthropology, communicology, and psychology. The thesis of this last chapter is simply the analogue logic (Both/And) combinatory thesis: "The prelogical and the mystic are co-existent with the logical."[8]

Here we come to the one item that may cause theoretical confusion. Littleton, in his introduction, counterposes Lévy-Bruhl's discussion of the "Law of Participation" to the "Law of Non-Contradiction" (namely, a thing cannot *both* be *and* not be at the same time/place).[9] Lévy-Bruhl is careful to always say "law of contradiction" (namely, one thing can not be *another* thing at the same time/place), that is derived from the "Law of Identity" (a thing is always itself in the same time/place). Littleton conflates the "Law of Contradiction" with the "Law of Non-Contradiction." It is an easy mistake for a non-logician. Let us be careful to note, then, that Lévy-Bruhl is making a clear argument in theory construction for the analogue logic rule of *differentiation by combination* which the Law of Non-Contradiction expresses (and not differentiation by exclusion, the digital logic rule for the Law of Contradiction).

Using Lévy-Bruhl's terminology, the *prelogical* (a thing can not) governs both the *logical* (both be) and the *mystic* (and not be) as a *person* (same time = memory) or *object* (same place = activity). Thus, the "illogical" construction, that the Law of Non-Contradiction grounds both the Law of Identity and the Law of Contradiction, is the Law of Participation. Abduction (Rule + Result = Case) replaces deduction (Rule + Case = Result) in this theoretical model. The paradigm of "social realty" (lifeworld) is counterposed to "reality" (theory world) therewith and conversely. To recall my previous example, such a participation construction (see figure 1) is at the very center of the extensive contemporary research into discourse by Foucault (hence his unique title "Professor of History and Systems of Thought" at the Collège de France), and, this same construction is latent in the work of Maurice Merleau-Ponty, also philosopher and human scientist at the Collège de France.

An English translation, by Lilian A. Clare, for the 1926 edition is reprinted in the present edition from Princeton University Press. One might assume that a new translation would help remove the negative response of a generation of anthropologists who fought against such terminology as "prelogical" and "primitive"—terms even Lévy-Bruhl discarded under pressure in later work—and the generations of their students who dismissed Lévy-Bruhl out of hand. But rather than a new translation, we need a careful reading of the first text and Littleton encourages us to it. Unquestionably such a reading will benefit those who participate in the current debate between qualitative and quantitative methodology, and in the theoretical competitions among semiotics, structuralism, phenomenology, poststructuralism, and hermeneutics. Indeed, the kind of reading Littleton suggests might create a space from which intercultural research in cultural studies, as well as social diversity, will emerge. This volume was written during the early twentieth century, at the beginning of a human science revolution called *sociology* (the first Latin and Greek compound term to name a discipline). It is now reprinted as a classic that can be read effectively at the end of the twentieth century, as we start another revolutionary discipline, one that we also name with a Latin-Greek term that describes and defines the theory and research on communication and culture: Communicology.

NOTES

1. Lucien Lévy-Bruhl, *How Natives Think (sic)*, trans. Lilian A. Clarke (Princeton: Princeton UP, 1985; original work published 1910), p. 361.
2. Lévy-Bruhl, p. 15.
3. Lévy-Bruhl, p. xvii.
4. Lévy-Bruhl, p. 76.
5. Lévy-Bruhl, p. 130.
6. Lévy-Bruhl, p. 106.
7. Gregory Bateson and Mary Catherine Bateson, *Angels Fear: Towards an Epistemology of the Sacred* (New York: Macmillan, 1987). In this posthumous text of Gregory, completed by Mary Catherine, the following definition is given: "Abduction: That form of reasoning in which a recognizable similarity between A and B proposes the possibility of further similarity. Often contrasted by Gregory Bateson with two other, more familiar types of reasoning, deduction and induction." (p. 206; see also page 37).
8. Lévy-Bruhl, p. 386.
9. Lévy-Bruhl, p. ix.

Communicology: An Encyclopedic Dictionary of the Human Science

INTRODUCTION FOR USERS

Entries in the encyclopedic dictionary follow the motivated sequence of figure 14, "Chart: Theory and Methodology in the Human Sciences." "Theory" on the chart branches into "eidetic" and "empirical," however, the meaning of "theory" is dependent upon the distinction between "praxis" and "poiesis" so these two definitions immediately follow the "theory" entry. There is also a categorical distinction to be made between "theory" and "methodology," so the methodology entry comes next. With all contextual definitions now presented, the categorical division between "eidetic" and "empirical" can occur with the next entries which are "eidetic" and "empirical" respectively. Thus, the sequence of entries in the encyclopedic dictionary conforms to the outline suggested by the figure 14 chart. But you can find particular entries quickly by using the alphabetical index below.

All encyclopedic dictionary terms are listed alphabetically and refer to their entry number location (not page number). There are total of 80 entries. *Primary entries* are designated by a plain number, for example: 25. Where there are useful secondary definitions that occur within the context of a cognate entry, such *secondary entries* are indicated by a parenthetical number, for example: (14). Many, but not all, of these secondary entries have full definitions (but did not merit a separate primary entry by themselves). The actual listing of terms in the encyclopedic dictionary occurs according to a motivated

197

logic sequence in which the immediately preceding or succeeding terms(s) from an ideational group. Thus, it is always useful to examine the entries around the one you located initially.

INDEX OF ENTRIES

D

O

Object	(33)
Object language	(78)
Observation	(37)
Ontic	(9)
Ontological	(8)
Opposition	(2), (65)
Ordinary language	(77)
Otherness	(35), (71), (76)

P

Pairing	(72), (79)
Paradigm	(4), (69)
Paradigmatic axis	56, 61, (69), (75)
Paradox	(26)
Parole	(70), (78)
Peirce, Charles S.	(33)
Perception	(44)
Perspective	(35)
Pharmakon	(2)
Particularize	19, (45)
Phatic	77
Phenomena	(21), (23)
Phenomenology	45, (1), (2), (40), [see Figs. 14 & 15]
Phenomenon	(22), (23), [see Fig. 15]
Plato	(34)
Poiesis	6, (see Fig. 15]
Poetic	76, (6)
Position	(65)
Possibility	(2), (26), (33)
Postulate	(33)
Praxis	5, [see Fig. 15]
Probability	(25), (32)
Process	51, (43)
Proposition	(36)
Propositional calculus	(33)
Précis	(13)
Predecessors	(23)
Problematic	39
Procedure	(7)
Process	(4)
Prototype	(7)
Puzzle	(26)

Q

QED	(16)
QEF	(14)

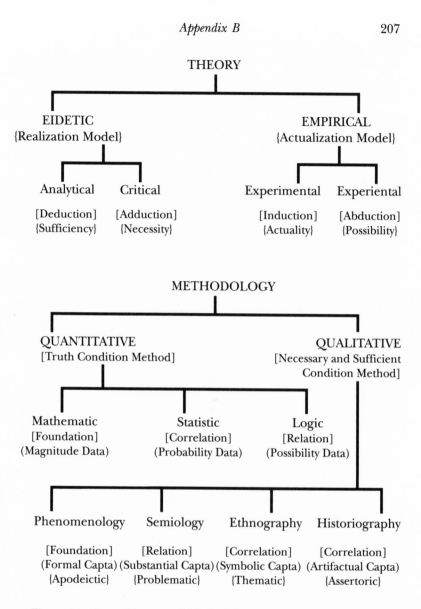

THEORY

EIDETIC
{Realization Model}

Analytical   Critical

[Deduction]   [Adduction]
{Sufficiency}   {Necessity}

EMPIRICAL
{Actualization Model}

Experimental   Experiental

[Induction]   [Abduction]
{Actuality}   {Possibility}

METHODOLOGY

QUANTITATIVE
[Truth Condition Method]

QUALITATIVE
[Necessary and Sufficient
Condition Method]

Mathematic   Statistic   Logic
[Foundation]   [Correlation]   [Relation]
(Magnitude Data) (Probability Data) (Possibility Data)

Phenomenology   Semiology   Ethnography   Historiography

[Foundation]   [Relation]   [Correlation]   [Correlation]
(Formal Capta) (Substantial Capta) (Symbolic Capta) (Artifactual Capta)
{Apodeictic}   {Problematic}   {Thematic}   {Assertoric}

Figure 14. Chart: Theory and Methodology in the Human Sciences.

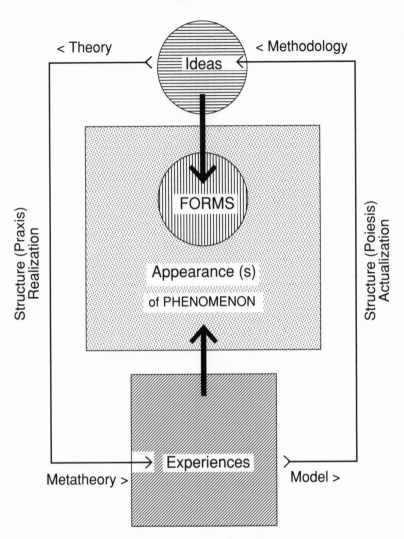

Figure 15. Phenomenology: The Form and Structure of Appearance.

Note: To understand the diagram, think of Ideas as the "word" entries in a Dictionary. Think of Experiences as the "essay" entries in an Encyclopedia. Thus, every word in a dictionary has Form (Idea), and, every "essay" entry in an encyclopedia has a Structure (Experience). Dictionaries tell you how to use words (forms; ideas), but not what word to use; hence, you tend to go from word to word (Appearances) trying to decide which one is the best description (counts as an experienced Phenomenon), but the dictionary cannot tell you what idea to choose!

Encyclopedias tell you what facts to use (structures; experiences), but not how to use them; hence, you tend to reread the essay going over and over the facts (Appearances) trying to decide how to define an experience (make a Phenomenon), but the encyclopedia cannot tell you how to think! Combining these activities yields (1) the Encyclopedic Dictionary which is the Realized idea of an experience or a Theory, and (2), the Illustrated Dictionary that is the Actualized experience of an idea or a Model. Using the encyclopedic dictionary [e.g., an almanac or "what-is-it book" is an exercise in Metatheory; the use of the illustrated dictionary [e.g., a "textbook" or "how-to book"] is the practice of Methodology.

PART 1. ENTRY TERMS BY LANIGAN

1. COMMUNICOLOGY = the discipline that studies the discourse of human communication; the term was first used in the late 1950's in the United States and is associated (1) with the early founders of the International Communication Association, especially Franklin H. Knower and Elwood Huey Allen Murray, and (2) with Wendell Johnson, a major scholar in the theory of General Semantics. The term was first used in a textbook title by Joseph A. Devito, *Communicology: An Introduction to the Study of Communication* (Harper & Row, 1978). Later, Devito offered this definition in his *The Communication Handbook: A Dictionary*: "*Communicology: The study of the processes involved in the sending and receiving of messages; the study of speech and language disorders and therapy*" (New York: Harper & Row, 1986, p. 65). The first usage in a theory book is Richard L. Lanigan, *Phenomenology of Communication: Merleau-Ponty's Thematics in Communicology and Semiology* (Duquesne University Press, 1988). A précis of ideas in the present glossary was presented by Lanigan as "Communicology: Paradigm Dialogue Position Thesis" at the May 1985 conference of the International Communication Association held at Honolulu, Hawaii.

There has been some use of the term in France (*communicologie*) and an occasional use of the term as an appropriate translation of the German *Kommunikationsgemeinschaft*. Communicology, as a word composed of both a Latin term (*communis*) and a Greek term (*logos*) follows the precedent established by the disciplinary name of "sociology." The meaning of "communicology" is founded on its historic connection to the "ideographic" (particularizing) emphasis in theory construction and application found within the *Geisteswissenschaft* (human science) tradition, especially the tradition associated with phenomenology, both American (Peirce, James, Urban) and European (Cassirer, Jakobson, Jaspers, Merleau-Ponty, Foucault).

Basic Reference books include: (1) Herbert Spiegelberg, *The Phenomenological Movement: A Historical Introduction*, third revised and enlarged edition, Boston: Martinus Nijhoff Publishers, 1984, especially "Part Five—The Essentials of the Phenomenological Method." (2) Donald Polkinghorne, *Methodology for the Human Sciences: Systems of Inquiry*, Albany: State University of New York Press, 1983; (3) Richard L. Lanigan, *Phenomenology of Communication: Merleau-Ponty's Thematics in Phenomenology and Semiology*, Pittsburgh: Duquesne University Press, 1988; and, (4) E. F. Kaelin and C. O. Schrag (Eds.), *American Phenomenology: Origins and Developments* (Vol. 26: Analecta Husserliana: The Yearbook of Phenomenological Research), Boston: Kluwer Academic Publishers, 1989.

2. COMMUNICATION THEORY = binary analogue logic that constitutes *possibility* differentiation (i.e., certainty) by combination; simply formulated as "a choice of context"; strictly formulated as "the choice of a context by relation which entails a choice by correlation"; formalized as:

{Both [Both/And] And [Either/Or]}

Note: In discourse, communication theory is exemplified primarily by declarative sentences with action verbs, e.g., "You won the Nobel Prize for Peace," and secondarily by imperative sentences, e.g., "Come in!". Use of the verb of being ("is"), rather than an action verb, in declarative sentences shifts the message from a "communication theoretic" meaning to an "information theoretic" signification, e.g., "You are the winner of the Nobel Prize for Peace" or "You are saying 'come in'." The shift phenomenon is also known as the "is/ought" paradox, i.e., information (ontic) versus communication (deontic).

Historical Note: Michel Foucault suggests that the "law of communication" (see Jakobson Note below) is demonstrated by reversing the hierarchy of Aristotle's "laws of thought" (i.e., shifting from a deductive to an ad- or abductive logic) and giving primacy to understanding (*savior*) the Law of Non-Contradiction: "Something cannot both be and not be at the same time." To understand this LN-C, human beings first intuit that the reverse must be true, otherwise one would not understand the exclusion the law describes. This is Foucault's idea of *rupture* in a system that both defines the old system (Jakobson's "marked term") and gives birth to a new system (Jakobson's "un-marked term"). Thus, what we understand is {Something both [is and is not possible] and [either can or cannot] be}. For example, there is Plato's famous illustration of the *pharmakon*, or drug: {Something *both* [is a medicine and a poison] and [either can or cannot] be healthy}.

Jakobson Notes: (1) "Two outstanding linguistic achievements in particular are based on the existence of invariant semantic values: the ability to introduce words into new context and the ability to translate. We cannot use or understand a word in a new context unless we are already familiar with certain components of the context, i.e., unless these components possess an invariant semantic value. In translation as well, we orient ourselves on the basis of the invariant values of the signs" (Holenstein, p. 98). (2) "Opposition is a binary relation in which one term 'univocally, reversibly, and necessarily' calls for another" (p. 122); "A *phenomenological analysis* differs from a purely logical one by not only examining each datum as it is 'in itself,' but also as it is given in consciousness, 'for us'. From this phenomenological point of view, *opposition* appears as both an exclusion and an inclusion" [p. 124; my emphasis].

3. INFORMATION THEORY = digital logic that constitutes *probability* differentiation (i.e., reduces uncertainty) by exclusion; simply formulated as "a context of choice"; strictly formulated as "the context of a choice by correlation which entails a context by relation"; formalized as:

{Either [Either/Or] Or [Both/And]}

Note: In discourse, information theory is exemplified primarily by interrogative sentences with the verb of being, e.g., "Are you the winner of the Nobel Prize for Peace?" and, secondarily in exclamatory sentences, e.g., "Fire!" Use of an action verb, rather than the verb of being ("is"), in interrogative sentences shifts the message from an "information theoretic" signification to a "communication theoretic" meaning, e.g., "Tell me if you know the winner of the Nobel Prize for Peace" or "Stop yelling fire!"

4. THEORY = *propositions*; statements expressing the *complete normative criteria* for choosing or selecting contexts of judgment; a set of process *rules*. For Aristotle, the sciences of *theória* deal with the metaphysical question of *how to understand what is always or is for the most part*; there are three such sciences: philosophy, mathematics, and physics. Where the criteria are limited (incomplete), they constitute a model. Where there is only one criterion, it is a construct. A metatheory is a theory used as the process (see Hjelmslev terms) of poiesis. Thus, a metatheory model is known as a paradigm for its constructs which are *data* or *capta*.

5. PRAXIS = conduct; *"doing," how to choose among the relative goods*, based on the Greek concepts of *praktike* (practical sciences; for Aristotle there are two: ethics [the good person] and politics [the good city]); an activity that has a goal within itself; theory

used in a particular context (typically *analytical* or *experimental*),
usually a theory specifying a problem in order to derive a
solution, i.e., a *Case*. Praxis is the opposite of *poiesis*.

6. POIESIS = *procedure, production, performance; "making," how to make
   things*, based on the Greek concepts of *poietike* (productive sciences; for Aristotle there are three: *Topics*, how to make a good
   argument; *Rhetoric*, how make a good speech; *Poetics*, how to
   make a good poem) and its subcategory *téchné* (craft, skill, art,
   applied science); an activity with an external goal, it brings into
   existence something distinct from the activity itself; a particular
   approach (typically *critical* or *experiential*) to a problem, usually
   to normalize a particular solution, i.e., a *Case*. A modern synonym for *poiesis* is method, as used in the phrase "method acting"
   or "scientific method."
   Note: "method" usually implies an atheoretical condition,
   i.e., either the phenomena are too complex for a theory or the
   phenomena are presumed to be too obvious to require a theory.
   Also in recent years, qualitative researchers (especially in
   sociology) adopted the adjective "poetic" as a code word to
   signal their anti-positivist (or neo-marxist) position in theory
   debates. Do not confuse this usage with Jakobson's "poetic
   function" (which is equal to *poiesis*).

7. METHODOLOGY = *practices;* actions expressing the *complete normative
   context (*usually *eidetic*) for making a choice(s); a system for the
   constitution or production of *Results*. Where the context is
   limited (incomplete), it constitutes a *procedure*. Where there is
   only one known context, it is an *exemplar*. A *methodology* is praxis
   used as a *system (*see Hjelmslev terms) of *poiesis*. Thus, a methodological procedure is known as a *prototype* for its exemplars
   which are *data* or *capta*. In short, methodology is "theory by
   analogy" where "practice" usually implies a knowledge of, or
   belief in, an action (procedure), rather than the performance
   per se (e.g., "scientific method" is invoked frequently by researchers who are not actually using it as their research procedure).

8. EIDETIC = *thinking;* a conceptual or ideational process; to make
   sense, to be conscious of; realizing/realization. Eidetic theory
   construction is tested reflexively by empirical theory construction. The Greek term *eidos* means appearance, constitutive
   nature, form, type, species, and idea.
   Historical Note: In Heidegger's existential phenomenology,
   the term *ontological,* and in Husserl's transcendental phenomenology, the term *noesis (noetic),* is used to designate eidetic

phenomena and now has general use as a term in the human sciences.

9. EMPIRICAL = *experiencing;* a performance process or actions; the activity of doing; to make significant, to be engaged with; actualizing/actualization. Empirical theory construction is tested reflexively by eidetic theory construction. The Greek term *empirikos* means experience gained through practice.

Historical Note: In Heidegger's existential phenomenology, the term *ontic,* and in Husserl's transcendental phenomenology, the term *noema (noematic),* is used to designate empirical phenomena and now has general use as a term in the human sciences.

10. REALIZATION = *capability; consciousness of experience;* the process of constituting a subject/object of consciousness; what can be thought by a person.

11. ACTUALIZATION = *ability; experience of consciousness;* the process of constituting a subject/object of experience; what can be lived by a person.

Historical Note: Aristotle referred to the process as *entelechy,* which means "actualization from potential." For Aristotle, *poetic discourse* moves from the actual to the potential, whereas in *rhetoric* the discourse moves from the potential to the actual.

12. EXPLICATION = method of analysis or criticism; from the French *explication de texte,* literally the "explication of a text," i.e., reconstituting a concrete message by analysis or criticism. For example, if an argument has the form of a thesis (I) with three subpoints (A, B, C), then an explication demonstrates by necessary (analysis) or sufficient (criticism) condition that subpoints (Z, X, Y) also apply to the thesis (I). The idea with this methodology is that the choices of *content* (what is explicit) all adhere to the s*tructure (*relationship) implicit in the thesis (argument being made). The structural characteristics of (A, B, C) must be shown to occur in (Z, X, Y). For example in this case, (A, B, C) literally belong to the Roman alphabet, there is a hierarchy of letters in this alphabet (A=first, B=second, C=third), and, all the letters are capitals. Such a content and structure is explicated by an *analysis* where the new (Z, X, Y) content and structure matches the original (A, B, C). Thus, (Z, X, Y) also belong to the Roman alphabet, have the same differential hierarchy (Z=first [to last], X=second [to last], Y=third [to last]), and, all the letters are capitals.

A similar result occurs with *criticism* by explication. Thus, within the Roman alphabet, A is a primary beginning and Z is a primary ending, B and Y are secondary, while C and X are tertiary respectively, and, both sets of printed capital letters present a precise differentiation from (1) each other as letters per se, (2) from each other as sets of letters, and (3) each other simultaneously as individual letters and letter sets by contrast to both lower case letters and script letters.

A more familiar, but complex example, is in the category of semantic meaning where *connotation* (*intension*) is an explication by analysis and *denotation* (*extension*) is an analysis by criticism. Thus, encyclopedias help you analyze meaning, while dictionaries help you critique meaning.

Still another example of explication is the comparison between an "envoi" and a "coda" (both terms originally taken from "literary or rhetorical criticism"). An *Envoi* (French for 'message') is a message sent to the reader at the end of a written document, a sort of explicit "moral of the story"; technically, it is a message defined by "same structure, different content" that "says" the same thing as the original message (recall the analytic or critical comparison example of A-B-C and Z-Y-X above). A *Coda* (Latin for "tail" as in "the tail that wags the dog") is a "reversing" message sent to the reader at the end of a written document, (also a sort of explicit "moral of the story"); technically, it it is a message defined by "same content, different structure" that "says" something *different* from the original message (review the analytical or critical comparison above, but substitute X-Y-Z, a new structure for Z-Y-X, (an old structure *because* it is the old structure already present in A-B-C).

13. EXPLANATION = method of experience or experiment; from the French *réduction de texte*, literally "reduction of the text," i.e., reconstituting an experience (as a form of *précise*) or experiment (as a form of *imaginative variation*). As explanation by experience, a familiar example of the précise (or "summary" experience) is the usual "book review" that one finds in professional journals, i.e., a scaled down version of the structure and content of the original full-length book that provides the same approximate experience of the full-length book. Turning to explanation by experiment, a familiar example of imaginative variation is the usual "book review essay" on a given book (or topic among several books) in a journal, i.e., the statement of the book(s) main thesis (argument and evidence; structure and content) contrasted and compared to the reviewer's thesis as an "imagination" that "varies" the original thesis by changing or modifying the original argument and evidence. Most authors would prefer a positive précise as the "review" of their

book, but frequently all they get is a negative imaginative variation "review" (which usually prompts a letter to the journal editor from the author claiming the reviewer did not understand the book).

14. ACTA = is that "which was to be done" (*Q.E.F.* = *quod erat faciendum*). That which is *created* as evidence either by *convention* or *invention*. In Alfred Schütz's phenomenology, acta is associated with capta (acting; an action) and data (activity; an act).

15. CAPTA = is that "which was to be found out" *(Q.E.I.* = *quod erat inveniendum)*. That which is *taken* as evidence or *discovery (disclosure)*. Discovery is associated with truth as the usual translation of the Greek *aletheia* (lit. uncovering or "clearing"). In Alfred Schütz's phenomenology, capta is associated with the *in-order-to-motive* marked by the future perfect verb from, i.e., what "shall have been" the case (the *terminus ad quem* or movement toward a destination point as a boundary condition; borrowed from Cicero's *De Oratore*). In Merleau-Ponty's phenomenology, capta is "transcendent"; capability, "I can; I am able to —"

Note: Capta and the discovery-disclosure process are especially well illustrated by Studs Terkel, the noted Chicago writer and radio interviewer, who uses a semiotic phenomenological approach to interviewing. He explains his method ("Interviews and Interviewers" [August 1970], Audiotape BB-2550, Pacifica Tape Library, Los Angeles, Calif.) by saying that he has two rules for interviewing: (1) Respect the Person; and (2) Listen. You respect the person by understanding that s/he (a) has "no rule" for answering, (b) is accepting "vulnerability" by talking, and (c) finds the experience a "surprise." You listen by hearing the *"revelatory phrase,"* i.e., that (a) the phrase is a signifier, it names the experience for the first time (surprise), (b) the phrase is a signified, it defines the experience (vulnerability), and (c) the phrase is a sign; the experience is reflexive self-consciousness (No Rule).

16. DATA = is that "which was to be demonstrated" (*Q.E.D.* = *quod erat demonstrandum)*, that which is *given* as evidence or *invention*. In Alfred Schütz's phenomenology, data is associated with the *because-motive* marked by the pluperfect verb form, i.e., what "had been" the case (the *terminus a quo* or movement away from a starting point as a boundary condition, borrowed from Cicero's *De Oratore*). In Merleau-Ponty's phenomenology, data is "immanent"; ability, "I think, I feel" (à la Descartes).

17. CONCRETE = The *coherence* of a whole or category before anything is abstracted from it. For example, because a declarative sen-

tence shows the coherence of a complete (whole) thought, it can be abstracted into the parts of speech (whole = the parts of subject and predicate), or alternatively, into the parts of grammar (whole = the parts of nouns, verbs, adjectives, conjunctions, etc.).

18. ABSTRACT = The *selection* of parts (empirical) or aspects (eidetic) from a whole or category upon which to focus attention. Note: "abstract" does not mean something that lacks existence in reality.

19. PARTICULARIZE = To *reduce* an initial class or category to *exclude* (more) *dissimilar* items.

20. GENERALIZE = To *extend* a particularized class or category to *include* (more) *similar* items.

21. TYPOLOGY = *phenomena* (Gk., plural); the class, set, or group to which a typification belongs; the typology is *eidetic* where the original typification is constituted by a necessary condition; the typology is *empirical* where the original typification is constituted by sufficient condition.

    Note: Eidetic typology is the counterpart to deductive *demonstration* in logical or mathematical research method (sometimes called *interpolation*); empirical typology is the counterpart to inductive *generalization* in statistical research method (sometimes called *extrapolation*).

22. TYPIFICATION = *phenomenon* (Gk., singular); the appearance (of the subject, object) which has *meaning* as a direct result of being (expressed, perceived as) a referent by necessary or sufficient condition.

    Note: See the *capta* entry, especially the *revelatory phrase* which is an example of typification. Other examples are Freud's notions of a "slip of the tongue" in speaking, "a slip of the pen" in writing, and the "dream symbol" in thinking. In grammar, the "parts of grammar" such as nouns, pronouns, verbs, adverbs, adjectives, prepositions, and conjunctions function as typifications by *naming* a function ("parts of speech") that is a necessary condition (i.e., the "subject"; whatever you "think") and a sufficient condition (i.e., the "predicate"; whatever you "say" or "write" after or before you "think"). See also the *explication* entry.

23. ANALYTICAL = use of *deductive logic* [Rule + Case = Result]. In the s*ame* context {Rule} two phenomena {Case} are *internally* compared {Result}; Analysis requires *sufficiency* (see "Sufficient Condition") as a standard of judgment, i.e., the *eidetic* claim that the

comparison holds true for this and subsequent cases (particular *tokens* and *types* cannot be distinguished) and that the truth of the claim *(tonality)* is dependent on the case(s) chosen. Analytical models of theory construction are tested reflexively by Critical models (an internal test) and by Experiential models (an external test).

Note: Two *different* "phenomena" may be the *same* phenomenon at different times/places. This is a key point in the study of discursive phenomena, especially with regard to Alfred Schütz's temporal model of interpersonal communication: (1) Predecessors = persons who never can share time/space, e.g., you and your great-grand parents; (2) Consociates [Associates] = persons who do share time/space, e.g., you and your classmates; (3) Contemporaries = persons who share time, but not space, e.g., you and the President of France; and (4) Successors = persons who do not share time/space, but can, e.g., you and your great-grand children.

24. CRITICAL = use of *adductive* logic [Rule + Result = Case (universal; a priori)]. In *different* contexts {Rule}, an *external* comparison {Result} establishes the identity of two phenomena {Case}; criticism requires *necessity* (see "Necessary Condition") as a standard of judgment, i.e., the eidetic claim that the comparison holds true in all *types* of the case (universal; no exceptions, all *tokens* fit all types) and that the truth of the claim (*tonality*) is obvious *before* it is experienced (a priori). Critical models of theory construction are tested reflexively by Analytical models (an internal test) and by Experimental models (an external test).

25. EXPERIMENTAL = use of *inductive* logic {Case + Result = Rule}. With two phenomena {Case}, an *internal* comparison {Result} establishes the same context {Rule}. Experimentation requires actuality as a standard of judgment. Actuality is the empirical presence/absence of a phenomena which validates the presence/absence of another phenomena. An experiment requires *actuality as a function of probability* as a standard of judgment, i.e., the e*mpirical* claim that the comparison holds true for this and subsequent cases (particular *tokens* and *types* cannot be distinguished) and that the truth of the claim (*tonality*) is dependent on the case(s) chosen. Experimental models of theory construction are tested reflexively by Experiential models (an internal test) and by Critical models (an external test).

Note: Experimentation is information theoretic, i.e., probability can make you more and more certain of *how* you are choosing, but it never tells you (defines) *what* you are choosing or have chosen. See the *statistic* entry.

26. EXPERIENTIAL = use of *abductive* logic [Rule + Result = Case (Particular; a posteriori)]. In the *same* context {Rule}, an *internal* comparison {Result} establishes the identity of two phenomena {Case}. Experience requires *possibility* as a standard of judgment, i.e., the empirical claim that the comparison holds true for this *type* of case (particular; all *tokens* fit the definition of the type) and that the truth of the claim (*tonality*) is obvious after it is experienced (a posteriori). Experiential models of theory construction are tested reflexively by Experimental models (an internal test) and by Analytical models (an external test).

   Note: Something is logically either possible or it is not. POSSIBILITY should not be confused with the positivist idea of "low probability"; rather, possibility is a "claim for immediacy" meaning that you can think of (eidetic possibility) or experience (empirical possibility) one completely describable case of the phenomenon. For example, you can draw a picture of the mythical animal called a "unicorn" (eidetic possibility of the empirical), you can say that "Buddha" is the name of god (empirical possibility of the eidetic), you can say that your great-grandchildren will have been girls (eidetic possibility of the eidetic), and you can say that "John and Mary" will have been the names of two of your great-grandchildren (empirical possibility of the empirical).

   Note: Experience is communication theoretic, i.e., possibility can make you more and more certain of *what* you are choosing, but it never tells you (defines) *how* you are choosing or have chosen. Thus, most puzzles, ambiguities, and paradoxes rely on the fact that compared phenomena are incorrectly and simultaneously thought to be both eidetic and empirical.

27. SUFFICIENT CONDITION = The logical criterion by which the *actualization* of one phenomenon is constituted, validated, and confirmed by the *actualization* of another phenomenon.

   Eidetic Example: Within Information Theory, either a "yes" or "no" choice provides the same information, i.e., affirms the existence of the context; each choice is a sufficient condition for the other choice.

   Empirical Example: Answer the following questions: "Can you tell a lie?" Every answer is a sufficient condition for any other, regardless of what you said. Note that replies like "maybe" and "I don't know" function the same way as "yes" and "no" because all replies *do not have any meaning*, each one merely signifies you have chosen and, therefore, confirms that you recognize and adhere to the context within which you are supposed to choose. You know *how* to play the game, but you still do not *what* the game is, e.g., finding the word you want in a *dictionary*.

28. NECESSARY CONDITION = The logical criterion by which the *realization* of one phenomenon is constituted, validated, and confirmed by the *realization* of another phenomenon.

    Eidetic Example: Within Communication Theory, any choice provides its own context of meaning; the choice is a necessary condition for the meaning.

    Empirical Example: Respond with a complete declarative sentence to the following question: "What is your name, age, and place of birth?" This question and your answer are a necessary condition for the meaning of each other, regardless of what you said. All human beings know before they respond to this question that it will have meaning (the *a priori* characteristic of *what* is said) and that the particular meaning cannot be changed once it is expressed (the *universal* characteristic of what is said). You know *what* the game is, but you do not know *how* to play, e.g., finding the meaning you want in an *encyclopedia*.

29. TRUTH CONDITION = The logical criterion by which the *realization* of one phenomena is constituted, validated, and confirmed by the *actualization* of another phenomenon. All judgments are either "true" or "false."

    Eidetic Example: "I always speak the truth, especially now that you are listening."

    Empirical Example: "Tomorrow's sunrise will be the same as today's sunrise."

    Note: The general failure of deduction in the physical and social sciences as a truth conditional method led to the current use of induction where only judgments of *falsity* (argument by counter-example) can be demonstrated as an empirical possibility (the "theory of falsification") or statistical probability (the "null hypothesis").

30. QUANTITATIVE METHODOLOGY = the practice of using a truth condition method in order to compare and contrast choices made within a given context of magnitude, probability, or possibility data. The natural science tradition or *Naturwissenschaft* approach of *systematic* judgment, i.e., the procedure of moving from (1) *hypostatization,* to (2) *verisimilitude,* to (3) *explanation,* to (4) *statement.* This procedure is frequently, if carelessly, referred to as "experimental" or "scientific" method.

31. MATHEMATIC = a truth condition methodology which measures *magnitudes* (difference by degree, e.g., a small versus a large), usually from a known or assumed reference point (*a foundation*) to a new point of reference (that which is "grounded").

Empirical Example: "My breadbox is larger than your apartment" or "When it comes to cars, bigger is better."

Eidetic Example: "Literal meaning allows for easy translation in a foreign language."

Note: In the arts and humanities context, the tropes of *metonymy* (substance/attribute comparison) and *synecdoche* (part/ whole comparison) exemplify a magnitude measure in discourse. See *tropic* entry. Also, a difference by degree in logic is known as a *deontic logic*, usually marked by the presence of the word "should" in a statement, e.g., "This should be a good movie." In this logical context, sociologists often use the name "grounded theory."

32. STATISTIC = a truth condition methodology which measures *probability* (difference by kind and degree, e.g., two small versus one large), usually from two assumed reference points ("dependent variables") to two new points ("independent variables"). The usual format is a "two-by-two" matrix (e.g., either "two" or "one"; either "small" or "large") and is information theoretic (either/or choice).

Empirical Example: "A small bird in the hand is worth two big birds in the bush."

Eidetic Example: "Either my translation is literal or metaphorical and it will be understood that way or not."

Note: In the arts and humanities context, the tropes of *simile* (positive part/attribute comparison) and *irony* (negative part/ attribute comparison) exemplify a probability measure in discourse. Also, contemporary notions of *causality* in both the humanities and the sciences rely on "Mill's Method" of inductive logic (John Stuart Mill, *System of Logic*, 1843):

(1) *Method of Agreement*, when two things happen together, one is the cause and one is the effect;

(2) *Method of Difference*, when two things happen together, except for one aspect in each thing, one aspect is the cause and the other is the effect;

(3) *Method of Agreement and Difference*, when two things happen together, have *nothing* in common except for one aspect in each thing, one aspect is the cause and the other is the effect;

(4) *Method of Concomitant Variation*, when two things *change* in the same way, one is the cause and the other is the effect; and

(5) *Method of Residues* [or "residues by mistake"], when all the causes/effects are know about two things, except for two aspects, one aspect is the cause and the other is the effect.

Because the methods are information theoretic, *how* cause

and effect work is known, but *what either the cause or the effect is* remains unknown.

33. LOGIC = a truth condition methodology which measures *possibility* (difference by kind, e.g., an edible orange versus a rotten apple), usually from a known or assumed reference point (a *class* or *type* such as "edible") to a new point (that which is a *member* of the class such as "orange" or "apple"), e.g., "One rotten apple will spoil the barrel" or "The best translation is the one that communicates." The trope of *metaphor* (substance/whole comparison) exemplifies a possibility measure in discourse.

Note: A discussion of "possibility" occurs in the glossary entry for *experiential.*

Historical Note: In the human sciences and philosophy, the logics of Charles Sanders Peirce (*Collected Works*, 2.619 – 644) are a standard of reference; he called them "normative semiotic models":

(1) Deduction: Rule + Case = Result.*
(2) Induction: Case + Result = Rule. [see *statistic* entry]
(3) Abduction: Rule + Result = Case. {particular; a posteriori}
(4) Adduction: Rule + Result = Case. {universal; a priori}

*Theory Construction frequently follows a formal deductive model and is known as a *Propositional Calculus* composed of (1) primitive symbols to represent foundational concepts, (2) rules of formation to connect the symbols, (3) axioms (or postulates), i.e., foundational concepts that are not provable and, therefore, must be (a) consistent, (b) complete, and (c) independent of one another, (4) rules of transformation that allow for (a) substitution and (b) inference, and (5) theorems, i.e., concepts that are proven by transforming axioms. See Joseph G. Brennan, *A Handbook of Logic*, 2nd. ed., New York: Harper and Row, 1961, p. 126 ff.

From the perspective of semiotic phenomenology, the following general relations of terminology and procedure can be treated as equivalents:

Merleau-Ponty	*Husserl*	*Peirce* (2.227–229)	
DESCRIIPTION =	HORIZON =	RULE =	OBJECT
REDUCTION =	FIELD =	RESULT =	GROUND
INTERPRETATION =	CORE (FOCUS) =	CASE =	INTERPRETANT*

interpretant = a sign of a sign; "interpreter" = a person who uses an "interpretant" to make a judgment, either eidetic or empirical; the interpretant is the same concept as Gregory Bateson's *deutero-learning* or "learning how to learn"; and, it is similar to Michel Foucault's *savior* or "understanding; know how."

34. RHETORIC = *discourse as praxis;* following the general discussion in Plato's dialogue *Sophist,* there are four rhetorics considered as structures (like logic) of thought and expression:

    Maieutic: questions that give (data) or take (capta) answers.
    [maieutic is a form of the tropes simile and irony]

    Rhetoric: Answers that give (data) or take (capta) questions.
    [rhetoric is a form of the trope metaphor]

    Sophistic: Answers that give (data) or take (capta) answers.
    [sophistic is a form of the trope metonymy]

    Dialectic: Questions that give (data) or take (capta) questions.
    [dialectic is a form of the trope synecdoche]

35. TROPIC = *discourse as poiesis;* "tropic logic" in the USA is associated with the Kenneth Burke model of "master tropes" and their "literal or realistic applications" (metaphor = perspective, metonymy = reduction, synecdoche = representation, irony = dialectic); in Europe, it is associated with the concept of "le même et l'autre" that translates from the French as *both* "self and other" *and* "same and different" thereby yielding the ratio {Self: Same :: Other : Different}. For Merleau-Ponty, the Self-Other ratio is the relation of c*hiasm.* For Foucault, the Same-Different ratio is the relation of *interstices.* In the semiotic phenomenology of Michel Foucault, poiesis operates the "law of communication" within the *"quadrilateral model of discourse"* as interpreted by Lanigan (see figure 8).

36. QUALITATIVE METHODOLOGY = the practice of using a necessary and/or sufficient condition method in order to compare and contrast choices made within a taken context of artifactual, symbolic, substantial, or *Formal Capta.* The human science tradition or *Geisteswissenschaft* approach of *systemic* judgment, i.e., the procedure of moving from (1) *hypothesis,* to (2) *verification,* to (3) *explication,* to (4) *proposition.* This procedure is frequently, if carelessly, referred to as "artistic," "humanistic," or "naturalistic" method. The use of "naturalistic" is especially unfortunate since it is the positivist view of science that is based on "nature." This is one reason why "cultural studies" and "interpretive studies" (hermeneutics) are becoming standard synonyms for qualitative research.

37. ASSERTORIC = *observation* and its logic, rhetoric, and tropic application, especially as Historiography; consciousness of what is actual or occurring; the study of *Artifactual Capta;* discourse that relies on *synecdoche* as a tropic structure. In research application, an assertoric often leads to an apodeictic in praxis (see the *praxis* entry).

Empirical Example: "The anthropologist in the midst of a field study grabs a s*tone* by the edge of a small stream of water." S/he has observed (consciousness) this object as a "stone"; s/he has taken (capta) this object out of nature (fact) and into culture (*artifact* = human mediation) by *either* picking it up (experience) *or* not, in which case it remains part of nature.

Eidetic Example: "27 August 1789, Declaration of the Rights of Man and of Citizens, by the National Assembly of France, Article 15: Every community has a right to demand of all its agents an account of their conduct." In the midst of the French Revolution, the men and women observed (consciousness) themselves as generic beings "[Hu-] Man"; therefore, they took (capta) themselves out of the revolution (fact = "Declaration of Rights") and into government (*artifact* = "National Assembly") by their very action of "27 August 1789" (experience). If there were no action, Culture would remain constant.

Historical Note: Contemporary science generally holds the nineteenth century view of *neutral* or *mental monism* offered by Ernst Mach: "nature" is a construct of mind, therefore, in methodological terms nature cannot be known directly; it is known only by human observation. Therefore, nature (an "external" system) and mind (an "internal" system,) are treated alike as the product of *inferences about human experience.*

38. THEMATIC = *knowledge* and its logic, rhetoric, and tropic application, especially as Ethnography; consciousness of what is real or occurred; the study of *Symbolic Capta.* (Schutz: the "because-motive" or "what had been"); discourse that relies on *simile* or *irony* as a tropic structure. In research application, a thematic often leads to a problematic in praxis (see the *praxis* entry).

Empirical Example: "The anthropologist in the midst of a field study grabs a *tool* by the edge of a small stream of water." S/he has observed (consciousness) this object as a "cleaved stone for cutting"; s/he has taken (capta) this object out of nature (fact = broken stone) and into culture (*symbolic artifact* = self consciousness: cleaved edges cut) by picking it up (experience) as *either* self-evident (to one's Self) *or* as evidence for another being (an Other).

Eidetic Example: "27 August 1789, Declaration of the Rights of Man and of Citizens, by the National Assembly of France, Article 15: Every community has a right to demand of all its agents an account of their conduct." In the midst of the French Revolution, the men and women observed (consciousness) themselves as *politically* generic beings "Citizens"; therefore, they took (capta) themselves out of the revolution (fact = "Rights") and into government (*symbolic artifact* = "community") by their very action of "Article 15" (experience).

39. PROBLEMATIC = *intuition* and its logic, rhetoric, and tropic application, especially as Semiology; consciousness of what is ideal or is capable of occurring; the study of *substantial capta.* (Schutz: the "in-order-to-motive" or "what shall have been"); discourse that relies on *metonymy* as a tropic structure. In research application, a problematic often leads to a thematic in poiesis (see the *poiesis* entry).

Empirical Example: "The anthropologist in the midst of a field study grabs a *knife* by the edge of a small stream of water." S/he has observed (consciousness) this object as a "stone cleaved on *two* sides for *particular* cutting"; s/he has taken (capta) this object out of nature (fact = stone broken in a *particular manner indicating purpose*) and into culture (*substantial symbolic artifact* = self consciousness: a double-edge makes cutting easier) by picking it up (experience) as *both* evidence of my Self and another being (an Other *like my Self).*

Eidetic Example: "27 August 1789, Declaration of the Rights of Man and of Citizens, by the National Assembly of France, Article 15: Every community has a right to demand of all its agents an account of their conduct." In the midst of the French Revolution, the men and women observed (consciousness) themselves as *politically empowered* generic beings "[Hu-] Man *and* Citizens"; therefore, they took (capta) themselves out of the revolution (fact = "an account") and into government (*substantial symbolic artifact* = "*every* community") by their very action "to demand" (experience).

40. APODEICTIC = *understanding* and its logic, rhetoric, and tropic application, especially as Phenomenology; consciousness of what is factual or must occur; the study of *Formal Capta.* (Husserl's *factum*); discourse that relies on *metaphor* as a tropic structure. In research application, an apodeictic often leads to an assertoric in poiesis (see the *poiesis* entry).

Empirical Example: "The anthropologist in the midst of a field study grabs a *weapon* by the edge of a small stream of water." S/he has observed (consciousness) this object as a "stone cleaved on *two* sides for *penetrating* and cutting *skin";* s/he has taken (capta) this object out of nature (fact = stone broken in a *sharp point)* and into culture (*formal substantial symbolic artifact* = self consciousness: a sharp point makes *killing* easier) by picking it up (experience) as evidence of another being (the *conscious* experience of an Other *like my Self).* Note that "Self" is the *foundation* or reference point of judgment [see *Mathematical* entry]; this is also the logic of Husserl's famous thesis that "Subjectivity is Intersubjectivity."

Eidetic Example: "27 August 1789, Declaration of the Rights of Man and of Citizens, by the National Assembly of France, Article 15: Every community has a right to demand of all its agents an account of their conduct." In the midst of the French Revolution, the men and women observed (consciousness) themselves as *politically empowered and embodied* generic beings, i.e., "Agents"; therefore, they took (capta) themselves out of the revolution (fact = "an account *of*") and into government (*formal substantial symbolic artifact* = "every community *has a right*") by the exemplar of "their conduct" (experience).

41. HISTORIOGRAPHY = Assertoric narrative using artifactual capta with a qualitative logic, rhetoric, or tropic of correlation; by tradition *(Geistesgeschichte)* in the discipline of History, an assertoric narrative is *analytical,* therefore, validity is obtained in the application of a *critical* review. Historiography is the systemic study of human cultures with particular attention to "time binding" (Ruesch & Bateson) relationships of an individual *(Lebenswelt)* and the community *(Gemeinschaft).*

42. ETHNOGRAPHY = Thematic narrative using symbolic capta with a qualitative logic, rhetoric, or tropic of correlation; by tradition *(Kulturwissenschaft)* in the discipline of Anthropology, a thematic narrative is *experiential,* therefore, validity is obtained in the application of an *experimental* review. Ethnography is the *systematic* study of human cultures with particular attention to "space binding" (Ruesch & Bateson) relationships of a society *(Gesellschaft)* and the culture *(Weltanschauung).*

43. SEMIOLOGY = Problematic narrative using substantial capta with a qualitative logic, rhetoric, or tropic of relation; by tradition *(Nomothetic Science = "generalizing" judgment)* in the discipline of Linguistics, a problematic narrative is *experimental,* therefore, validity is obtained in the application of an *experiential* review. In particular, semiology (the historical name) or *semiotics* (the contemporary human science name) is the study of codes (i.e., the system of representation); in general, it is the study of "sign production" or messages (i.e., the process of representation). "Semiotics" is a synonym for "communication" where communication includes the study of human, animal, and machine "languages" as icon, index, or symbol systems.

44. SIGN = (1) in American phenomenology ("the theory of categories"), the famous definition is that of Charles Sanders Peirce (*Collected Papers,* 2.228), "A sign, or *representamen,* is something which stands to somebody for something in some respect or

capacity." Peirce's definition translates the Medieval Latin definition of the sign from the perspective of Scholastic philosophy: *"aliquid stat pro aliquo."* There are many types of signs, but the most common are:

"An *Icon* is a sign which refers to the Object that it denotes merely by virtue of characters of its own, and which it possesses, just the same, whether any such object actually exists or not" (2.247).

"An *Index* is a sign which refers to the Object that it denotes by virtue of really being affected by that Object" (2.248).

"A *Symbol* is a sign which refers to the Object that it denotes by virtue of a law, usually an association of general ideas, which operates to cause the Symbol to be interpreted as referring to that Object" (2.249).

(2) In European structuralism, the famous definition is that of Ferdinand de Saussure, "I call the combination of a concept and a sound-image a *sign.* . . ." "I propose to retain the word *sign [signe]* to designate the whole and to replace *concept* and *sound-image* respectively by *signified [signifié]* and *signifier [signifiant]*" (*Course in General Linguistics,* p. 67).

Note: "Signifier" (Sr) refers to the process of expression; the correct translation of "signifiant" is *signifying.* "Signified" (Sd) refers to the process of perception. In Merleau-Ponty's semiotic phenomenology, the Sr and Sd are multiple and reversible, as are signs; in the context of phenomenological intentionality, signifiers are "subjects of consciousness" and signifieds are "objects of consciousness."

45. PHENOMENOLOGY = Apodeictic narrative using formal capta with a qualitative logic, rhetoric, or tropic of foundation; by tradition *(Ideographic Science = "individualizing" judgment)* in the discipline of Philosophy, an apodeictic narrative is *critical,* therefore, validity is obtained in the application of an *analytical* review. In Merleau-Ponty's phenomenology, a reflexive three step methodology of (1) description, (2) reduction, and (3) interpretation of intentionality (the subject and object of consciousness; "consciousness of - - -"). *Semiotic Phenomenology* is a human science approach to research consisting of (1) the description of the sign, (2) reduction of the signifier, and (3) interpretation of the signified.

46. FORM = a particular *system* (see *system* entry). To illustrate the idea, a dictionary entry gives a complete description of *how* something is described so that you can recognize what *each of its characteristics do not have in common* and you understand that each characteristic is definitional. The individual "how" is a

PROBLEMATIC:

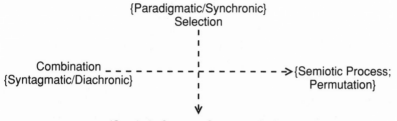

{Paradigmatic/Synchronic}
Selection

Combination
{Syntagmatic/Diachronic} → {Semiotic Process;
Permutation}

{Semiotic System; Commutation}

THEMATIC:

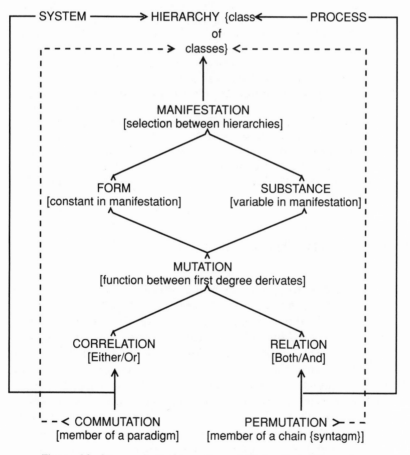

SYSTEM → HIERARCHY {class ← PROCESS
of
classes} ←

MANIFESTATION
[selection between hierarchies]

FORM
[constant in manifestation]

SUBSTANCE
[variable in manifestation]

MUTATION
[function between first degree derivates]

CORRELATION
[Either/Or]

RELATION
[Both/And]

< COMMUTATION
[member of a paradigm]

PERMUTATION >
[member of a chain {syntagm}]

Figure 16. Saussure's Problematic and Hjelmsllev's Thematic.

form; in semantics it is called a *denotation* and in logic it is called an *intension* (note spelling; not "intention").

Eidetic Example: **A a** *A* a A characters here are all forms of the first letter of the Roman alphabet. Your ability to recognize form allows you to decode the handwriting of most people.

Empirical Example: Apples, oranges, bananas and tomatoes are all forms of fruit. Your ability to recognize form allows you to decode what you consider edible.

47. STRUCTURE = a particular *process* (see *process* entry). To illustrate the idea, an *encyclopedia* entry gives a complete description of *what* something is so that you can recognize what *all of its characteristics have in common* and you understand that one characteristic (the *tone*) is definitional for the *typology*, although that particular characteristic does not define the *token*. The common "what" is a structure; in semantics it is called a *connotation* and in logic it is called an *extension*.

Eidetic Example: **A** *A* A A all have a "pointed top" (tone) which defines a "capital or upper case" (typology) first letter (token) of the Roman alphabet; and, **a** *a* a a all have a "rounded top" that defines "lower case" letters.

Empirical Example: Gothic architecture is recognized by its display of vertical "points" of weight stress; Gothic style is "pointedness", i.e., all artifacts display points, especially print with letters like these: A W M K X Z V N. Renaissance architecture is recognized by its display of vertical weight stress on "round" arches; Renaissance style is "roundness", i.e., artifacts display curvature on top, especially "Renaissance print just like all this."

PART 2. ENTRY TERMS FROM LOUIS HJELMSLEV

These terms are taken from the glossary (indexed) in Louis Hjelmslev's *Prolegomena to a Theory of Language*, F. J. Whitfield, Trans.; Revised English Edition (Madison: University of Wisconsin Press, 1961). See figure 16: "Saussure's Problematic and Hjelmslev's Thematic."

While the *Prolegomena* has proved to be a deductive failure as a "science of linguistics," the work is a positive success in describing communication conduct and performance as an abductive logic. The terms have become standard referents in theory construction in the human sciences generally. See especially the three works by Anthony Wilden: (1) *System and Structure: Essays in Communication and Exchange*, 2nd ed. (Tavistock Publications: Metheun, Inc., 1980); (2) *The Rules Are No*

Game: The Strategy of Communication (New York: Routledge & Kegan Paul, 1987); (3) *Man and Woman, War and Peace: The Strategist's Companion* (New York: Routledge and Kegan Paul, 1987).

48. RELATION = Both/And function.

49. CORRELATION = Either/Or function.

50. SYSTEM = Correlational hierarchy.

51. PROCESS = Relational hierarchy.

52. FUNCTION = Dependence that fulfills the conditions for an analysis (analysis: description of an object by the uniform dependencies of other objects on it and on each other).

53. FUNCTIVE = Object that has function to other objects.

54. FORM = The constant in a manifestation.

55. SUBSTANCE = The variable in a manifestation.

56. PARADIGMATIC = Semiotic system.

57. SYNTAGMATIC = Semiotic process.

PART 3. ENTRY TERMS FROM ROMAN JAKOBSON

These terms, in addition to figures 3 and 4, are taken from the standard reference work on Jakobson's theory of communication and the human sciences, Elmar Holenstein, *Roman Jakobson's Approach to Language: Phenomenological Structuralism* (Bloomington: Indiana University Press, 1976). All bracketed page numbers refer to this book. For "classic" applications of the theory see especially "Principles of Human Communication" and "Synopsis of the Theory of Human Communication" in Jurgen Ruesch, *Semiotic Approaches to Human Relations* (The Hague & Paris: Mouton, 1972; and, "Individual, Group, and Culture: A Review of the Theory of Human Communication" in Jurgen Ruesch and Gregory Bateson, *Communication: The Social Matrix of Psychiatry* (New York: W. W. Norton & Co., 1987; first published 1951).

58. COMMUNICATION = "The *addresser* sends a *message* to the a*ddressee*. To be operative, the message requires a *context* referred to ("referent" in another, somewhat ambiguous, nomenclature), seizable by the addressee, and either verbal or capable of being verbalized; a *code* fully, or at least partially common to the addresser and addressee (or in other words, to the encoder and decoder of the message); and, finally, a *contact*, a physical

channel and psychological connection between the addresser
and addressee, enabling both of them to enter and stay in communication." [p. 153] A schematic diagram [p. 154] is presented in figure 3.

59. ELEMENT = the necessary conditions for (1) communication (addresser, addressee, context, message, contact, code), (2) for the
inherent category of distinctive features in the phoneme that
consists of (a) *sonority,* (b) *protensity,* and (c) *tonality.*

60. FUNCTION = the sufficient conditions for (1) communication (emotive, conative, referential, poetic, phatic, metalinguistic), and
(2) for the *prosodic* category of distinctive features in the phoneme
that consists of (a) *force,* (b) *quantity,* and (c) *tone.*

61. PARADIGMATIC AXIS = *discours (discourse);* the "vertical" category
operation of *Selection, Substitution, Similarity, and Metaphor* [p.
139]. The category is *in absentia,* constitutes *langue (code),* and
displays *synchrony (statics)* [p. 141]. Parenthetical terms are
Jakobson's substitutes for Saussure's original terms.

62. SYNTAGMATIC AXIS = *langage (grammar; language);* the "horizontal"
category operation of *Combination, Contexture, Contiguity, and
Metonymy* [p. 139]. The category is *in presentia,* constitutes *parole
(messages),* and displays *diachrony (dynamics)* [p. 141]. Parenthetical terms are Jakobson's substitutes for Saussure's original
terms.

63. DISTINCTIVE FEATURES = the qualities of phonemes; there are two
groups with three subcategories each: (1) inherent features:
sonority, protensity, and tonality; and (2) prosodic features:
force, quantity, and tone [p. 178].

64. REDUNDANCY FEATURES = the formations [significative, coded
units] that *result from transformations* [significative, coded *matrices*] between the paradigmatic and syntagmatic axes; the *effect*
of poetic function; in general, the transformations of all the
communication *functions,* i.e., the "thesis of the creativity of
language" [p. 9], "Language is a highly redundant means of
communication" [p. 94], "The code at the disposal of [hu-
mans] for intersubjective communication is a convertible code,
a transformational system by means of which a message can be
translated from subcode to subcode, from sign system to sign
system" [p. 42].

65. MARKED TERM = "Statement of P" [p. 131]; a position (or opposition); a first term explains itself, hence "marks" itself in a

position which simultaneously opposes it to the other possible positions of similar terms. In *Communication Theory,* "the choice of a context" (statement of) "for choosing" (P). For example, what a dictionary does for words/ideas: Word entries mark themselves by their definitions (ideas) and simultaneously oppose themselves to the other word entries in the dictionary. In the sentence "Socrates is mortal," the word "Socrates" is marked by the definition "mortal." See the *abstract* entry; marked terms are abstractions.

66. UNMARKED TERM = "(1) General Meaning: nonstatement of P"; (2) "Specific Meaning: statement of non-P' [p. 131]; an *apposition;* a second term explains a first term, hence the "unmarked" second term explains the now "marked" first term. In *Information Theory,* there is first General Meaning in which "the context of choice" (non-statement of) restricts the "choosing" (P), or secondly, there is a Specific Meaning in which "the choice of context" (statement of) restricts the "not choosing" (non-P). Under the conditions of General Meaning, Information Theory (signification) entails Communication Theory (meaning); whereas, under the conditions of Specific Meaning, Communication Theory (meaning) entails Information Theory (signification). In short, marked meaning and specific unmarked meaning stand in an apposition in which Communication Theory (choice of context) entails Information Theory (choice in context). Apposition, for example, is what an encyclopedia does for words/ideas: Unmarked ideas are explained by marked definitions (words). In the sentence "He flies to New York, and/or she swims from Paris," all ideas are defined by word placement. "He" is marked as "masculine" by the expression later in the sentence of the word "she" which is unmarked [specific meaning: the statement of non-he]. Thus in this specially constructed example sentence, all marked terms [he, flies, to, New York, and] take on their "marking" or meaning by direct apposition to the subsequent expression of their respective "unmarked" terms [she, swims, from, Paris, or]. Apposition is the construction of a distinction after two things have been *combined* and thereby a comparison constructs a contrast: he/she, flies/swims, to/from, New York/Paris, and/or. Now you know why you can never decided between "and" and/or "or" and thus just write (like I just did!) "and/or." For further discussion, see the *concrete* entry; unmarked terms are concretions. Marking and unmarking may be used as a "poetic function" to introduce time and space hierarchies of reference. For example, we may substitute the word "when" for the conjunction "and/or" in our example sentence, so it now reads: "He

flies to New York when she swims from Paris." The result is to introduce a marked (in praesentia) time term ("when") which indexes an unmarked (in absentia) time reference of *simultaneity*. A spatial marking of direction now applies inasmuch as "to New York" and "from Paris" as marked conjointly by "when" now refer to their opposite, respective destinations which are unmarked. In the original example employing "and/or" we know someone is arriving in New York (but the "in absentia" city of origin is unknown) and someone is leaving from Paris (but the "in praesentia" city of termination is unknown). Depending on the natural language and its cultural referents, many levels of transformation and hierarchical reference are possible. Note that in Medieval logic, *syncategorematical* words (like prepositions, conjunctions, etc. that point to categories) were thought to be secondary to *categorematical* words (like nouns, verbs, etc. that name categories of meaning). But in contemporary discourse theories the reverse is true, and this suggests the basis of Jakobson's marked/unmarked distinction since the syncategorematical function is that of "marking" (primary) what categorematical function is "unmarked" (secondary) in use—virtually a definition of *rhetoric* or a *tropic logic*.

67. ADDRESSER = The person who [interpersonal] or the consciousness which [intrapersonal] constitutes a message (encoding) by engaging (expression) the "units of language" in the paradigmatic axis moving in the message's "ascending scale of freedom [choice]"; from "text/utterance > sentence > phrase > word > morpheme > phoneme > distinctive feature" [p. 165].

68. ADDRESSEE = The person who [interpersonal], or the experience which [intrapersonal], constitutes a code (decoding) by engaging (perception) the "units of language" in the syntagmatic axis moving in the code's "descending scale of code dependence [context]; from "distinctive feature > phoneme > morpheme > word > phrase > sentence > text/utterance" [p. 165].

69. CONTEXT = paradigmatic relation [unit = paradigm]; Jakobson's replacement for the term "reference"; *designated* [p. 159] or part of a semiotic system (following Peirce): *icon* or "factual similarity," *index* or "factual contiguity," and *symbol* or "imputed, learned contiguity" [p. 158].

Note: Jakobson *rejects* the Saussurian principle of arbitrariness; signs have a relative motivation to each other (Peirce's *interpretant*). Jakobson rejects the Saussurian principle of the linear signifier. He adopt's Peirce's diagrammatic (iconic) relation of the signifier and signified, i.e., "a diagram is a sign whose own constitution reflects the relational structure of the thing represented,"i.e., "intersemiotic translation" [pp. 157–9]. See Edward Hall's model in Appendix E.

70. MESSAGE = diachronic relation; expression, speaking *(parole);* consists of (1) linguistic utterance, (2) language as individual, private property, and (3) the individualizing, centrifugal aspect of language [p. 160].

71. CONTACT = syntagmatic relation [unit = syntagm]; the performative function in discourse that is both *physical* (interpersonal) and *psychological* (embodied; intrapersonal); refers to Husserl's thesis that "subjectivity is intersubjectivity" (differentiation by combination); a human (existential) performance of Self and Other; "All phonemes designate nothing but mere *otherness*" [p. 172].

72. CODE = synchronic relation, apperception, social language *(langue);* consists of (1) linguistic norm, (2) language as supraindividual, social endowment, and (3) the unifying, centripetal aspect of language [p. 160].

73. EMOTIVE = *expression;* process of exchange systems; state of the speaker, Addresser: (1) implementation of cognitive acts, (2) indication on phonic, grammatical, and lexical levels of distinctive features, and (3) performance of the speech act.

TYPE	SIGN*	REFERENT	
Linguistic (Distinctive Features)	F/F	Message Form (referring to)	Message Form
Semiotic (Redundancy Features)	S/S	Message Structure	Message Structure
Anthropologic & Economic	F/S	Message Form	Message Structure
Biologic	S/F	Message Structure	Message Form

*These illustrate Peirce's notion of the *interpretant;* see the *logic* entry.

74. CONATIVE = *value choice;* orientation towards the Addressee; existential motivation to act with purpose *(conatus);* redundancy features are manifest in grammar as the vocative (noun) capacity *to name* and the imperative (verb) capacity *to do;* occurs earliest in language acquisition [p. 155]; Husserl's *ego* and Merleau-Ponty's *radical cogito:* "I can; I am able to. . . ."

TYPE	SIGN*	REFERENT	
Taxonomy (Static; Systematic):			
Eidetic	P/P	Purpose (referring to)	Purpose

Empirical	Cd/Cd	Conduct	Conduct

Taxonomy (Dynamic; Systemic):

Teleological (Goal-Intended)	P/Cd	Purpose	Conduct
Teleonomic (Goal-Directed)	Cd/P	Conduct	Purpose

*These illustrate Peirce's notion of the *interpretant;* see the *logic* entry.

75. REFERENTIAL = There are two types of reference (circularity and overlapping) and they are reflexive [= four typologies]; paradigmatic relationship. Jakobson replaces the general concept of "reference" with that of *context.*

TYPE	SIGN*	REFERENT	
Circularity	M/M	Message (referring to)	Message
	C/C	Code	Code
Overlapping	M/C	Message	Code
	C/M	Code	Message

*These illustrate Peirce's notion of the *interpretant;* see the *logic* entry.

76. POETIC = the operation of the paradigmatic and syntagmatic axes are *reversible;* diachronic relationship. See the *poiesis* entry; the phenomenological concept of *reversibility.* An extrapolation of Jakobson's theory using Merleau-Ponty's phenomenology is:

TYPE	SIGN*	REFERENT	
Embodiment:			
Self	Ar/Ar	Addresser (referring to)	Addresser
Other	Ae/Ae	Addressee	Addressee
Intentionality:			
Thetic	Ar/Ae	Addresser	Addressee
Operative	Ae/Ar	Addressee	Addresser

* These illustrate Peirce's notion of the *interpretant;* see the *logic* entry.

77. PHATIC = the purpose of "establishing, prolonging, checking, confirming or discontinuing the communication" [p. 155]; syntagmatic relationship.

Note: In the discipline of philosophy, "ordinary language philosophers" have concentrated on this behavioral data as a means of inferring communicative intention; the theory is usually associated with Austin's "phenomenology of speech," Searle's "speech act theory," and Grice's "conversational implicature." In the disciplines of sociology and speech communication "conversational analysis" has taken a similar behavioristic, but atheoretical, approach that is often critiqued as "naive positivism" or "neo-linguistics."

An extrapolation of Jakobson's theory using Hall's phenomenology is:

TYPE	SIGN*	REFERENT	
Sociocentric Culture	Ct/Ct †	Contact (referring to)	Contact
	Cx/Cx #	Context	Context
Egocentric Culture	Ct/Cx ≠	Contact	Context
	Cx/Ct #	Context	Contact

*These illustrate Peirce's notion of the *interpretant;* see the *logic* entry.

†Edward Hall's concept of a "High Context" culture where "groups" provide an "information theoretic" environment; # Hall's "Middle-Context" culture (following Margaret Mead; Appendix C) where interacting "generations" represent groups versus individuals in a contest to "define the situation"; ≠ Hall's "Low Context" culture where "individuals" provide a "communication theoretic" environment. See Hall's *Beyond Culture,* Garden City, NY: Anchor/Doubleday, 1977, pp. 85–103); see Appendix E)

78. METALINGUISTIC = every science has both an *object language* (discourse about extralinguistic entities) and a *metalanguage* (discourse about linguistic entities) [p. 159]; synchronic relationship; also known as "double articulation."

Note: Jakobson *replaces* Saussure's *langue* with "code" [me-talinguistic function] and *parole* with "message" [poetic function]. Saussure's static dichotomy (digital logic) becomes Jakobson's dynamic differentiation (analogue logic): (a) "For the speaker the paradigmatic operation of selection supplies the basis for encoding"; (b) "while the listener engages the syntagmatic combination in decoding the message" [p. 161].

TYPE	SIGN*	REFERENT	
Verbal Communication:			
Object Language (Signifier or Signified)	OL/OL	Language (referrring to)	Referents
Metalanguage (Signifier and Signified)	ML/ML	Language	Language
"Nonverbal" Communication:			
Object Semiotic (Signifier or Signified)	OS/OS	Sign	Referent
Metasemiotic (Signifier and Signified)	MS/MS	Sign	Sign

*These illustrate Peirce's notion of the *interpretant;* see the *logic* entry.

79. SPEECH ACT = The progressive phases: intention > innervation > gradual production > transmission > audition {apperception; Husserl's "pairing"} > perception > comprehension [p. 179]. "The uniqueness of human speech lies in

 (1) its creativity (in animal languages the entire corpus of messages is tantamount to their code);

 (2) its ability to handle abstractions, fictions, or, generally speaking, that which is not present in the situation of the speaker;

 (3) its hierarchical structure of constitutive elements as in the dichotomy of distinctive and significative units and the division of the grammatical system in words and sentences or coded units and coded matrices;

 (4) its use of propositions (affirmations and negations); and

 (5) its reversible hierarchy of diverse function" [pp. 189–90]."

80. HUMAN SCIENCES = "Three integrated sciences encompass each other and present three gradually increasing degrees of generality: 1. Study in communication of verbal messages = *Linguistics*. 2. Study in communication of any messages = *Semiotics* (communication of verbal messages implied). 3. Study in communication = *Social Anthropology* jointly with *Economics* (communication of messages implied)." 4. "Study in ways and forms of communication used by manifold living things" = *Biology* [science of life]" [p. 186–7]. A schematic diagram [p. 187] is presented in figure 4.

Mead's Model of Cultural Transmission

Source: Margaret Mead, *Culture and Commitment: A Study of the Generation Gap.*
Garden City, NY: Doubleday & Co., Inc., 1970

THREE TYPES OF CULTURE:

The continuity and survival of all cultures require the *living presence* of at least three generations who engage in group communication.

1. Postfigurative Culture:

a. Children learn primarily from their forebears.

b. Elders cannot conceive of change; reality is the **Past**.

c. Each person embodies the whole culture.

d. All communication, oral and gestural, reflects itself in synthetic forms.

e. Lack of written communication allows the quick assimilation of the new by the old forms.

2. Cofigurative Culture:

a. Children and adults learn from their peers.

b. Difference and change is a normal expectation; reality is the **Present**.

c. Cofiguration begins with the breadkdown of postfigurative culture; no society is known to have preserved exclusively the cofiguration model through the generations.

d. Cofiguration is typical in groups forced to migrate [in space] and learn new (second) languages and cultural practices.

e. Cultural continuity is directly linked to fashion and practices of dress; sexual roles are stereotypic; embodiment is symbolic.

[Notes on cofigurative culture:
1. Technology stimulates postfigurative rupture.
2. "Retirement" or similar social practices indicate the acceptance of cofiguration.
3. The two-generation "nuclear family" creates a prference for digital choice.]

3. *Prefigurative Culture*:

   a. Adults learn from their children
   b. The new and unexpected is a normal expectation; reality is the **Future** ["So, as the young say, The Future is Now."].
   c. Prefiguration begins with the breakdown of cogifurative society; is Mead's hypothesis for emerging cultures, whether first, second, or third world.
   d. Prefiguration is typical in group forced to assimilate or accommodate technology [migrate in time] and learn second (new) values in language and cultural practices.
   e. Cultural continuity is linked to immediacy of experience, especially where media technology is used to manipulate or manage time.

Definitions for Figure 1: Cultural Values Communication Model

I. AWARENESS CATEGORIES (Ontological Orientation):

(1) CULTURE: The development of human abilities ("intellect") and capabilities ("morality") as an individual achievement ("understanding"; Lebenswelt) in language/speech (sign-systems; e.g., "learning") and as a group accomplishment ("knowledge"; Weltanschauung) in communication behavior (intersemiotic translation; e.g., "learning to learn").

(2) CIVILIZATION: The stage of human development where practice (actual comportment) is recorded as a symbol (substitute behavior) in a semiotic system, e.g., the invention of "writing" (substitute behavior) to make a universal record [Weltanschauung] of "speaking" (actual practice) by an individual person [Lebenswelt]; or, the shift from "farming" ("rural") as actual behavior to the symbolic behavior of "managing" ("urban") as a record of the shift from "community" [Gemeinschaft] to "society" [Gesellschaft].

(3) NATURE: The inherent character, essence, and basic constitution of a person or thing in the experiential ("natural") world, i.e., the Weltanschauung.

(4) CONSCIOUSNESS: A person's awareness (both as expression and perception) of similarity in the form of oneself ("embodiment"; Lebenswelt) or an awareness of alterity in the form of another person ("subjectivity"; Gemeinschaft) or things as "real" ("objectivity"; Gesellschaft) or "ideal" ("objectivity"; Weltanschauung).

II. JUDGMENT CATEGORIES (Axiological Orientation):

(5) HUMAN VALUES: The mediation [culture practice] of Consciousness and Culture, i.e., "morality" as form of understanding ("ethics") and as a form of knowledge ("desire") in communication. The mediation is a process of "derivation" (Foucault) that functions as a "rule" of "communication choice" {see nos. 5a and 5b below}. Example: Mead's "postfigurative culture" model of cultural transmission (see Appendix C).

(5a) PERSON: A human being, an individual who is humane (ethics). *Rule of Cultural Practice:* The absolute mediation of Culture by Consciousness. The mediation process of consciousness "derives" an "element" (Foucault) of what is "different" in the Cultural situation. Example: The success of Mead's "postfigurative culture" model of cultural transmission (see Appendix C).

(5b) XENOPHOBIA: The fear and hatred of strangers or foreigners or anything that is strange or foreign (desire). *Rule of Cultural Practice:* The absolute mediation of Conciousness by Culture. The mediation process of culture "derives" a "combination" (Foucault) of what is "different" in the other person/thing that consciousness encounters; the "combination" is not acceptable. Example: The failure of Mead's "postfigurative culture" model of cultural transmission (see Appendix C).

(6) GROUP VALUES: The mediation [culture practice] of Culture and Civilization, i.e., "politics" as form of understanding ("power") and as a form of knowledge ("law") in communication. The mediation is a process of "designation" (Foucault) that functions as a "game" [closed system; McFeat's "Group – Ordering" Group Model in his *Small-Group Cultures* (Pergamon 1974)] of "communication choice" {see nos. 6a and 6b below}. Example: Mead's "cofigurative culture" model of cultural transmission (see Appendix C).

(6a) SOCIETY: The association, companionship, and community of other persons (power). *Game of Cultural Practice:* The absolute mediation of Culture by Civilization. The mediating process of civilization "designates" a "substitution" (Foucault) in other people of what is the "same" as ourselves [McFeat's "Content-Ordering" Group Model]; the egocentric individual symbolizes the group (the ideal peson appears) or the sociocentric group symbolizes the individual (the ideal group appears). Example: The success of Mead's "cofigurative culture" model of cultural transmission (see Appendix C).

(6b) ALIENATION: The isolation and estrangement of a person from a position or object of former attachment; a loss of powers or rights (law). *Game of Cultural Practice:* The absolute mediation of Civilization by Culture. The mediating process of culture "designates" a "substitution" (Foucault) in ourselves of what is the "same" as other people [McFeat's "Task – Ordering" Group Model]; the egocentric group symbolizes the individual (the real person disappears), or, the sociocentric individual symbolizes the group (the real group disappears). Example: The failure of Mead's "cofigurative culture" model of cultural transmission (see Appendix C).

(7) MATERIAL VALUES: The mediation [communication choice] of Civilization and Nature, i.e., "aesthetics" as a form of understanding ("mentifact"; appreciated idea) and as a form of knowledge ("artifact"; appreciated object) in culture. The mediation is a process of "articulation" (Foucault) that functions as a "habit" of "culture practice" {see nos. 7a and 7b below}. Example: Mead's "prefigurative culture" model of cultural transmission (see Appendix C).

(7a) PHYSICAL REALITY: The material existence (artifact) of people and objects. *Habit of Communication Choice:* The absolute mediation of Civilization by Nature. The mediating process of nature "articulates" a "specification" (Foucault) of civilized experience for the Other person. Example: The success of Mead's "prefigurative culture" model of cultural transmission (see Appendix C).

(7b) ETHNOCENTRICISM: The attitude (mentifact) that one's own group is better, usually based in race, class, or caste as a central interest. *Habit of Communication Choice:* The absolute mediation of Nature by Civilization. The mediating process of civilization "articulates" a "specification" (Foucault) of experience according to the nature of the Other person (as uncivilized or barbarian). Example: The failure of Mead's "prefigurative culture" model of cultural transmission (see Appendix C).

(8) SPIRITUAL VALUES: The mediation [communication choice] of Nature and Consciousness, i.e., "theology" as a form of understanding ("belief") and as a form of knowledge ("norm") in culture. The mediation is a process of "attribution or proposition" (Foucault) that functions as a "ritual" of "culture practice" by the Self {see nos. 8a and 8b below}. Example: Mead's "postfigurative culture" model of cultural transmission (see Appendix C).

(8a) MYTH: The popular, traditional narrative that explains a worldview (Weltanschauung) or belief. *Ritual of Communication Choice:* The absolute mediation of Nature by Consciousness. The mediating process of Consciousness "attributes" a "representation" (Foucault) of the Self (Lebenswelt) as the proper (belief) view of the natural world. Example: The success of Mead's "postfigurative culture" model of cultural transmission (see Appendix C).

(8b) ANOMIE: The instability that results from a breakdown of social standards and values, especially as a personal experience. *Ritual of Communication Choice:* The absolute mediation of Consciousness by Nature. The mediating process of nature "proposes" a "representation" (Foucault) of the natural world as the proper (normal) view of the Self (Lebenswelt); the comparison of the proposal (change) versus the "belief" (stability of Nature) causes instability, anxiety, and the breakdown of normative experience. Example: The failure of Mead's "postfigurative culture" model of cultural transmission (see Appendix C).

APPENDIX E

Hall's "High – Low Context" Model of Cultural Communication

Source: Edward T. Hall, *Beyond Culture*.
New York: Anchor Press; Doubleday 1979, pages 88–89.

"Any transaction can be characterized as high-, low-, or middle-context. HC transactions feature preprogrammed information that is in the receiver and in the setting, with only minimal information in the transmitted message. LC transactions are the reverse. Most of the information must be in the transmitted message in order to make up for what is missing in the context (both internal and external).

"HC communications are frequently used as art forms. They act as a unifying, cohesive force, are long-lived, and are slow to change. LC communications do not unify; however, they can be changed easily and rapidly. This is why evolution by extension is so incredibly fast; extensions in their initial stages of development are low-context. To qualify this statement somewhat, some extensions are higher on the context scale than others. *** One wonders if it is possible to develop strategies for balancing two apparently contradictory needs: the need to adapt and change (by moving in the low-context direction) and the need for stability (high-context)."

Appendix E

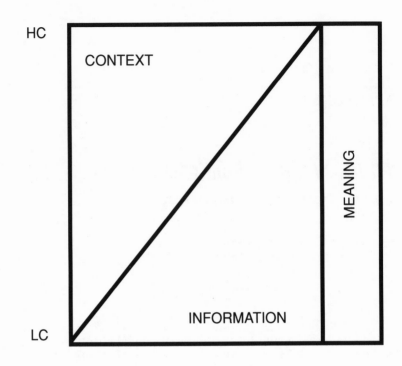

Notes

Chapter 1 – Communicology

1. Thomas Kuhn, *The Structure of Scientific Revolutions*, 2nd ed. rev. (Chicago: Chicago UP, 1970).

2. Charles S. Peirce, *Collected Papers of Charles Sanders Peirce*, 8 vols., ed. Charles Hartshorne & Paul Weiss, vols. 1–6; Arthur W. Burks, vols. 7–8 (Cambridge: Harvard UP, 1934–1935; 1958); Charles S. Peirce, *The New Elements of Mathematics*, 4 vols., ed. Carolyn Eisele (The Hague: Mouton, 1976).

3. Richard L. Lanigan, *Phenomenology of Communication: Merleau-Ponty's Thematics in Communicology and Semiology* (Pittsburgh: Duquesne UP, 1988).

4. Hubert G. Alexander, *The Language and Logic of Philosophy* (Washington, DC: UP of America, 1988); Lanigan, "Structuralism in the Human Science Context of Phenomenology and Semiology," in *Phenomenology of Communication*, 157–67.

5. M. S. Poole, D. R. Seibold, & R. D. McPhee, "Group Decision-Making as a Structural Process," *Quarterly Journal of Speech* 71.1 (1985): 74–102.

6. Tom McFeat, *Small-Group Cultures* (New York: Pergamon, 1974).

7. John Lyons, *Semantics*, 2 vols. (New York: Cambridge UP, 1977).

8. Vincent Descombes, *Modern French Philosophy*, trans. L. Scott-Fox & J. M. Harding (New York: Cambridge UP, 1980; Original work published 1979 as *Le Même et L'Autre*), 81.

9. Louis Hjelmslev, *Prolegomena to a Theory of Language*, rev. English ed., trans. F. J. Whitfield (Madison: Wisconsin UP, 1961; Original work published 1943).

10. Roland Barthes, *Image-Music-Text*, trans. S. Heath (New York: Hill & Wang, 1977); Barthes, *A Lover's Discourse: Fragments*, trans. R. Howard (New York: Hill & Wang, 1978; Original work published 1977).

11. Pierre Bourdieu, *Outline of a Theory of Practice*, trans. R. Nice (New York: Cambridge UP, 1977; Original work published 1972).

12. Jean Baudrillard, *Selected Writings*, trans. M. Poster (Stanford: Stanford UP, 1988).

13. E. F. Kaelin & C. O. Schrag, eds., *American Phenomenology: Origins and Developments*, Analecta Husserliana: The Yearbook of Phenomenological Research 26 (Boston: Kluwer Academic Publishers, 1989).

14. Poole, et al, "Group Decision-Making."

15. J. G. Manis & B. N. Meltzer, eds., *Symbolic Interaction*, 3rd ed.

(Boston: Allyn & Bacon, 1978) 11.

16. Manis & Meltzer, eds., *Symbolic Interaction*, 5.

17. Roman Jakobson, "Verbal Communication," *Communication*, a *Scientific American* book (San Francisco: W.H. Freeman, 1972) 39–44; Umberto Eco, *A Theory of Semiotics* (Bloomington: Indiana UP, 1979); Eco, *Semiotics and Philosophy of Language* (Bloomington: Indiana UP, 1984).

18. Richard L. Lanigan, *Speech Act Phenomenology* (The Hague: Martinus Nijhoff, 1977); Lanigan, *Phenomenology of Communication*.

19. Richard L. Lanigan, *Speaking and Semiology: Maurice Merleau-Ponty's Phenomenological Theory of Existential Communication*, Approaches to Semiotics 22 (The Hague & Paris: Mouton, 1972); Lanigan, *Semiotic Phenomenology of Rhetoric: Eidetic Practice in Henry Grattan's Discourse on Tolerance* (Washington, DC: Center for Advanced Research in Phenomenology; UP of America, 1984).

20. John R. Searle, *Speech Acts: An Essay in the Philosophy of Language* (Cambridge: Cambridge UP, 1969); Searle, *Intentionality: An Essay in the Philosophy of Mind* (Cambridge: Cambridge UP, 1983).

21. Maurice Merleau-Ponty, *Phenomenology of Perception*, trans. Colin Smith, revisions by Forrest Williams & David Guerrière (New York: Humanities, 1981; Original work published 1945); Michel Foucault, *Archaeology of Knowledge & The Discourse on Language*, trans. A. M. S. Smith (New York: Pantheon, 1982; Original works publishes 1969 & 1971).

22. Anthony Wilden, *System and Structure: Essays on Communication and Exchange*, 2nd ed. (New York: Tavistock/Methuen, 1980); Wilden, *The Rules Are No Game: The Strategy of Communication* (New York: Routledge & Kegan Paul, 1987); Wilden, *Man and Woman, War and Peace: The Strategist's Companion* (New York: Routledge & Kegan Paul, 1987).

23. Vincent Descombes, *Objects of All Sorts: A Philosophical Grammar*, trans. L. Scott-Fox & J. Harding (Baltimore: Johns Hopkins UP, 1986; Original work published 1983 as *Grammaire d'objects en tous genres*).

24. Alexander Comfort, "On the Biology of Religion," *Center Report*, Center for the Study of Democratic Institutions, Santa Barbara, California (October 1974), 16–19.

25. Algirdas Julien Greimas, *Structural Semantics: An Attempt at a Method*, trans. D. McDowell, R. Schleifer, & A. Velie (Lincoln: Nebraska UP, 1983; Original work published 1966); Greimas, *On Meaning: Selected Writings in Semiotic Theory*, trans. P. J. Perron & F. H. Collins (Minneapolis: Minnesota UP, 1987; Original works published in 1970 in *Du Sens I*, in 1976 in *Semiotique et Sciences Sociales*, and in 1983 in *Du Sens II*); Greimas, *The Social Sciences: A Semiotic View*, trans. P. Fabbri & P. Perron (Minneapolis: Minnesota UP, 1990; Original works published between 1970 and 1986); Greimas & J. Courtés, *Semiotics and Language: An Analytical Dictionary*, trans. L. Crist, et al. (Bloomington: Indiana UP, 1982; Original work published 1979).

26. Elmar Holenstein, *Roman Jakobson's Approach to Language: Phenomenological Structuralism*, trans. C. Schelbert & T. Schelbert (Bloomington: Indiana UP, 1976; Original work published 1974).

27. Emile Benveniste, *Problems in General Linguistics*, trans. M. E. Meek (Coral Gables: Miami UP, 1971; Original work published 1966); Benveniste, *Indo-European Language and Society*, trans. E. Palmer (Coral Gables: Miami UP, 1973; Original work published 1969).

CHAPTER 2 – GOFFMAN AND MASS MEDIA

1. Gregory Bateson & Mary Catherine Bateson, *Angels Fear: Towards an Epistemology of the Sacred* (New York: Macmillan, 1987).

2. Erving Goffman, *Frame Analysis: An Essay on the Organization of Experience* (Cambridge: Harvard UP, 1974) 10.

3. Goffman, *Frame Analysis*, 46.

4. Pierre Bourdieu, *Outline of a Theory of Practice*, trans. R. Nice (Cambridge: Cambridge UP, 1977; Original work published 1972) 78, 83.

5. Michel Foucault, *Power/Knowledge: Selected Interviews and Other Writings 1972–1977*, ed. Colin Gordon (New York: Pantheon, 1980) 196–7.

6. Claude E. Shannon & Warren Weaver, *The Mathematical Theory of Communication* (Urbana: Illinois UP, 1964).

7. Goffman, *Frame Analysis*, p. 10.

8. Bourdieu, *Theory of Practice*, pp. 82, 87, 93.

9. Charles S. Peirce, *Collected Papers of Charles Sanders Peirce*, 8 vols., ed. Charles Hartshorne & Paul Weiss, vols. 1–6; Arthur W. Burks, vols. 7–8 (Cambridge: Harvard UP, 1934–1935; 1958) codex 4.537.

10. Edmund Husserl, *Cartesian Meditations: An Introduction to Phenomenology*, trans. D. Cairns (The Hague: Martinus Nijhoff, 1969); Maurice Merleau-Ponty, *Phenomenology of Perception*, trans. Colin Smith; corrections, Forrest Williams & Daniel Guerrière (New York: Routledge & Kegan Paul, 1981; Original work published 1945).

11. See chapter 5; Anthony Wilden, *System and Structure: Essays on Communication and Exchange*, 2nd ed. (New York: Tavistock/Methuen, 1980); Wilden, *The Rules Are No Game: The Strategy of Communication* (New York: Routledge & Kegan Paul, 1987); Wilden, *Man and Woman, War and Peace: The Strategist's Companion* (New York: Routledge & Kegan Paul, 1987).

12. Edmund Husserl, "The Syllabus of the London Lectures," *J.B.S.P.: The Journal of the British Society for Phenomenology* 1.1 (1970): 23.

13. Michel Foucault, *The Birth of the Clinic: An Archaeology of Medical Perception*, trans. A. M .S. Smith (New York: Vintage; Random House, 1973); Foucault, *Discipline and Punish: The Birth of the Prison*, trans. A. Sheridan (New York: Vintage; Random House, 1979).

14. Erving Goffman, *Asylums: Essays on the Social Situation of Mental Patients and Other Inmates* (New York: Doubleday Anchor, 1961).

15. Michel Foucault, *The Archaeology of Knowledge*, trans. A. M. S. Smith (New York: Pantheon; Random House, 1972); Richard L. Lanigan, *Semiotic Phenomenology of Rhetoric: Eidetic Practice in Henry Grattan's Discourse on Tolerance* (Washington: Center for Advanced Research in Phenomenology; UP America, 1984).

16. See chapter 5.

17. Merleau-Ponty, *Phenomenology of Perception*; Richard L. Lanigan, *Speaking and Semiology: Merleau-Ponty's Phenomenological Theory of Existential Communication* (The Hague and Paris: Mouton, 1972); Lanigan, *Phenomenology of Communication: Merleau-Ponty's Thematics on Communicology and Semiology* (Pittsburgh: Duquesne UP, 1988).

18. Don Ihde, *Experimental Phenomenology: An Introduction* (New York: G. P. Putnam's Sons, 1977).

19. Elmar Holenstein, *Roman Jakobson's Approach to Language: Phenom-*

enological Structuralism, trans. C. and T. Schelbert (Bloomington: Indiana UP, 1976) 154; Richard L. Lanigan, *Speech Act Phenomenology* (The Hague: Martinus Nijhoff, 1977).

20. Umberto Eco, *A Theory of Semiotics* (Bloomington: Indiana UP, 1976) 68, 268.

21. Lanigan, *Phenomenology of Communication*.

22. Alfred Schütz, *The Phenomenology of the Social World*, trans. G. Walsh and F. Lehnert (Evanston: Northwestern UP, 1967) 97–136; Lanigan, *Semiotic Phenomenology of Rhetoric*, see chapter 5.

23. Goffman, *Frame Analysis*, p. 13.

24. Erving Goffman, *Forms of Talk* (Philadelphia: Pennsylvania UP, 1981), 197–327.

25. Christopher Ricks, "Phew! Oops! Oof! [Review of Erving Goffman's *Forms of Talk*]," *The New York Review of Books* 16 July 1981: 42–44.

26. Goffman, *Frame Analysis*, pp. 144–9.

27. Goffman, *Frame Analysis*, p. 145.

28. Goffman, *Frame Analysis*, p. 146.

29. Goffman, *Forms of Talk*, pp. 242–3.

30. Lanigan, *Speech Act Phenomenology*.

31. Ricks, "Phew! Oops! Oof!"

CHAPTER 3 – SILENT SCIENCE

1. Madeleine Mathiot, *Ethnolinguistics: Boas, Sapir and Whorf Revisited* (New York: Mouton, 1979).

2. Geoffery, G. Harpham, *The Ascetic Imperative in Culture and Criticism* (Chicago: Chicago UP, 1987) 220ff.

3. Lenore Langsdorf, "The Emperor Has Only Clothes: Toward a Hermeneutic of the Video Text," *Video Icons and Values*, ed. Alan M. Olson (Albany: State U. New York P., 1991).

4. G. E. Marcus & M. M. J. Fischer, *Anthropology as Cultural Critique: An Experimental Moment in the Human Sciences* (Chicago: Chicago UP, 1986).

5. Don Ihde, "The Technological Embodiment of Media," *Communication Philosophy and the Technological Age*, ed. Michael J. Hyde (University, AL: Alabama UP, 1982) 54–72; see Richard L. Lanigan, ed., *Semiotics and Phenomenology*, Special Issue, *Semiotica* 41.1–4 (1982): 1–335.

6. Tom McFeat, *Small-Group Cultures* (New York: Pergamon, 1974).

7. Donald Polkinghorne, *Methodology for the Human Sciences: Systems of Inquiry* (Albany: New York State UP, 1983).

8. Ib Bondebjerg, "Critical Theory, Aesthetics and Reception Theory," *The NORDICOM Review of Nordic Mass Communication Research* 1 (1988): 22.

9. Langsdorf, "The Emperor Has Only Clothes," p. 5.

10. Richard L. Lanigan, *Phenomenology of Communication: Merleau-Ponty's Thematics in Communicology and Semiology* (Pittsburgh: Duquesne UP, 1988), 203–222.

11. Maurice Merleau-Ponty, "Eye and Mind," *The Primacy of Perception and Other Essays on Phenomenological Psychology, the Philosophy of Art, History, and Politics*, trans. J. M. Edie, et al. (Evanston: Northwestern UP, 1964) 186.

12. D. R. Smith & L. K. Williamson, *Interpersonal Communication: Roles,*

Rules, Strategies, and Games (Dubuque, IA: Wm. C. Brown, 1977).

13. R. D. Laing, H. Phillipson & A. R. Lee, *Interpersonal Perception: A Theory and a Method for Research* (London: Tavistock; New York: Springer, 1966).

14. Burten L. Alperson, "In Search of Buber's Ghost: A Calculus for Interpersonal Phenomenology," *Behavioral Science* 20.3 (1973), 179–190.

15. Gail & Michele Meyers, *The Dynamics of Human Communication: A Laboratory Approach,* 4th ed. (New York: McGraw-Hill, 1985) 8.

16. Lanigan, *Phenomenology of Communication; Introduction,* trans. R. Hurley (New York: Vintage, 1980; Original work published in 1976 as *Volenté de savior*); Foucault, *Power/Knowledge: Selected Interviews and Other Writings 1972–1977,* ed. C. Gordon; trans. C. Gordon, et al. (New York: Pantheon, 1980); Foucault, "The Subject and Power," *Michel Foucault: Beyond Structuralism and Hermeneutics,* by H. L. Dreyfus & P. Rabinow (Chicago: Chicago UP, 1982) 208–226.

17. This view is corrected by Bill Nichols, *Ideology and the Image: Social Representation in the Cinema and Other Media* (Bloomington: Indiana UP, 1981).

18. Elmar Holenstein, *Roman Jakobson's Approach to Language: Phenomenological Structuralism,* trans. C. & T. Schelbert (Bloomington: Indiana UP, 1976).

19. Lanigan, *Phenomenology of Communication.*

20. Umberto Eco, "The Multiplication of the Media, *"Travels in Hyperreality: Essays,* trans. W. Weaver (New York: Harcourt, Brace, Jovanovich, 1986).

21. Briankle G. Chang, "Representing Representation: A Visual Semiotics of *Las Meninas,* " *Journal of Communication Inquiry,* 10.3 (1986), 3–13.

22. Arnold Isenberg, "Critical Communication," *Philosophy Looks at the Arts: Contemporary Readings in Aesthetics,* ed. Joseph Margolis (New York: Charles Scribners Sons, 1962) 143.

23. See Kaelin & Schrag, *American Phenomenology.*

24. Louis Hjelmslev, *Prolegomena to a Theory of Language,* trans. F. J. Whitfield, revised English ed. (Madison: University of Wisconsin UP, 1961; Original work published 1943).

25. See Lanigan, *Speech Act Phenomenology*; Umberto Eco, "Towards a Semiotic Inquiry into the Television Message," *Communication Studies: An Introductory Reader,* ed. John Corner & Jeremy Hawthorn (London: Edward Arnold, 1980) 131–149.

26. Polkinghorne, *Methodology for the Human Sciences,* p. 256.

27. Tom as P. O. Cluanáin, "Toward a Psychology of Imagination in Art and in Esthetics," *Imagination and Phenomenological Psychology,* ed. Edward L. Murray (Pittsburgh: Duquesne UP, 1987) 78–108.

28. Meyers, *The Dynamics of Human Communication,* pp. 341–2;

29. Jean Baudrillard, *In the Shadow of the Silent Majority,* trans. P. Foss, et al. Trans.). (New York: Semiotext(e), 1983) 97–8.

30. Charles S. Peirce, *Collected Papers of Charles Sanders Peirce,* 8 vols., ed. Charles Hartshorne & Paul Weiss, vols. 1–6; Arthur W. Burks, vols. 7–8 (Cambridge: Harvard UP, 1934–1935; 1958) codex 2.619; Gregory & Mary Catherine Bateson, *Angels Fear: Towards an Epistemology of the Sacred* (New York: Macmillan, 1987), 36ff.

31. Lanigan, *Phenomenology of Communication,* pp. 144–53.

32. See Lanigan, *Phenomenology of Communication.*

33. Brewster Ghiselin, ed., *The Creative Process: A Symposium* (New York: Mentor; New American Library, 1955) 62–4.

34. Marshall McLuhan, *Understanding Media: The Extensions of Man* (New York: Signet, 1964) 247; see Marshall & Eric McLuhan, *Laws of Media: The New Science* (Toronto: Toronto UP, 1988).

35. Michel Foucault, *This Is Not a Pipe; with Illustrations and Letters by René Magritte,* ed. & trans. J. Harkness (Berkley: California UP, 1983).

36. See chapters 5 and 6.

37. Jean-Paul Ribes, "*Le Vrai Visage de Max* [Max's True Face]," *L'Express* 24 Juin 1988: 9; my translation.

38. Michel Foucault, *The Order of Things: An Archaeology of the Human Sciences,* trans. anon. (London: Tavistock, 1970; Original work published in 1966 as *Les Mots et les Choses* [Words and Things]) 116. Foucault has noted subsequently that the English translation title is a more accurate aphorism of his thesis in the book.

39. Tzvetan Todorov, *The Fantastic: A Structural Approach to a Literary Genre,* trans. R. Howard (Ithaca, NY: Cornell UP, 1975; Original work published 1970) 174.

40. See Eco, n. 25 above; Anthony Wilden, "Changing Frames of Order: Cybernetics and the Machina Mundi," *The Myths of Information: Technology and Postindustrial Culture,* ed. Kathleen Woodward (Madison: Coda Press, 1980) 219–41.

41. Jacques Gerstlé, "*La Communication et la Dualité Public/Privé.* [Communication and the Public/Private Duality]. *Revue Francaise de science politique,* 37.5 (1987), 659; my translation.

42. Jean Baudrillard, "The Implosion of Meaning in the Media and the Implosion of the Social in the Masses," *The Myths of Information: Technology and Postindustrial Culture,* ed. Kathleen Woodward (Madison: Coda Press, 1980) 141, 183.

43. David A. Ross, "Nam June Paik's Videotapes," *Transmission: Theory and Practice for a New Television Aesthetics,* ed. Peter D'Agostino (New York: Tanam, 1985) 152.

44. Ihde, "The Technological Embodiment of Media," p. 72.

45. Christopher Finch, "Communicators 1" and "Communicators 2," *Image as Language: Aspects of British Art 1950–1968* (Baltimore: Penguin, 1969) 153–67.

46. Hal Himmelstein, "Television Culture," *Transmission: Theory and Practice for a New Television Aesthetics,* ed. Peter D'Agostino (New York: Tanam, 1985) 43–54.

47. Lucien Lévy-Bruhl, *How Natives Think,* trans. L. A. Clarke (Princeton: Princeton UP, 1985) 13; see appendix A.

48. Claude Lévi-Strauss, *The Elementary Structures of Kinship,* trans. J. H. Bell & J. R. von Sturmer (Boston: Beacon, 1969; Original work published 1949) 478–97.

49. Lévy-Bruhl, *How Natives Think,* p. 361.

50. Michel Foucault, *The Archaeology of Knowledge (sic) & The Discourse on Language (sic),* trans. A. M. S. Smith (New York: Pantheon, 1972) 62, 151–3.

51. John Fiske, B. Hodge, & G. Turner, *Myths of Oz: Reading Australian Popular Culture* (Boston: Allen & Unwin, 1987) 54; see John Fiske, *Television Culture* (New York: Routledge, 1987). The shift in the ontology and epis-

temology of the art museum and the ethnographical museum is analyzed phenomenologically by James Clifford, *The Predicament of Culture Twentieth-Century Ethnography, Literature, and Art* (Cambridge: Harvard UP, 1988), esp. "Part Three: Collections."

52. Lévy-Bruhl, *How Natives Think,* pp. 361–2.

53. Maurice Merleau-Ponty, *Phenomenology of Perception,* trans. Colin Smith; corrections, Forrest Williams & Daniel Guerrière (New York: Routledge & Kegan Paul, 1981; Original work published 1945); Merleau-Ponty, *In Praise of Philosophy,* trans. J. Wild & J. M. Edie (Evanston: Northwestern UP, 1963; Original work published 1953); see chapters 5 and 6; cf. a contrary view by Paul Heyer, *Communications and History: Theories of Media, Knowledge, and Civilization* (New York: Greenwood, 1988).

54. Lévy-Bruhl, *How Natives Think,* p. 76.

55. John Fiske, B. Hodge, & G. Turner, *Myths of Oz,* pp. 144–55.

56. Richard Ross, *Museology* (Santa Barbara: Aperture Foundation, 1989).

57. Nam June Paik, *Family of Robot: Mother, Family of Robot: Father, & Connection,* Exhibit & Exhibit Catalog, Chicago International Art Exposition, May 8–13 (Cincinnati: Carl Solway Gallery, Inc., 1986).

58. Edward Kienholz & Nancy Redden, *The Art Show,* 1963–1977, Exhibit & Exhibit Catalog, Museum of Contemporary Art, 7 September 1985 to 2 February 1986 (Chicago: Museum of Contemporary Art, 1986).

59. Merleau-Ponty, "Eye and Mind," p. 167.

60. Vilem Flusser, "Two Approaches to the Phenomenon, Television," *The New Television: A Public/Private Art,* ed. Douglas Davis & Allison Simmons (Cambridge: MIT UP, 1977), 243–4; see Ihde, "The Technological Embodiment of Media," p. 66.

61. Jenny L. Nelson, "The Other Side of Signification: The Semiotic Phenomenology of Televisual Experience," Ph.D. diss., Dept. of Speech Communication, Southern Illinois University, 1986; see Nelson, "On Media and Existence," *Critical Studies in Mass Communication* 4.3 (1987): 311–18.

62. Flusser, "Two Approaches to the Phenomenon, Television," p. 239.

63. See Michel Foucault, *The Order of Things;* Foucault, *This Is Not a Pipe;* and Foucault, *Death and the Labyrinth: The World of Raymond Roussel,* trans. C. Ruas (New York: Doubleday, 1986).

64. Merleau-Ponty, "Eye and Mind"; Merleau-Ponty, *Phenomenology of Perception.*

65. Merleau-Ponty, "Eye and Mind," p. 170; see Foucault, *The History of Sexuality,* p. 98; cf. Chang, "Representing Representation."

66. Foucault, *The Order of Things,* p. 4.

67. Anthony Wilden, *The Rules Are No Game: The Strategy of Communication* (New York: Routledge & Kegan Paul, 1987) 67; see Wilden, *Man and Woman, War and Peace: The Strategist's Companion* (New York: Routledge & Kegan Paul, 1987) and Wilden, *System and Structure: Essays on Communication and Exchange,* 2nd ed. (New York: Tavistock/Methuen, 1980).

68. See Nelson, "The Other Side of Signification."

69. Foucault, *The History of Sexuality,* p. 83.

70. Eco, "The Multiplication of the Media," pp. 145–6.

71. Foucault, *The Archaeology of Knowledge,* pp. 62, 151–3; Wilden, *System and Structure,* p. 188 et passim.

72. See McFeat, *Small-Group Cultures.*

73. Foucault, *Death and the Labyrinth*; Foucault, *This Is Not a Pipe*; see Richard L. Lanigan, *Speaking and Semiology: Maurice Merleau-Ponty's Phenomenological Theory of Existential Communication*, Approaches to Semiotics 22 (The Hague & Paris: Mouton, 1972); Lanigan, *Speech Act Phenomenology* (The Hague: Martinus Nijhoff, 1977); Lanigan, Richard L. (1984); *Semiotic Phenomenology of Rhetoric: Eidetic Practice in Henry Grattan's Discourse on Tolerance* (Washington, DC: Center for Advanced Research in Phenomenology & UP America, 1984).

74. Maurice Merleau-Ponty, "The Child's Relation with Others," *The Primacy of Perception and Other Essays on Phenomenological Psychology, the Philosophy of Art, History, and Politics*, trans. J. M. Edie, et al. (Evanston: Northwestern UP, 1964), 96–155.

75. Foucault, *Death and Labyrinth*, p. 25.

76. Foucault, *The Archaeology of Knowledge*, p. 215.

77. Foucault, *The Order of Things*, p. 118.

78. Foucault, "The Subject and Power," p. 208.

79. Baudrillard, "The Implosion of Meaning in the Media," p. 145.

80. Foucault, *The History of Sexuality*, p. 92ff.

81. Foucault, *Death and the Labyrinth*, p. 16.

82. Longinus, *On Great Writing (On the Sublime)*, trans. G. M. A. Grube (New York: Liberal Arts, 1957; Original work written circa 3rd century A.D.) 29.

83. John G. Handhardt, "Watching Television," *Transmission: Theory and Practice for a New Television Aesthetics*, ed. Peter D'Agostino (New York: Tanam, 1985) 57–61.

84. Baudrillard, "The Implosion of Meaning in the Media," p. 148.

85. Foucault, *This Is Not a Pipe*, p. 28.

CHAPTER 4 – SAUSSURE

1. Jonathan Culler, *Ferdinand de Saussure* (New York: Penguin, 1977).

2. A. J. Greimas & J. Courtés, *Semiotics and Language: An Analytical Dictionary*, trans. L. Crist, et al. (Bloomington: Indiana UP, 1982; Original work published 1979) 308–310.

3. Roman Jakobson, *Language in Literature* (Cambridge: Harvard UP, 1987) 444.

4. Ferdinand de Saussure, *Course in General Linguistics*, ed. by C. Bally & A. Sechehaye with A. Riedlinger; trans. by Wade Baskin (New York: McGraw-Hill, 1966). The more recent 1986 translation by Roy Harris published by Open Court, La Salle, Illinois, is, in my opinion, spurious and to be avoided.

5. Louis Hjelmslev, *Prolegomena to a Theory of Language*, rev. English ed., trans. F. J. Whitfield (Madison: Wisconsin UP, 1961; Original work published 1943).

6. Elmar Holenstein, *Roman Jakobson's Approach to Language: Phenomenological Structuralism*, trans. C. & T. Schelbert (Bloomington: Indiana UP, 1976).

7. Richard L. Lanigan, *Phenomenology of Communication: Merleau-Ponty's Thematics in Communicology and Semiology* (Pittsburgh: Duquesne UP, 1988).

8. Michel Foucault, *The Order of Things: An Archaeology of the Human Sciences*, trans. anon. (London: Tavistock, 1970) 115, 200.

9. Michel Foucault, *The Archaeology of Knowledge (sic) & The Discourse*

on Language (sic), trans. A. M. S. Smith (New York: Pantheon; Random House, 1972), 158; see Hayden White, "Foucault Decoded: Notes from Underground," *Tropics of Discourse: Essays in Cultural Criticism* (Baltimore: Johns Hopkins UP, 1978), 230–260.

10. White, "Foucault Decoded," p. 162.

11. Foucault, *Order of Things*, p. 116.

12. Maurice Merleau-Ponty, *Phenomenology of Perception*, trans. C. Smith; revisions by F. Williams & D. Guerrière (New York: Humanities, 1981; Original work published 1945).

13. Roland Barthes, *Elements of Semiology*, trans. A. Lavers & C. Smith (New York: Hill & Wang, 1967).

14. Lanigan, *Phenomenology of Communication*.

15. Claude Lévi-Strauss, *The Elementary Structures of Kinship*, trans. by J. Bell & J. R. von Sturmer (Boston: Beacon, 1969) 478ff.

16. Jacques Lacan, *Écrits: A Selections*, trans. A. Sheridan (New York: W. W. Norton, 1977) 234. (Original work published 1966); John Muller and William J. Richardson, *Lacan and Language: A Reader's Guide to Écrits* (New York: International Universities, 1982); the example of Gregory Bateson's patient and a generalization of Lacan's symbolic, imaginary, and real model can be found in the work of Anthony Wilden, see chapter one, n. 22.

17. Julia Kristeva, *Revolution in Poetic Language*, trans. M. Waller (New York: Columbia UP, 1984); the place of rhetoric is discussed in Kristeva, *Language, The Unknown: An Initiation into Linguistics*, trans. A. M. Menke (New York: Columbia UP, 1989; Original work published 1981) 278ff.

18. Jacques Derrida, *Of Grammatology*, trans. by G. C. Spivak (Baltimore: Johns Hopkins UP, 1974; Original work published 1967).

19. Emile Benveniste, *Problems in General Linguistics*, trans. by M. E. Meek (Coral Gables: Miami UP, 1971) 205ff.

20. Richard Kearney, ed., *Dialogues with Contemporary Continental Thinkers: The Phenomenological Heritage* (Manchester, UK: Manchester UP, 1984) 20–21.

21. Pierre Bourdieu, *Outline of a Theory of Practice*, trans. R. Nice (New York: Cambridge UP, 1977; Original work published 1972).

22. Pierre Bourdieu, *The Logic of Practice*, trans. Richard Nice (Stanford: Stanford UP, 1990; Original work published 1980 as *Le sens pratique*) 26; the same point (apparently little noticed) is made by Vincent Descombes, *Modern French Philosophy*, trans. L. Scott-Fox & J. M. Harding (New York: Cambridge UP, 1980; Original work published 1979 as *Le Même et L'Autre*) 81.

23. Michel Foucault, *L'ordre du discours: Leçon inaugural au Collège de France prononcée le 2 décembre 1970* (Paris: Éditions Gallimard, 1971), 7–8; my translation; See n. 9 above for a complete translation of the work in English.

CHAPTER 5 – SOMEBODY IS NOWHERE

1. Calvin O. Schrag, *Communicative Praxis and the Space of Subjectivity* (Bloomington: Indiana UP, 1986) 11; see Hayden White, *Tropics of Discourse: Essays in Cultural Criticism* (Baltimore: Johns Hopkins UP, 1978); Richard L. Lanigan, *Speaking and Semiology: Maurice Merleau-Ponty's Phenomenological Theory of Existential Communication* (The Hague: Mouton, 1972); Lanigan, *Speech Act Phenomenology* (The Hague: Martinus Nijhoff, 1977).

2. Schrag, *Communicative Praxis*, p. 2.

3. Calvin O. Schrag, *Radical Reflection and the Origin of the Human Sciences* (West Lafayette, Indiana: Purdue UP, 1980); Michel Foucault, *The Order of Things: An Archaeology of the Human Sciences*, trans. anon. (London: Tavistock, 1970; Original work published 1966).

4. Schrag, *Communicative Praxis*, p. 3.

5. Schrag, *Communicative Praxis*, p. 2.

6. Julia Kristeva, *Language: The Unknown*, trans. Anne M. Menke. (New York: Columbia UP, 1989; Original work published 1981); see especially the discussion of "Orators and Rhetors" in chapter 21 entitled "The Practice of Language"; for Foucault's theory of rhetoric, see his *Death and the Labyrinth: The World of Raymond Roussel*, trans. C. Ruas (Garden City: Doubleday, 1986; original work published 1963).

7. Schrag, *Communicative Praxis*, p. 3.

8. Michel Foucault, "The Subject and Power," afterword, *Michel Foucault: Beyond Structuralism and Hermeneutics; with an Afterword by Michel Foucault*, by Hubert L. Dreyfus & Paul Rabinow (Chicago: Chicago UP, 1982) 212.

9. Michel Foucault, *Power/Knowledge: Selected Interviews and Other Writings 1972–1977*, ed. Colin Gordon (New York: Pantheon 1980) 85.

10. Kristeva, *Language*, p. 221; see n. 22 in chapter 4.

11. John S. Nelson, "Tropal History and the Social Sciences: Reflections on Stuever's Remarks," *History and Theory* 19 (1984): 80–101; Nelson basically repeats the criteria formulated by Umberto Eco, *A Theory of Semiotics* (Bloomington: Indiana UP, 1976) especially his "anti-Ockhamistic principle: *entia sunt multiplicanda propter necessitatem*" [phenomena are multiplied by reason of necessity], p. viii.; see Richard L. Lanigan, *Semiotic Phenomenology of Rhetoric: Eidetic Practice in Henry Grattan's Discourse on Tolerance* (Washington, DC: Center for Advanced Research in Phenomenology & UP of America, 1984).

12. Schrag, *Communicative Praxis*, pp. 6 (my emphasis), 181.

13. Michel Foucault, *The Archaeology of Knowledge (sic) & The Discourse on Language (sic)*, trans. A. M. Sheridan Smith (New York: Pantheon, 1972; original work published 1969) 162.

14. Foucault, *Archaeology*, pp. 149–55.

15. Schrag, *Communicative Praxis*, p. 52.

16. Larry Shiner, "Foucault, Phenomenology and the Question of Origins," *Philosophy Today* 26 (1982): 319.

17. Maurice Merleau-Ponty, *Themes from the Lectures at the Collège de France 1952–1960*, trans. John O'Neill (Evanston: Northwestern UP, 1970; original work published 1968) 4; my insertions.

18. Maurice Merleau-Ponty, *In Praise of Philosophy*, trans. J. Wild and J. M. Edie (Evanston: Northwestern UP, 1963; original work published 1953).

19. Maurice Merleau-Ponty, "On the Phenomenology of Language," *Signs*, trans. R. C. McCleary (Evanston: Northwestern UP, 1964; original work published 1960).

20. Maurice Merleau-Ponty, *Phenomenology of Perception*, trans. C. Smith; corrections by Forrest Williams & David Guerrière (New Jersey: Humanities, 1981; original work published 1945).

21. Richard L. Lanigan, *Phenomenology of Communication: Merleau-Ponty's Thematics in Communicology and Semiology* (Pittsburgh: Duquesne UP, 1988).

22. A. J. Greimas & J. Courtés, *Semiotics and Language: An Analytical*

Dictionary, trans. L. Cris & Daniel Patte (Bloomington: Indiana UP, 1982; original work published 1979) 307–8.

23. Greimas & Courtés, *Semiotics and Language*, pp. 105, 157.

24. Greimas & Courtés, *Semiotics and Language*, p. 362.

25. Foucault, *Archaeology*, pp. 86–7; my emphasis.

26. Foucault, *Archaeology*, p. 28; my insertions.

27. Jürgen Habermas, "IX. The Critique of Reason as an Unmasking of the Human Sciences: Michel Foucault" and "X. Some Questions Concerning the Theory of Power: Foucault Again," *The Philosophical Discourse of Modernity*, trans. Frederick Lawrence (Cambridge: MIT, 1987; original work published 1985).

28. Foucault, *Archaeology*, p. 44.

29. Schrag, *Communicative Praxis*, p. 8.

30. Kristeva, *Language*, pp. 10–11.

31. Foucault, *Archaeology*, p. 57.

32. J. M. Miller, M. H. Prosser, & T. W. Benson, eds., *Readings in Medieval Rhetoric* (Bloomington: Indiana UP, 1973) 170–1; cf. George A. Kennedy, *Classical Rhetoric and Its Christian and Secular Tradition from Ancient to Modern Times* (Chapel Hill: North California UP, 1980) 138, 158, 191.

33. Umberto Eco, *Semiotics and the Philosophy of Language* (Bloomington: Indiana UP, 1984) 130–63, esp. 148–9. A complete history of the method is given in Winfried Noth, *Handbook of Semiotics* (Bloomington: Indiana UP, 1990), pp. 334–337.

34. Umberto Eco, *Foucault's Pendulum*, trans. William Weaver (New York: Harcourt Brace Jovanovich, 1989) 599.

35. Anthony Wilden, *The Rules Are No Game: The Strategy of Communication* (New York: Routledge & Kegan Paul, 1987) 274.

36. Eco, *Foucault's Pendelum*, p. 4.

37. Foucault, *Archaeology*, p. 58.

38. Richard L. Lanigan, "Thomas D'Aquin and the Practice of Discourse at L'Université de Paris," unpublished paper.

39. Eco, *Semiotics and the Philosophy of Language*, p. 153.

40. Foucault, *Archaeology*, p. 58.

41. Schrag, *Communicative Praxis*, p. 56.

42. Schrag, *Communicative Praxis*, p. 68.

43. Schrag, *Communicative Praxis*, p. 23.

44. Foucault, *The Order of Things*, pp. 117–8.

45. Foucault, *The Order of Things*, p. 84.

46. Foucault, *Archaeology*, p. 70.

47. Lanigan, *Phenomenology of Communication*, Chapter 17: "Semiotic Phenomenology in Plato's *Sophist*," See Lanigan, *Semiotic Phenomenology of Rhetoric*.

48. Schrag, *Communicative Praxis*, p. 22.

49. Foucault, *Archaeology*, pp. 31–2.

50. Schrag, *Communicative Praxis*, p. 54.

51. Schrag, *Communicative Praxis*, p. 57.

52. Foucault, *Archaeology*, p. 12.

53. Lanigan, *Semiotic Phenomenology of Rhetoric*.

54. Schrag, *Communicative Praxis*, p. 60.

55. Foucault, *Archaeology*, p. 33.

56. Schrag, *Communicative Praxis*, p. 54.
57. Foucault, *Archaeology*, p. 34.
58. Schrag, *Communicative Praxis*, p. 54.
59. Foucault, *Archaeology*, p. 35.
60. Schrag, *Communicative Praxis*, p. 54.
61. Foucault, *Archaeology*, p. 37.
62. Vincent Descombes, *Modern French Philosophy*, trans. L. Scott-Fox & J. M. Harding (New York: Cambridge UP, 1980; originally published 1979 as *Le Même et L'Autre*) 38.
63. Schrag, *Communicative Praxis*, p. 152.
64. Foucault, *Archaeology*, p. 62; my emphasis.
65. Foucault, *Archaeology*, p. 68.
66. Foucault, *Archaeology*, pp. 160–1.
67. Schrag, *Communicative Praxis*, p. 171.
68. Schrag, *Communicative Praxis*, p. 172.
69. Descombes, *Modern French Philosophy*, p. 12.
70. Schrag, *Communicative Praxis*, p. 180.
71. Wilden, *The Rules Are No Game*, pp. 107–8.
72. Schrag, *Communicative Praxis*, pp. 172–3.
73. Foucault, *Archaeology*, pp. 161–2.
74. Foucault, *Archaeology*, pp. 56–9.
75. Foucault, *The Order of Things*, p. 353.
76. Schrag, *Communicative Praxis*, pp. 38–9.
77. Michel Foucault, *This Is Not A Pipe*, trans. J. Harkness (Berkeley: California UP, 1983; original work published 1982).
78. Wilden, *The Rules Are No Game*.
79. Anthony Wilden, "Montage Analytic and Dialectic," *American Journal of Semiotics* 3 (1984): 25–47.
80. Wilden, *The Rules Are No Game*, p. 253.
81. Wilden, *The Rules Are No Game*, p. 245.
82. Wilden, *The Rules Are No Game*, p. 253.
83. Wilden, *The Rules Are No Game*, p. 255.
84. Wilden, *The Rules Are No Game*, pp. 276–7.
85. Wilden, *The Rules Are No Game*.
86. Schrag, *Communicative Praxis*, p. 173.
87. Wilden, *The Rules Are No Game*, p. 277.
88. Wilden, *The Rules Are No Game*, p. 254.
89. Jacques Derrida, "Structure, Sign, and Play in the Discourse of the Human Sciences," *Writing and Difference*, trans. Alan Bass (Chicago: Chicago UP, 1978; original work published 1967) 279.
90. Schrag, *Communicative Praxis*, p. 200.
91. Wilden, *The Rules Are No Game*, p. 276.
92. Foucault, *This Is Not A Pipe*, p. 29.
93. Foucault, *Archaeology*, p. 62; my insertions.
94. Foucault, *This Is Not A Pipe*, p. 20.
95. Foucault, *This Is Not A Pipe*, pp. 25–6.
96. Foucault, *This Is Not A Pipe*, p. 30.
97. Schrag, *Communicative Praxis*, pp. 206–7.
98. Jacques Derrida, "Signature Event Context," *Limited Inc.*, trans. Samuel Weber (Evanston: Northwestern UP, 1988; original work published 1977) 1–23; Derrida, "Plato's Pharmacy," *Dissemination*, trans. Barbara Johnson

(Chicago: Chicago UP, 1981; original work published 1972) 95ff. Foucault's own discussion of "signatures" occurs in *Archaeology*, pp. 25–30.

99. Schrag, *Communicative Praxis*, p. 89.

100. Michel Foucault, *Herculine Barbin: Being the Recently Discovered Memoirs of a Nineteenth-Century French Hermaphrodite*, trans. R. McDougall (New York: Pantheon, 1980; original work published 1978).

101. Schrag, *Communicative Praxis*, p. 174.

102. Foucault, *Archaeology*, p. 200.

103. Foucault, "The Subject and Power," p. 209; Foucault, *The History of Sexuality: Vol. I: An Introduction*, trans. Robert Hurley (New York: Vintage; Random House, 1980; original work published 1976) 60, 85.

104. Schrag, *Communicative Praxis*, p. 214.

105. Foucault, *Archaeology*, pp. 205–6.

106. Eco, *A Theory of Semiotics*, p. viii.

107. Schrag, *Communicative Praxis*, p. 144.

108. Schrag, *Communicative Praxis*, p. 152.

109. Schrag, *Communicative Praxis*, p. 143.

110. Schrag, *Communicative Praxis*; my emphasis of the neuter decentered space of subjectivity in this discourse about discourse.

111. Schrag, *Communicative Praxis*, p. 144.

112. Foucault, *Power/Knowledge*, p. 151.

113. Foucault, *"The Subject and Power,"* p. 225.

CHAPTER 6 – ALGEBRA OF HISTORY

1. Maurice Merleau-Ponty, *In Praise of Philosophy*, trans. John Wild and J. M. Edie (Evanston: Northwestern UP, 1963; original work published 1953) 52 (IPP).

2. Michel Foucault, *The Archaeology of Knowledge (sic) & The Discourse on Language (sic)*, trans. A. M. Sheridan Smith (New York: Pantheon; Random House, 1972; original works published 1969 and 1971) 224, AK Citations of French and retranslations are from *L'Ordre du discours*, Paris: Gallimard, 1971.

3. Charles B. Paul, *Science and Immortality: The Éloges of the Paris Academy of Sciences* (1699–1791) (Berkeley: California UP, 1980).

4. I am accounting for the signifying ambiguity of *l'histoire* by the double translation where "history" is narrative [figure of language; fiction] and "story" is equal to discourse [trope of speech; fable]. Thus, I am following the communicological distinction in discourse practice established by Emile Benveniste, "The Correlations of Tense in the French Verb," *Problems in General Linguistics*, trans. M. E. Meek (Coral Gables: Miami UP, 1971; original work published 1966) 205–16.

5. IPP, pp. 57–8.

6. IPP, p. 53; The trope *prosopopoeia* is a special case of *metonymy* in which there is a comparison by degree (binary analogue) of the *real* (substance) and the *imaginary* (attribute). Hence, prosopopoeia is a judgment of *narrative (nameless) voice*. In Aristotle's rhetoric this trope is parallel to the proof called *ethos*, i.e, a reason in argument derived from performance where embodiment in equal to "the forgetfulness of rationality" [Foucault's phrase] or *magikos*. "It is this global sense of *ethos*, involving traditions, attitudes, and

historicity of man's dwelling in the world, that was later degraded into the ethical as an autonomous branch of philosophy," Calvin O. Schrag, *Communicative Praxis and the Space of Subjectivity* (Bloomington: Indiana UP, 1986) 200; Thus, we understand Merleau-Ponty's provocative thesis on the existential phenomenology of embodiment as expression: "The relationship between my decision and my body are, in movement, magic ones," *Phenomenology of Perception*, trans. by Colin Smith; corrections by Forrest Williams and David Guerrière (New Jersey: Humanities, 1981; original work published 1945) 94.

Note that a "trope" creates a change in signification [change of meaning] whereas a "figure" gives emphasis to a signification [change in words]; see Lester Thonssen & A. Craig Baird, *Speech Criticism: The Development of Standards for Rhetorical Appraisal* (New York: Ronald, 1948) 420–23.

7. The trope *chiasm* (L. chiasmus; E. chasm) is a special case of *irony* (negative) or *simile* (positive) in which there is a comparison by degree (binary analogue) of presence (part) and absence (attribute). Hence, a chiasm is a judgment of reversibility. In Aristotle's rhetoric this trope is parallel to the proof called *pathos*, i.e., a reason in argument derived from silence or *mystos*.

The trope *persona* is a special case of *synecdoche* in which there is a comparison by degree (binary analogue) of the appearance (part) and the concrete (whole). Hence, persona is a judgment of *perceived (named) voice*. In Aristotle's rhetoric this trope is parallel to the proof called *enthymeme*, i.e., a reason in argument derived from the form and matter of the syllogism. See Richard L. Lanigan, *Semiotic Phenomenology of Rhetoric* (Washington, DC: Center for Advanced Research in Phenomenology & UP America, 1984), especially chapter 5; and my "Enthymeme: The Rhetorical Species of Aristotle's Syllogism," *Southern Speech Communication Journal* 40.2 (Winter 1975): 127–41.

8. Vincent Descombes, *Modern French Philosophy* trans. L. Scott-Fox and J. M. Harding (New York: Cambridge UP, 1980) 27; Original work published as *Le Même et L'Autre* (Paris: Les Editions de Minuit, 1979) 41; see Vincent Descombes, *Objects of All Sorts: A Philosophical Grammar*, trans. L. Scott-Fox and J. Harding (Baltimore: Johns Hopkins UP, 1986; original work published 1983).

9. Michel Foucault, "Behind the Fable," *Critical Texts* 5.2 (1988): 1–5; originally published in *L'Arc* 29 (1966) as "L'Arrière-Fable": "In every work of narrative form, we distinguish between *fable* and *fiction*. Fable is that which is told: episodes, characters, their functions in the narrative, events. Fiction is the realm of narrative [l'histoire; figure of language], or rather the various realms of the 'narrating'...." *** "Fable consists of elements placed in a certain order. Fiction is the web of relationships that has been established, by means of the speech [*discours*] itself, between the speaker and what is spoken. Fiction is an 'aspect' of fable [l'histoire; trope of speech]" (p. 1; my insertions); see Umberto Eco, "*Lector in Fabula*: Pragmatic Strategy in a Metanarrative Text," *The Role of the Reader: Explorations in the Semiotics of Texts* (Bloomington: Indiana UP, 1979) 200ff; also, see Michel de Certeau, "The Science of Fables," *The Practice of Everday Life*, trans. S. F. Rendall (Berkeley: California UP, 1984) 159ff.

10. The importance of rhetoric as a pedagogical influence on French intellectual thought is noted by Annie Cohen-Sola; *Sartre – A Life*,

trans. A. Cancogni (New York: Pantheon, 1987) 62; see Paul, *Science and Immortality.*

11. Elmar Holenstein, *Roman Jakobson's Approach to Language: Phenomenological Structuralism,* trans. C. and T. Schelbert (Bloomington: Indiana UP, 1976; original work published 1974) 138.

12. Holenstein, *Roman Jakobson,* p. 2.

13. Holenstein, *Roman Jakobson,* p. 137ff; This model of "rhetoric as a mechanism for meaning-generation" where "a trope is a semantic transposition from a sign *in praesentia* to a sign *in absentia*" is discussed by Yuri M. Lotman, *Universe of the Mind: A Semiotic Theory of Culture* (Bloomington: Indiana UP, 1990), 36ff.

14. Don Ihde, *Experimental Phenomenology: An Introduction* (New York: Capricorn; Putnam, 1977) 50.

15. The trope *catachresis* is a special case of *metaphor* in which there is a comparison by degree (binary analogue) of the *proper* (substance) and the *insipid* (whole). Hence, catachresis is a judgment of propriety. In Aristotle's rhetoric this trope is parallel to the proof called *logos,* i.e., a reason in argument derived from speech or *mythos.*

16. IPP, p. 9.

17. IPP, p. 14.

18. IPP, p. 15.

19. IPP, pp. 16, 18.

20. IPP, p. 18.

21. IPP, pp. 19–20.

22. IPP, p. 30.

23. IPP, p. 32.

24. IPP, pp. 22–3.

25. IPP, p. 34.

26. IPP, p. 39.

27. IPP, p. 36.

28. IPP, p. 41.

29. IPP, pp. 42, 44.

30. IPP, p. 44.

31. IPP, pp. 44–5.

32. Friedrich Nietzsche, *Human, All Too Human: A Book For Free Sprits,* trans. M. Faber (Lincoln: Nebraska UP, 1984) 187.

33. IPP, pp. 46–7.

34. IPP, p. 46; note that an "echo" is an empirical example of prosopopoeia while a "narrative consciousness" is an eidetic example, and the reversibility of these two examples is a chiasm. Another example might be the title of a book which reads (orally and visually) as a calligram: "Umberto Eco, *The Name of the Rose.*" The point has been rendered blunt by a subsequent hermeneutic calligram: *Foucault's Pendulum;* see chapter five where these novels by Eco are discussed.

35. IPP, p. 48.

36. IPP, p. 50.

37. AK, p. 229. Julia Kristeva, *Revolution in Poetic Language,* trans. M. Waller (New York: Columbia UP, 1984, original work published 1974); Kristeva announces her semiotic phenomenology by arguing that "We shall see that when the speaking subject is no longer considered a phenomenological

transcendental ego nor the Cartesian ego but rather a *subject in process / on trial [sujet en procès]*, as is the case in the practice of the *text.* . . ." (p. 37). And further, "The object of a particular science, the material where the subject and his knowledge are made, language is above all a *practice*. A daily practice that fills every second of our lives, including the time of our dreams, speaking and writing, it is a social function that is manifested and known through its exercise. The practice of ordinary communication: conversation and information. Oratory practice: political, theoretical, or scientific discource. Literary practice: oral folklore, written literature; prose, poetry, song, theater, etc. The list could be lengthened: language invades the entire field of human activity", Kristeva, *Language: The Unknown; An Initiation into Linguistics*, trans. Anne M. Menke (New York: Columbia UP, 1989; original work published 1981) 278.

38. IPP, p. 51. Kristeva, *Revolution in Poetic Language*, p. 87, "If these two terms—genotext and phenotext—could be translated into a metalanguage that would convey the difference between them, one might say that the genotext is a matter of topology, whereas the phenotext is one of algebra"; the respective allusion to Foucault and Merleau-Ponty is clear.

39. IPP, p. 54.

40. AK, p. 229.

41. IPP, p. 56.

42. IPP, pp. 57–8.

43. IPP, p. 58.

44. AK, p. 234.

45. IPP, p. 59.

46. IPP, p. 63.

47. Descombes, *Modern French Philosophy*, p. 3.

48. Michel Foucault, "The Subject and Power," afterword, H. L. Dreyfus and P. Rabinow, *Michel Foucault: Beyond Structuralism and Hermeneutics* (Chicago: Chicago UP, 1982) 208 (SP).

49. SP, p. 212.

50. SP, pp. 211, 222; Michel Foucault, *Power / Knowledge: Selected Interviews and Other Writings 1972–1977*, ed. Colin Gordon (New York: Pantheon, 1980). 83. Cf. Paul Heyer, *Communications and History: Theories of Media, Knowledge, and Civilization* (New York: Greenwood, 1988) 152–3.

51. Hayden White, "Foucault's Discourse: The Historiography of Anti-Humanism," *The Content of the Form: Narrative Discourse and Historical Representation*, (Baltimore: Johns Hopkins UP, 1987) 120. Cf. Hayden White, "Foucault Decoded: Notes from Underground," *Tropics of Discourse: Essays in Cultural Criticism* (Baltimore: Johns Hopkins UP) 230–60; the quadrilateral of language" is discussed in Michel Foucault, *The Order of Things: An Archaeology of the Human Sciences*, trans. anon. (London: Tavistock, 1970; original work published 1966 as *Les Mots et les choses*) 115 (OT); See AK, p. 158ff for the quadrilateral as "archaeology" and note that in later work the archaeological method is renamed "critical" method, AK, p. 233; and for the quadrilateral as "genealogy," see Michel Foucault, *The History of Sexuality: Vol. I. An Introduction*, trans. R. Hurley (New York: Vintage, 1980; original work published in 1976 as *Volenté de savior*) 92ff (HS).

52. AK, pp. 231–3.

53. Michel Foucault, *Death and the Labyrinth: The World of Raymond*

Roussel, trans. C. Ruas (New York: Doubleday, 1986) 16 (DL); citations of French and retranslations are from *Raymond Roussel* (Paris: Editions Gallimard, 1963).

54. Foucault, *Death and the Labyrinth,* p. 15.

55. Michel Foucault, *This Is Not A Pipe: With Illustrations and Letters by René Magritte,* trans. & Ed. J. Harkness (Berkeley: California UP) 20–1, 28 (TNP); AK, pp. 161–2, 227.

56. DL, p. 28.

57. TNP, p. 22.

58. AK, p. 216; A clear allusion to the semiotic order or experience and analysis offered in Plato's dialogue *Sophist* that Foucault is following; see Richard Lanigan, *Phenomenology of Communication: Merleau-Ponty's Thematics in Communicology and Semiology* (Pittsburgh: Duquesne UP, 1988) Chapter 17, "Semiotic Phenomenology in Plato's *Sophist.*"

59. AK, pp. 216, 237, an allusion to the *Sophist* in which the persona of the Statesman represents political rhetoric (knowledge of the future).

60. AK, pp. 216–7.

61. AK, p. 237; an allusion to the *Sophist* in which the persona of the Philosopher represents judicial rhetoric (knowledge of the past).

62. AK, p. 237; an allusion to the *Sophist* in which the persona of the Sophist represents evaluative rhetoric (knowledge of the present).

63. DL, p. 16.

64. AK, p. 220.

65. AK, p. 222.

66. DL, pp. 16–7; also see n. 84 below.

67. AK, p. 224.

68. AK, pp. 225, 228, 235.

69. AK, p. 226.

70. Chaim Perelman and L. Olbrechts-Tyteca, *The New Rhetoric: A Treatise on Argumentation,* trans. J. Wilkinson and P. Weaver (Notre Dame: Notre Dame UP, 1969) 1, et passim; Cf. Gérard Genette, *Figures of Literary Discourse,* trans. A. Sheridan (New York: Columbia UP, 1982) 10ff.

71. AK, p. 226.

72. AK, p. 227; Michel Foucault, "*Omnes et Singulatim*: Towards a Criticism of 'Political Reason',* *The Tanner Lectures on Human Values 1981, Vol. II.,* ed. Sterling M. McMurrin (Salt Lake City: Utah UP; Cambridge: Cambridge UP, 1981) 227.

73. DL, pp. 26–7; see Anthony Wilden, *The Rules Are No Game: The Strategies of Communication* (New York: Routledge & Kegan Paul, 1987) 245ff.

74. AK, p. 28.

75. AK, pp. 228, 231.

76. AK, p. 227.

77. White, *"Foucault's Discourse,"* p. 115.

78. AK, p. 227.

79. AK, pp. 222, 228.

80. AK, p. 235.

81. OT, p. 116; my emphasis; see n. 8 above, Descombes, *Les Même et l'Autre.*

82. Benveniste, op. cit., p. 215.

83. AK, p. 229. Cf. n. 59 above, the task of the Statesman in the *Sophist.*

84. AK, p. 220; "play" is a traditional human science metaphor for "communication theory" as "deutero-learning" or the logic of *abduction;* see Gregory Bateson and Mary Catherine Bateson, *Angels Fear: Towards an Epistemology of the Sacred* (New York: Macmillan, 1987), esp. 36ff; and see Charles Sanders Peirce, "Ampliative Reasoning," *Collected Papers of Charles Sanders Peirce,* ed. C. Hartshorne and P. Weiss (Cambridge: Harvard UP, 1931–60), codex 2.619.

85. AK, p. 218.

86. AK, p. 228.

87. AK, p. 215.

88. AK, p. 235. For a discussion of Canguilhem, see Gary Gutting, *Michel Foucault's Archaeology of Scientific Reason* (New York: Cambridge UP, 1989).

89. AK, p. 228.

90. AK, p. 228.

91. AK, p. 222.

92. AK, p. 229. Cf. n. 61 above, the task of the Philosopher in the *Sophist.*

93. AK, p. 220.

94. AK, p. 232.

95. AK, p. 228; see n. 58 above.

96. See n. 58 above, Aristotle's *Rhetorica,* 1358b.4–1359a.29, and Plato's *Sophist.*

97. AK, p. 231.

98. AK, p. 236.

99. AK, pp. 220, 229. Cf. n. 62 above, the task of the Sophist in the *Sophist.*

100. AK, pp. 231–2.

101. IPP, p. 14.

102. AK, p. 233.

103. SP, p. 208; AK, p. 229.

104. Michel Foucault, *Language, Counter-Memory, Practice: Selected Essays and Interviews,* ed. Donald F. Bouchard (Ithaca, NY: Cornell UP, 1977) 137–8.

105. AK, p. 229.

106. HS, p. 100.

107. HS, p. 99.

108. Ibid.

109. AK, p. 230.

110. HS, p. 98.

111. AK, p. 215; trope name insertions are mine.

112. IPP, p. 39.

CHAPTER 7 – CHINESE ENCYCLOPEDIA

1. Michel Foucault, *The Order of Things: An Archaeology of the Human Sciences,* trans. anon. (London: Tavistock, 1970; original work published in 1966 as *Les Mots et les Choses*).

2. Michel Foucault, *The Archaeology of Knowledge (sic) & The Discourse on Language (sic),* trans. A.M. Sheridan Smith (New York: Pantheon; Random

House, 1972; original works published as *L'Archaéologie du Savior* in 1969 and as *L'Ordre du Discours* in 1971).

3. Erroneously translated as "The Archaeology of Knowledge"; the translation ignores the *connaissance* [knowledge; "know"] and *savior* [understanding; "know how"] distinction so fundamental to Foucault's thought in distinguishing the analytic method of *archaeology* and the critical method of *genealogy*.

4. Foucault, *The Order of Things*, p. 4.

5. Richard L. Lanigan, *Semiotic Phenomenology of Rhetoric: Eidetic Practice in Henry Grattan's Discourse on Tolerance* (Washington, D.C.: Center for Advanced Research in Phenomenology; UP America, 1984).

6. Foucault, *The Order of Things*, p. 115; Foucault, *Archaeology* p. 158.

7. Foucault, *The Order of Things*, p. xv; my translation.

8. Foucault, *Archaeology*, p. 162.

9. Michel de Certeau, *The Practice of Everyday Life*, trans. Steven F. Randall (Berkeley: California UP, 1984; original work published (n.d.) as *Arts de Faire*) 159.

10. Foucault, *The Order of Things*, p. 116.

11. Umberto Eco, "*Lector in Fabula*: Pragmatic Strategy in a Metanarrative Text, "*The Role of the Reader: Explorations in the Semiotics of Texts* (Bloomington: Indiana UP, 1979) 223.

12. Umberto Eco, "Dictionary vs. Encyclopedia," *Semiotics and the Philosophy of Language* (Bloomington: Indiana UP, 1984), 46–86.

13. Umberto Eco, *A Theory of Semiotics* (Bloomington: Indiana UP, 1976) 7, 162.

14. Foucault, *The Order of Things*, p. 230.

15. Michel Foucault, *Death and the Labyrinth: The World of Raymond Roussel*, trans. Charles Ruas (Garden City: Doubleday, 1986; original work published 1963 as *Raymond Roussel*) 15–6; Foucault, *The Order of Things*, pp. 113–4; Foucault, *Archaeology*, pp. 58, 60–62.

16. Foucault, *Archaeology*, pp. 108–9.

17. Maurice Merleau-Ponty, *Phenomenology of Perception*, trans. Colin Smith; corrections by Forrest Williams and David Guerrière (New Jersey: Humanities, 1981; original work published 1945).

18. Pierre Bourdieu, *Outline of a Theory of Practice*, trans. Richard Nice (New York: Cambridge UP, 1977; original work published 1972 as *Esquisse d'une théorie de la pratique, précédé de trois études d'ethnologie*); and on Maurice Merleau-Ponty as the influence for his phenomenological sociology, see Bourdieu, "Fieldwork in Philosophy," *In Other Words: Essays Towards a Reflexive Sociology*, trans. Matthew Adamson (Stanford: Stanford UP, 1990) 3–33.

19. Emmanuel Levinas, "Reality and Its Shadow," *The Levinas Reader*, ed. Seán Hand (Oxford: Blackwell, 1989) 135.

20. Levinas, "Reality and Its Shadow."

CHAPTER 8 – FOUCAULT'S PHENOMENOLOGY

1. Michel Foucault/Maurice Blanchot, *Maurice Blanchot: The Thought from Outside* by Michel Foucault, trans. B. Massumi; *Michel Foucault as I Imagine Him* by Maurice Blanchot, trans. J. Mehlman (New York: Zone, 1987; original work published 1986), 10.

2. Michel Foucault, "Behind the Fable," *Critical Texts* 5.2 (1988): 2.

3. Maurice Merleau-Ponty, *Phenomenology of Perception*, trans. Colin Smith; corrections by Forrest Williams and David Guerrière (New Jersey: Humanities, 1981; original work published 1945), 392.

4. Richard L. Lanigan, *Phenomenology of Communication: Merleau-Ponty's Thematics in Communicology and Semiology* (Pittsburgh: Duquesne UP, 1988).

5. Martin Heidegger, *The Basic Problems of Phenomenology*, trans. Albert Hofstadter (Bloomington: Indiana UP, 1982; original work published 1975), 267; see Richard L. Lanigan, *Speech Act Phenomenology* (The Hague: Martinus Nijhoff, 1977).

6. Anthony Wilden, *Man and Woman, War and Peace: The Strategist's Companion* (New York: Routledge & Kegan Paul, 1987), 12 et passim.

7. Merleau-Ponty, *Phenomenology of Perception*, p. 419.

8. Umberto Eco, *A Theory of Semiotics* (Bloomington: Indiana UP, 1976) viii.

9. Merleau-Ponty, *Phenomenology of Perception*, p. xix; Merleau-Ponty's emphasis in italics, mine in bold type.

10. Lanigan, "Structuralism and the Human Science Context of Phenomenology and Semiology," *Phenomenology of Communication*, p. 157ff.

11. Eco, *A Theory of Semiotics*, p. 7.

12. Michel Foucault, *The Order of Things: An Archaeology of the Human Sciences*, trans. anon. (London: Tavistock, 1970; original work published 1966 as *Les Mots et les choses*) 361–2; English translation title change approved by Foucault; my emphasis and insertions.

13. Michel Foucault, *The Archaeology of Knowledge (sic) & The Discourse on Language (sic)*, trans. A. M. Sheridan Smith (New York: Pantheon; Random House, 1972; original works published 1969 and 1971) 155, 162.

14. Merleau-Ponty, *Phenomenology of Perception*, p. 197; see Richard L. Lanigan, *Speaking and Semiology: Maurice Merleau-Ponty's Phenomenological Theory of Existential Communication* (The Hague & Paris: Mouton, 1972).

15. Claude Hagège, *The Dialogic Species: A Linguistic Contribution to the Social Sciences*, trans. Sharon L. Shelly (New York: Columbia UP, 1990) 93.

16. Elmar Holenstein, *Roman Jakobson's Approach to Language: Phenomenological Structuralism*, trans. Catherine & Tarcisius Schelbert (Bloomington: Indiana UP, 1976; original work published 1974).

17. Merleau-Ponty, *Phenomenology of Perception*, p. 426.

18. Merleau-Ponty, *Phenomenology of Perception*, p. 427, Merleau-Ponty's emphasis.

19. Michel Foucault/Maurice Blanchot, p. 58.

20. Anthony Wilden, "Analog and Digital Communication: On Negation, Signification, and Meaning," *System and Structure: Essays in Communication and Exchange* (New York: Tavistock, 1972) 155ff.

21. Eco, *A Theory of Semiotics*, p. viii.

22. Maurice Merleau-Ponty, *The Structure of Behavior*, trans. A. L. Fisher (Boston: Beacon, 1963; original work published 1942) 176; my insertions.

23. Foucault, *The Order of Things*, p. 80.

24. Foucault, *Archaeology*, p. 234; my emphasis and insertions.

25. Foucault, *Archaeology*, p. 155.

26. Michel Foucault, *Foucault Live (Interviews 1966/84)*, trans. J. Johnston (New York: Semiotext(e); Columbia University, 1989), 89.

27. Foucault, "Behind the Fable."

28. Foucault, *The Order of Things*, p. 116; for the insertion on "generation and generalization" see Jacques Derrida, "Signature, Event, Context," *Limited, Inc.*, trans. S. Weber & J. Mehlman (Evanston: Northwestern UP, 1988; original work published 1977) 11.

29. Lester Thonssen & A. Craig Baird, *Speech Criticism: The Development of Standards for Rhetorical Appraisal* (New York: Ronald, 1948), 420.

30. Foucault, *Archaeology*, p. 230, et passim.

31. Foucault, *The Order of Things*, p. 18.

32. Foucault, *The Order of Things*, p. 19.

33. Foucault, *The Order of Things*, p. 21.

34. Foucault, *The Order of Things*, p. 23.

35. Foucault, *The Order of Things*, pp. 23–4.

36. Foucault, *The Order of Things*, p. 25.

37. Foucault, *The Order of Things*, p. 27.

38. Foucault, *The Order of Things*, p. 28.

39. Derrida, "Signature, Event, Context," *Limited, Inc.*, p. 21.

40. Foucault, *The Order of Things*, p. 127.

41. Anthony Wilden, *The Rules Are No Game: The Strategy of Communication* (New York: Routledge & Kegan Paul, 1987), 316, et passim.

42. Foucault, *Archaeology*, p. 171.

43. Maurice Merleau-Ponty, *In Praise of Philosophy*, trans. John Wild & James Edie (Northwestern UP, 1963; original work published 1953), 57.

44. Hayden White, *Tropics of Discourse: Essays in Cultural Criticism* (Baltimore: Johns Hopkins UP, 1978), 230ff.

45. Foucault, *Archaeology*, p. 168.

46. Merleau-Ponty, *In Praise of Philosophy*, pp. 57–8.

47. Michel Foucault, *The History of Sexuality: Vol. I. An Introduction*, trans. R. Hurley (New York: Vintage; Random House, 1980; original work published 1976) 98–100; see Richard L. Lanigan, *Semiotic Phenomenology of Rhetoric: Eidetic Practice in Henry Grattan's Discourse on Tolerance* (Washington, DC: Center for Advanced Research in Phenomenology & UP America, 1984).

48. Foucault, *Archaeology*, pp. 155–6.

49. Foucault, *Archaeology*, p. 169.

50. Emmanuel Levinas, *The Levinas Reader*, ed. Seán Hand (Oxford: Basil Blackwell, 1989) 158; my insertions.

51. Merleau-Ponty, *Phenomenology of Perception*, pp. 400–1; see Michel Foucault, "The Subject and Power," *Michel Foucault: Beyond Structuralism and Hermeneutics* by Hubert L. Dreyfus & Paul Rabinow (Chicago: Chicago UP, 1982).

CHAPTER 9 – CULTURE AND COMMUNICATION

1. Satischandra Chatterjee & Dhirendramohan Datta, *An Introduction to Indian Philosophy*, 6th ed. (Calcutta: Calcutta UP, 1960) 10.

2. Chatterjee & Datta, An Introduction.

3. G. W. F. Hegel, *The Phenomenology of Mind*, trans. J. B. Baille (New York: Harper & Row, 1967; original work published 1807) 660–1; my insertions.

4. Friedrich Nietzsche, *Human, All Too Human*, trans. M. Faber

(Lincoln: Nebraska UP, 1984); aphorism 221 is itself a commentary on Nietzsche's debt to the French literary tradition of the aphorism.

5. Ananda K. Coomaraswamy, *Christian and Oriental Philosophy of Art* (New York: Dover, 1956) 133.

6. Chatterjee and Datta, *An Introduction to Indian Philosophy*, p. 10.

7. J. N. Mohanty, "On Husserl's Theory of Meaning," *Southwestern Journal of Philosophy* 5 (1974): 243.

8. Ananda K. Coomaraswamy, *The Transformation of Nature in Art* (New York: Dover, 1956; original work published 1934) 85.

9. Edmund Husserl, "The Syllabus of the London Lectures," *JBSP: The Journal of the British Society for Phenomenology* 1.1. (January 1970): 18.

10. J. N. Mohanty, "Indian Philosophy" in *Encyclopedia Britannica*, 15th ed. (New York: Encyclopedia Briticanna, 1974) 1: 334.

11. Maurice Merleau-Ponty, "On the Phenomenology of Language," *Signs*, trans. R. C. McCleary (Evanston: Northwestern UP, 1964; original work published 1960) 86. See R. L. Lanigan, *Speaking and Semiology: Merleau-Ponty's Phenomenological Theory of Existential Communication* (The Hague and Paris: Mouton, 1972).

12. J. N. Mohanty, "Communication, Interpretation, and Intention," a lecture presented in the Department of Communication, Southern Illinois University, 4 February 1985, xerox copy, p. 1.

13. Merleau-Ponty, "On the Phenomenology of Language," p. 92.

14. Merleau-Ponty, "On the Phenomenology of Language," p. 13.

15. Michel Foucault, *The History of Sexuality: Volume 1: An Introduction*, trans. Robert Hurley (New York: Vintage; Random House, 1980; original work published 1976) 62.

16. Merleau-Ponty, "On the Phenomenology of Language," p. 95.

17. Merleau-Ponty, "On the Phenomenology of Language," pp. 95–96.

18. Foucault, *The History of Sexuality*, p. 61.

19. Merleau-Ponty, "On the Phenomenology of Language," p. 97.

20. Foucault, *The History of Sexuality*, p. 143.

21. William Gerber, ed., *The Mind of India* (Carbondale: Southern Illinois UP, 1977; original work published 1967) 12.

22. Richard L. Lanigan, "Semiotic Phenomenology in Plato's *Sophist*," *Phenomenology of Communication: Merleau-Ponty's Thematics in Communicology and Semiology* (Pittsburgh: Duquesne UP, 1987) 223–45.

23. Merleau-Ponty, "On the Phenomenology of Language," p. 97. See the very insightful analysis by Lester E. Embree, "Toward a Phenomenology of Theoria," *Life-World and Consciousness: Essays for Aron Gurwitsch* (Evanston: Northwestern UP, 1972) 191–207.

24. Maurice Merleau-Ponty, *Phenomenology of Perception*, trans. Colin Smith; revisions and corrections by Forrest Williams & David Guerrière (New Jersey: Humanities, 1981; original work published 1945) 345.

Index

Note: Entries marked by the letter "B" will also be found in Appendix B: "Communicology: An Encyclopedic Dictionary of the Human Science" beginning on page 197. Only selected terms from Appendix B are included in this Index.